Challenges of the Agrarian Transition in Southeast Asia (ChATSEA)

Gambling with the Land

The Contemporary Evolution of
Southeast Asian Agriculture

Challenges of the Agrarian Transition in Southeast Asia (ChATSEA)

The shift from rural societies dependent upon agricultural livelihoods to predominantly urbanized, industrialized and market-based societies is one of the most significant processes of social change in the modern world. The Challenges of the Agrarian Transition in Southeast Asia (ChATSEA) project examines how the transformation is affecting the societies and economies of Southeast Asia. Headed by Professor Rodolphe De Koninck, holder of the Canada Chair in Asian Research at the University of Montreal, and sponsored by the Social Sciences and Humanities Research Council of Canada, the ChATSEA project includes publications by senior academics as well as junior scholars.

Gambling with the Land

The Contemporary Evolution of Southeast Asian Agriculture

Rodolphe De Koninck

Jean-François Rousseau

NUS PRESS
SINGAPORE

Published by:

NUS Press
National University of Singapore
AS3-01-02, 3 Arts Link
Singapore 117569

Fax: (65) 6774-0652
E–mail: nusbooks@nus.edu.sg
Website: http://www.nus.edu.sg/nuspress

ISBN 978-9971-69-561-3 (Case)

National Library Board, Singapore Cataloguing-in-Publication Data

De Koninck, Rodolphe.
    Gambling with the land: the contemporary evolution of Southeast Asian agriculture / Rodolphe De Koninck, Jean-François Rousseau. – Singapore: NUS Press, 2012.
    p. cm.
    Includes bibliographical references and index.
    ISBN: 978-9971-69-553-8 (pbk.)

    1. Agriculture – Economic aspects – Southeast Asia. 2. Land use, Rural – Southeast Asia. I. Rousseau, Jean-François. II. Title.

HD2075.8
338.10959 — dc23   OCN786447188

Printed by: Mainland Press Pte Ltd

Contents

List of Figures

List of Maps

List of Appendices

Preface

This book is part of a series resulting from a five-year international research project (2005–10) funded by the Social Sciences and Humanities Research Council of Canada (SSHRC). Titled "Challenges of the Agrarian Transition in Southeast Asia", it has involved collaboration between scholars, faculty and graduate students from Indonesia, Malaysia, the Philippines, Thailand, Vietnam and Singapore as well as Canada, the UK, France and Australia.

We therefore wish to thank the SSHRC for its financial support as well as the Asia Research Institute at the National University of Singapore and, in Paris, the Fondation Maison des sciences de l'homme, the Maison Suger and the Institut des études avancées. Several individuals were also very helpful. These include Marc Girard, from the Geography Department at the Université de Montréal, who prepared the maps that illustrate the book, Julie Drolet, Martine Ignat, Ariane and Annie Pelé, and Étienne Turgeon-Pelletier as well as all members of the ChATSEA project, particularly Stéphane Bernard, Jean-François Bissonnette, Rob Cramb, Steve Déry, Derek Hall, Pham Thanh Hai, Phil Hirsch, Phil Kelly, Danielle Labbé, Jean-Philippe Leblond, Tania Li, Gilles Maillet, Melissa Marschke, Lesley Potter, Jonathan Rigg, Steffanie Scott, Pujo Semedi, Louis Tanguay, Bruno Thibert, Sarah Turner, Peter Vandergeest, Chusak Wittayapak and Doracie Zoleta-Nantes. We also wish to thank the anonymous referees of the manuscript, whose comments and recommendations have been very useful. Of course, none of these persons is responsible for any of the mistakes or inaccuracies that may be found in our book.

CHAPTER 1

Introduction:
Assessing the Dynamism of
Southeast Asian Agriculture

"Such coincidence of policy across several centuries and, in the modern period, across very different types of regime is prima facie evidence that something fundamental about state making is at work."

(Scott 2009: 79)

"A third line of reasoning would look at the ways in which the village economy is tied to supra-village or even national economic structures"

(Hüsken 1989: 327)

Studying Southeast Asian Agricultures since the 1960s

This book is one among several being prepared in the context of a collaborative research project titled "Challenges of the Agrarian Transition in Southeast Asia" (De Koninck 2004). Its specific purpose is to provide an overall interpretation of the dominant trends in agriculture throughout the region between the early 1960s and the latter years of the first decade of the twenty-first century.

Why since the early 1960s? First, because that period corresponds to the beginning of the post-colonial era, with several of the region's major countries being involved in intensive state making (Map 1). Second, and more specifically, this involved adopting major new policies in state monitoring of the agricultural sector. Such policies were not necessarily adopted concurrently, nor were they implemented in exactly the same manner and with the same rhythm; but some 50 years later — by which time the region's political map had stabilized (Map 2) — their impact had become quite evident. Nearly everywhere, they consisted of incentives to both intensify and expand territorially the agricultural domain, as they were meant, at least officially, to provide answers to widespread problems of low productivity in agriculture and poverty among rural populations, particularly those involved in farming.

The identification of these problems as well as the solutions envisaged to solve them can be traced back to the late colonial and early postcolonial literature, when most observers appeared pessimistic in their assessments of Southeast Asia's agriculture (De Koninck 2003).[1] This was the case with Dumont, as early as 1935 (p. 32), and Gourou in 1936 (p. 574–7). In later works, including in his very influential *Les pays tropicaux*, first published in 1947 and reedited several times, Gourou repeated, referring to Vietnamese peasants, that cultural as well as ecological constraints were such that there was little hope for an improvement in their livelihoods. Dobby (1960: 359) and Geertz (1963:

144–7) were equally pessimistic about other peasantries in the region. All emphasized the demographic problem, claiming that throughout most of the region, the lowlands were densely overpopulated and population grew faster than food production. Several, notably Gourou in 1953, Robequain in 1958, Burling in 1965 and Fisher in 1966, suggested that part of the solution might be found in moving people to less populated areas, particularly to the highlands. Charles Robequain (1958: 440) was particularly clear about it: "Besides, there must be a transfer of population from overpopulated districts and a real internal colonization of empty spaces". As for Charles Fisher (1966: 179), his concern appeared more geopolitical: "although many of the governments are conscious of the maldistribution of population within their national territory, it is probably true to say that most of them are more worried by the relative emptiness of their lands which it is feared may arouse the cupidity of overcrowded neighbours."

These statements underscore a major feature of Southeast Asia's geography, which is characterized by an intricate network of lowlands and uplands, both on the continent and in the archipelago (Maps 3 and 4). The Southeast Asian lowland and upland domains are themselves differentiated by a number of different ecological, demographic and cultural features. While real and complex, these have often been referred to and made use of in a simplistic and deterministic manner during both the precolonial and the postcolonial periods.

Thus, the call for population redistribution from the lowlands towards the less densely populated uplands through agricultural expansion was generally made for a number of socioeconomic or geopolitical purposes. It was also frequently motivated by the claim that the minority hill people's practice of swidden agriculture was environmentally destructive. References to the "backwardness" of the ethnic minorities inhabiting the uplands have remained frequent throughout much of the colonial literature, as well as in more recent writings, as have

---

[1] The following paragraphs resemble closely some of those contained in "A Half Century of Agrarian Transformations in Southeast Asia, 1960–2010", authored by De Koninck, Rigg and Vandergeest. That article is an introductory chapter to another book emanating from the ChATSEA project, *Revisiting Rural Places: Pathways to Poverty and Prosperity in Southeast Asia*. Edited by Rigg and Vandergeest, it has been published by NUS Press as part of the ChATSEA series.

Map 1 Southeast Asia: Political map in 1960

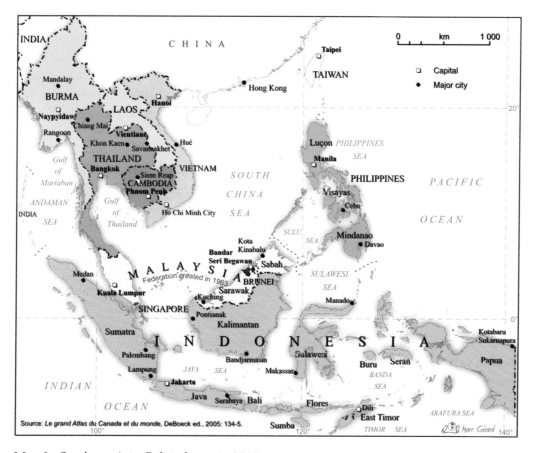

Map 2 Southeast Asia: Political map in 2010

accusations as to the supposedly environmentally destructive consequences of their agricultural practices, particularly their reliance on swiddening. Although repeatedly and eloquently refuted — for example by Pelzer (1945), Spencer (1966), Dove (1983), Pouchepadass (1993), Thrupp *et al.* (1997), Fox (2000), Cramb (2007) and Scott (2009) — these allegations are still made in several countries, notably Indonesia, Malaysia and Vietnam, as a political argument to justify sedentarization of the minorities and, increasingly, land-grabbing, which, it so happens, has largely been achieved through agricultural expansion involving population redistribution from the lowlands (De Koninck and Déry 1997).

In addition to the need to expand the agricultural domain, observers as well as policymakers emphasized the need to increase the productivity of agricultural practices — i.e., crop yields — particularly those of food crops, first and foremost rice. This was in tune with the recommendations from leading economists regarding poverty alleviation, in particular Gunnar Myrdal's *Asian Drama: An Inquiry into the Poverty of Nations* (1971). Although the three volumes resulting from Myrdal's massive inquiry were published only in 1971, the study had been launched in 1957 and its recommendations reflected the dominant thinking among development economists of the post-World War II decades: governments had to step in and massively support the so-called modernization of agricultural practices. This is precisely what happened in several of the major Southeast Asian countries, in particular the Philippines, Malaysia and Indonesia and, to some extent Thailand, where by the 1960s financial support for innovation, in particular in rice cultivation, as well as diversified agricultural extension services were made available to peasant producers. And while state help to the plantation sector was much less significant, the latter was gradually induced to improve yields in a context where it had to compete with or to make the best of the expansion of the state-supported smallholder sector.

A key point here is that, notwithstanding several episodes of peasant unrest and some attempts at agrarian reform, particularly in Luzon and Java (Mortimer 1972, Kerkvliet 1977), the policy choice had become increasingly clear. Rather than advocating agrarian transformation through land reform or land redistribution, as had occurred or was occurring in capitalist East Asian countries such as Japan, South Korea and Taiwan (Kay 2002), Southeast Asian governments supported massive technological innovation through a reliance on the green revolution, along with a systematic increase in the territorial extent of the national agricultural domain. In short, they supported agricultural intensification and expansion.

These transformations did not proceed evenly or concurrently. With the exception of Thailand, the participation of mainland Southeast Asian countries in these two processes was somewhat delayed. In particular, the peasantries of the former French colonies of Vietnam (Tonkin, Annam and Cochinchina), Laos and Cambodia were subjected to various attempts at land reform (Taillard 1983). In the cases of Laos and particularly Vietnam, these attempts were socialist inspired, while in Cambodia they took a particularly violent turn under the Khmer Rouge regime (1975–79). But in all cases, the reforms turned out to be ephemeral, each of these countries having since been gradually drawn into the market economy. This occurred through a combination of vigorously enacted state policies, notably in Vietnam after 1986 and, increasingly, market driven incentives, including, more recently, in Cambodia and Laos.

The consequences of these policies and of other factors, including peasant initiatives and market forces, have been considerable although far from uniform. It should be remembered that, as stated earlier, state policies — in particular those favouring agricultural intensification and expansion — have been implemented throughout the region following very different time frames and with great geographical unevenness within each of the respective countries. For example, in Indonesia, in the 1960s and 1970s, green revolution policies were applied first and with greatest intensity in densely populated Java, where rice yields were already significantly higher than in the so-called outer islands; while territorial expansion took place essentially in the latter islands. But, overall, even if yields are nowadays still higher in Java, they have been catching up in several other regions of the country. In Vietnam, where meaningful yield increases began only in the 1980s, the same type of evolution has taken place. Rice yields in the Mekong Delta have been

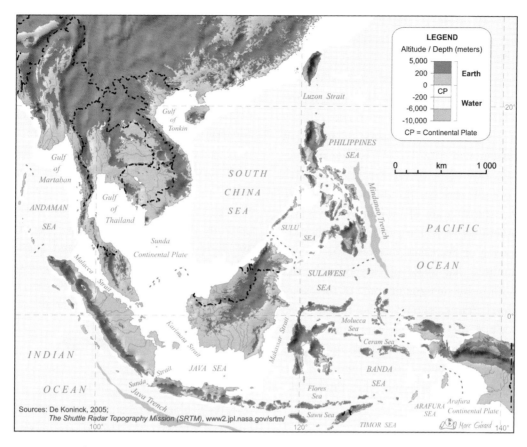

Map 3 Southeast Asia: Topography, 200m and above

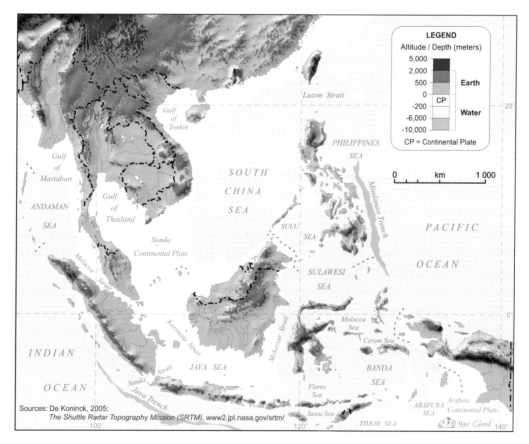

Map 4 Southeast Asia: Topography, 500m and above

catching up with those in the Red River Delta, traditionally much more intensively cultivated (Gourou 1936).

However, looking at national-level data as we do in this book does not allow us to investigate the substantial differences that may exist between the smallholder and plantation sectors in terms of yields, for instance in palm oil and rubber production; nor do these data reveal the share of each sector in overall national production. In short, national-level statistics are of little use in investigating the sometimes very sharp differences that are either increasing or decreasing between the regions and communities that make up any country. But they are useful in the analysis of some of the essential macro-level trends ongoing in Southeast Asian agriculture since the 1960s in every one of the eight major agricultural countries in the region, namely Burma, Thailand, Laos, Cambodia, Vietnam, Malaysia, Indonesia and the Philippines (Maps 5 and 6).[2]

General and Specific Objectives

Our general purpose is to identify, illustrate as well as interpret the above-described major trends in themselves, as their understanding is indispensable to a better interpretation of the rapid agrarian transformations occurring throughout the region at all scales. Such transformations are both taking place and articulated not only at the local, farm and household levels but also at the national, regional and international levels.

Our specific objectives can be grouped under three headings. The exceptional resilience and growth of the agricultural sector in nearly all countries of the region, which are at various stages of industrialization and urbanization, deserve to be better documented and interpreted. Our first objective is to contribute to this documentation and interpretation. Doing so allows us to pursue a second objective, that is, to further analyze the specific nature and role of agricultural transformations within the agrarian transition itself, as it unfolds

throughout Southeast Asia. For example, why does agriculture, while rapidly ceding its place to industry as the dominant realm of production and accumulation and the leading engine of economic growth in Southeast Asia, continue to diversify and expand, including territorially, while such continuing expansion has been — and still is — rare elsewhere? Why is land, particularly agricultural land, still a major locus of activity, investment and competition? What are the reasons as well as the implications of what we call gambling with the land and even gambling or betting on the land? Our third objective in addressing these issues and questions — if only by way of raising additional questions — is to provide tools useful to the further analysis of Southeast Asian agrarian issues, at all scales.

Sources and Methodology

In order to achieve our objectives, we chose to look at the evolution of several key aspects of agriculture, particularly intensification, expansion, production and exports, but also at a number of related domains, including urbanization and industrialization, demography, employment and fishing.

For this we opted to rely on national-level statistics only, primarily those made available online by the Food and Agriculture Organization of the United Nations, commonly and henceforth referred to as the FAO. For a number of topics not strictly agricultural, we use data provided by other United Nations agencies: UNCTAD (United Nations Conference on Trade and Development); UNEP (United Nations Environment Programme), particularly its GEO Data Portal; UNESCO (United Nations Educational, Scientific and Cultural Organization); UNPOP (United Nations Population Division); and UNSTATS (United Nations Statistics Division). The World Bank's World Development Indicators (WDI) database was also very useful as was the database of the Nelson Institute for Environmental Studies (N.I.E.S.) at the University of Wisconsin-Madison. Finally, for Figure 2.7, we relied on the Instituto Brasiliero de Geographica e Estatistica database.

---

[2] In this study we are leaving out Singapore, Brunei and East Timor, for several reasons, ranging from the limited importance of agriculture in the first two cases to the lack of sufficient longitudinal data available for East Timor.

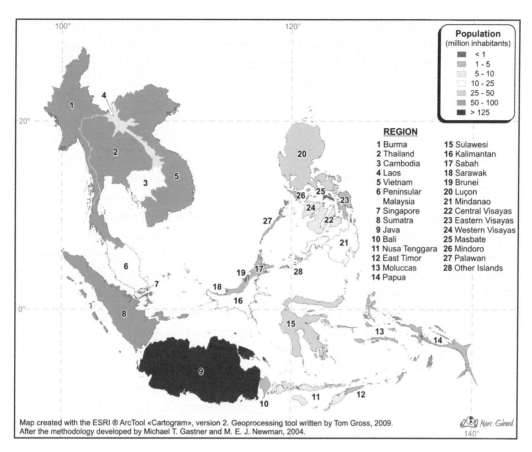

Map 5 Southeast Asia: Countries and islands, population in 2010

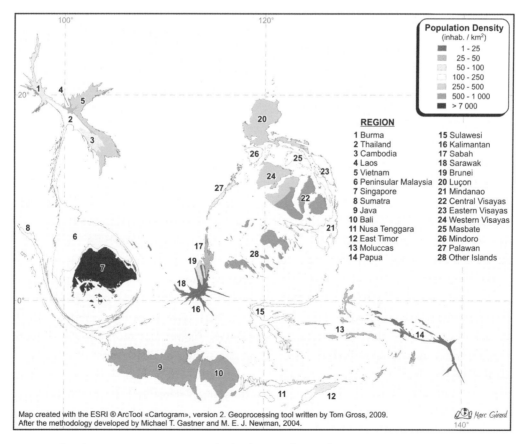

Map 6 Southeast Asia: Countries and islands, population density in 2010

Since 2008, when we began the systematic collection of statistics to produce the graphs at the core of our study, two of these databases have been the object of mergers. First, the World Bank's WDI database — one of our essential sources — was merged with the Bank's other databases to form a single one, the World dataBank. Second, the UNCTAD Commodity Price Statistics, from where we retrieved most price data, does not exist as such anymore, having been integrated within the organization's UNCTAD stats database. Also notable is that when we undertook this research, accessing both the World Bank and the UNCTAD former databases required subscription. These sources are now accessible free of charge on the Internet.

We are fully aware that national-level statistics provided by these bodies, particularly by the FAO, our principal source, are not always entirely reliable. That is understandable, given the magnitude of the databases assembled, the nature and diversity of the topics covered (from employment to fruit production), and, more important, the nature of the sources — generally national reporting — and the difficulty inherent in data collection in less developed countries. In other words, we fully agree with the view that official statistics are "not simply (...) 'social facts', but social and political constructions which may be based upon the interests of those who commissioned the research in the first instance" (May 1997: 71). As most political regimes in place in the region over the time period we focus on have weak records in terms of accountability and information sharing, a substantial proportion of the data we have used cannot be readily taken for granted. The problem is serious in the case of some of the region's current authoritarian regimes, particularly in Burma but also in Laos and Vietnam.

In order to minimize the risk of using unreliable data, we followed a series of self-imposed guidelines. First, consistency in the data retrieved was the guiding criterion that determined which indicator we could use. Second, to be retained, statistical series had to cover a sufficient number of years so as to allow for real longitudinal analyses. Third, statistical series had to include enough entries so that we could get a sense of the regional picture and its evolution. This was because, fourth, inconsistencies are much more detectable when the data examined are longitudinal.

We were also faced with the questionable reliability of monetary indicators, the use of which we chose to refrain from as much as possible. Values of national currencies against the dollar fluctuate, sometimes dramatically — for example, during and following the 1997–98 Asian financial crisis — while the value of the US dollar itself also changes. In addition, several of the major statistical databases that we consulted do not even provide systematic data in both current and constant dollars. To cope with this problem, we relied on price indexes whenever possible. Consequently, fifth, when compelled to refer to monetary values and again to maintain consistency, we prioritized current dollar values over constant dollar ones as often as possible, the former being more readily available. To this must be added that we are more concerned with — and more confident in — data concerning area measurements and volumes of production, as over the years hectares remain hectares and tonnes remain tonnes. In order to measure the evolution of agricultural yields and production, those indicators are definitely more eloquent than dollar values.

As stated earlier, we have substantive reasons to use the early 1960s as a benchmark. It also happens that data concerning earlier decades are much thinner. Most of the major international organizations now providing near universal databases were established during the late 1940s and the 1950s, and nearly a decade had elapsed before they were able to get their act together, so to speak.

As our collection of data spanned a period of nearly three years, from early 2008 until mid-2010, we constantly had to revise previously assembled statistics, tables and graphs. This is because we came to notice that figures had frequently been revised inside the very databases that we were consulting (FAOSTATS, UNSTATS, World dataBank, etc.). Our readers should be aware of this. Should they be interested in adding to our time series, they may discover that some of the numbers we reproduce here have since been modified in the original sources. As our last round of data update occurred in the spring of 2010, most of our statistical series reach 2007–8. When they do not, it means that the sources consulted did not provide more recent material.

At times we noticed discrepancies between some of our sources, so we had to make choices on the basis of our own judgment. In the case of the most significant discrepancy, the one concerning land use statistics provided by FAO and N.I.E.S., we worked with both versions (Figures 2.1–2.9). In fact, N.I.E.S data collection methods share little with the FAO's, which partly explains the differences between their datasets. Ramankutty and Foley (1999: 998), who contributed to the setting up of the N.I.E.S. database, explain that what they call "cropland" corresponds to "the Food and Agriculture Organization (FAO) definition of 'arable lands and permanent crops'".[3] We also had to be particularly careful in handling production and export figures in cases where there were differences between the products harvested and the commodities processed and exported. This concerned in particular rubber, oil palm fruit, sugar cane and coconut.

The Contents of the Book

The core of this book consists of seven chapters, each grouping several plates, the number of which varies between as few as four and as many as 18, for a total of 67. The relative importance of the respective chapters is largely related to our desire to focus on the intensification and expansion of Southeast Asian agricultures since the early 1960s.[4] We actually began by compiling a larger number of graphs and tables, much larger than we care to admit. But for several reasons, including lack of confidence in some data and the difficulty of having to constantly update numbers and reconstruct graphs, we decided to reduce the "harvest" to a more manageable size.

Each plate contains graphs, under which are presented summary tables and, on the opposite page, comments and interpretations of the evolutionary processes illustrated in the figures. Unlike the graphs, the tables do not present annual data, but preferably triennial averages, which, for reasons of space, are generally interspaced on a decade basis. This explains why the actual curves on the graphs, which are based on annual figures, appear at the same time more accurate and more entangled — largely because of the vagaries of agricultural cycles — than the numbers in the tables. The graphs on the one hand generally provide a simpler, more synthetic picture of the evolutionary processes commented upon. But, on the other hand, the actual numbers presented in the tables appear sometimes more telling and allow for a more balanced interpretation. These tables are themselves a summary of the detailed tables we compiled and from which the graphs were produced.

In most cases, graphs and tables regroup the eight Southeast Asian countries studied under two geographical realms, termed "mainland" and "archipelago". We are aware that the first group, made up of Burma, Thailand, Laos, Cambodia and Vietnam, is often referred to as peninsular Southeast Asia, while what we designate the archipelago, consisting of Malaysia, Indonesia and the Philippines, corresponds to what many authors call insular Southeast Asia or peninsular and insular Southeast Asia. None of these designations, including our own, is fully adequate, largely because of the dual territorial nature of Malaysia. We simply had to make a choice and stick to it, which did not prevent us from occasionally referring, in the comments, to peninsular or insular countries. Another choice that we had to make concerns the extent of statistical detail. Thus, whenever a given commodity, for example palm oil,

---

[3] The FAO definition of arable land is "land under temporary agricultural crops (multiple-cropped areas are counted only once), temporary meadows for mowing or pasture, land under market and kitchen gardens and land temporarily fallow (less than five years). The abandoned land resulting from shifting cultivation is not included in this category. Data for "arable land" are not meant to indicate the amount of land that is potentially cultivable"; and the definition for permanent crops is "crops planted once, and then occupy the land for some years and need not be replanted after each annual harvest, such as cocoa, coffee and rubber. This category includes flowering shrubs, fruit trees, nut trees and vines, but excludes trees grown for wood or timber" (FAOSTAT).

[4] Regarding expansion, Chapter 2 carries the same title — "Southeast Asian Agricultural Expansion in Global Perspective" — as the first chapter of another ChATSEA book titled *Borneo Transformed: Agricultural Expansion on the Southeast Asian Frontier*, edited by De Koninck, Bernard and Bissonnette and published by NUS Press in 2011. The contents of that chapter, authored by De Koninck, overlap partially with those of the present chapter, in which, however, the figures are in greater number, updated and more elaborately commented on.

is not produced in significant quantity in all eight countries, we only present the data concerning the four countries where it is.

We are also very much aware of the huge differences and contrasts that exist in territorial as well as demographic terms between — and even within — the eight countries examined, particularly Indonesia (Maps 5 and 6). Considering the scale at which our material was collected, there was not much we could do about this, except that in our comments and interpretation we tried to take these differences into consideration whenever possible.

Finally, why a plate on Brazil? Simply because, as made clear in the comments on Figures 2.7–2.9, the huge agricultural-cum-forested South American giant provides a good mirror image of some of the key processes of the ongoing Southeast Asian agrarian transition, particularly in Indonesia — to such an extent that we originally assembled enough

material to devote an entire chapter to that comparison. That was also trimmed down, but we hope to return to it in future work.

For the moment, our goal remains modest and limited to providing, without further delay, a broad picture of the evolution of the agricultures of Southeast Asia since the early 1960s as well as preliminary interpretations of this picture. We also hope that others will use, criticize and perfect our study, while helping us move on to more focused representations and analyses of the multiple and complex trajectories followed by Southeast Asian communities in their own agrarian transition. In case we have not been clear enough about it, we are fully aware of the need to look into — as achieved in other ChATSEA volumes, such as Hall, Hirsch and Murray Li's (2011) as well as Rigg and Vandergeest's (2012) — processes that operate at scales different from the national one.

CHAPTER 2

Southeast Asian Agricultural Expansion in Global Perspective

"Besides, there must be a transfer of population from overpopulated districts and a real internal colonization of empty spaces. Experience has shown that spontaneous migration would not adequately achieve the desired transfer."

(Robequain 1958: 440)

"It is the settlers themselves who by their own exertions open and develop the land, and it must be clearly understood that they have as permanent a stake in the welfare of the country as any mine or estate owner."

(Anonymous 1940: 73)

Plate 1

Until the sixteenth century, throughout the world, cropland* expansion remained moderate, as did population growth. Things began to change following European explorations of the sixteenth and seventeenth centuries, themselves followed by colonial expansion. By the early eighteenth century cropland expansion, along with population growth, was already going strong. This was observed not only in Europe and Russia but also in the northeastern portion of the United States as well as in China. Rapid agricultural expansion continued in all these regions during the first half of the nineteenth century, but by the middle of the century it had begun to level off in Europe. The opposite occurred in the United States, where new land openings accelerated noticeably with the conquest of the West. In Russia, strong expansion lasted for centuries, also accelerating towards the middle of the nineteenth century, with even a massive spurt following a relapse during World War II. In China and South Asia, while the nineteenth century witnessed a relative reduction in the pace of cropland expansion, the pace remained strong until the middle of the twentieth century. In China, expansion peaked at the time of the communist takeover, but since the 1950s the country has been losing some of its agricultural land. The same has been occurring in Russia and Europe since the 1960s, but at a slower pace in the latter case. As for South Asia, cropland expansion continued during the second half of the twentieth century, with a noticeable reduction in pace since the 1960s, India and Bangladesh having by then attained exceptionally high ratios of cultivated land — over 50 per cent and 60 per cent respectively.

Within South America, European-induced cropland expansion began at different times, depending on the region. On average, it remained very modest throughout the eighteenth and nineteenth centuries, accelerating only noticeably at the turn of the twentieth century, first in the southernmost realm, particularly in the pampas, then in the northern countries, notably in Brazil, where expansion was massive from the 1950s until the 1980s. Cropland expansion was somewhat comparable in Canada: modest during the eighteenth and nineteenth centuries and accelerating during the twentieth, but never at a pace comparable to that reached by countries to the south, whether the United States or Latin American countries. However, a reduction in agricultural land has been a characteristic common to most of the American realm, from Canada to the pampas, with the exception of Central America and, more recently, Brazil. In the United States, it actually began in the 1930s, with a few ephemeral expansion spurts since then. In the Central American domain, cropland expansion seems to have definitely levelled off in the 1990s. In Tropical Africa, the expansion of cropland remained modest throughout the eighteenth and nineteenth centuries and began to accelerate noticeably only by the 1940s. Since then, expansion has continued at a pace well over the world's average. The same applies, somewhat surprisingly, to North Africa and the Middle East, which have also been the object of sustained cropland expansion, particularly since the 1920s, with Turkey at the forefront.

Regarding mid- and late-twentieth century agricultural expansion, two other major regions stand out: so-called Pacific developed countries — essentially Australia and New Zealand — and Southeast Asia. In Australasia, noticeable agricultural expansion began during the last quarter of the nineteenth century. It accelerated slowly during the first half of the twentieth century, then very rapidly during the 1950s and 1960s. However, it has since levelled off. That has not been the case in Southeast Asia, where contemporary agricultural expansion and intensification have unique implications that need to be better understood.

---

* N.I.E.S. data collection methods share little with the FAO's, which partly explains the differences between their datasets. Ramankutty and Foley (1999: 998), who assembled the N.I.E.S. database, explain that what they call cropland corresponds to "the Food and Agriculture Organization (FAO) definition of 'arable lands and permanent crops'" (Cf. Chapter 1, footnote 3).

Figure 2.1 Estimated global population growth and cropland expansion, 1700–2007*

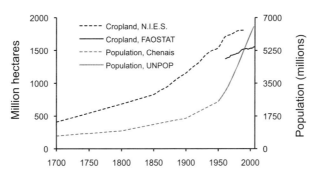

Sources: Chenais 1991; FAOSTAT 2010; N.I.E.S. 2010; UNPOP 2010.

Figure 2.2 Estimated cropland expansion in selected regions and countries, 1700–2007*

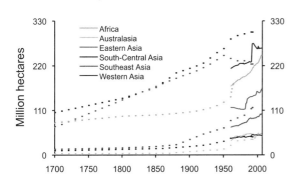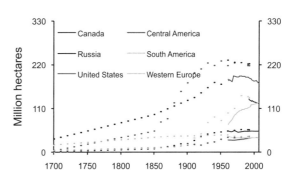

Sources: FAOSTAT 2010; N.I.E.S 2010.   Sources: FAOSTAT 2010; N.I.E.S 2010.

Cropland (million hectares)*

	1700	1800	1900	1950	2000	2007
Southeast Asia	407	684	1,155	1,543	1,536	1,554

Population (million)†

	1700	1800	1900	1950	2000	2005
Southeast Asia	680	954	1,634	2,529	6,115	6,512

Cropland expansion (million hectares)*

	1700	1800	1900	1950	2000	2007
Africa	79	95	105	129	225	247
Australasia	0.3	3	7	14	51	47
Canada	0.4	5	21	50	52	52
Central America	4	8	17	32	35	35
Eastern Asia	70	135	200	244	155	163
Russia	33	74	130	171	126	123
South America	3	7	19	79	120	126
South-Central Asia	105	140	214	262	262	264
Southeast Asia	14	17	38	66	94	101
United States	3	36	174	229	178	173
Western Asia	10	13	20	33	48	46
Western Europe	17	30	40	42	35	35

* Data for 1700–1950 from N.I.E.S.; data for 2000 and 2007 from FAOSTAT
† Data for 1700–1900 from Chenais (1991); data for 1950–2005 from UNPOP

Plate 2

During the eighteenth century, at a time when only the Philippines and limited portions of what was to become Indonesia were under colonial administration, cropland expansion in Southeast Asia remained relatively modest. Between 1700 and 1800, Southeast Asia's total cropland area grew by less than 25 per cent, from about 14 million to about 17 million hectares. During the first half of the nineteenth century, as population grew at an average annual rate of 0.7 per cent, from ~28 million to ~40 million inhabitants (Neville 1979: 54), cropland did not even keep pace as it increased at an average annual rate of less than 0.3 per cent, covering a total of only about 20 million hectares by 1850. During the second half of the century, the average annual rate of population growth accelerated substantially, reaching 1.5 per cent. Over the same period, the rate of cropland expansion also increased significantly, but never surpassed the demographic growth rate. However, from the 1880s onwards, agricultural expansion truly picked up. During the first half of the twentieth century, as population continued to grow at an average rate of 1.5 per cent per annum, cropland grew at an average rate of 1 per cent. Between 1950 and 1990, cropland expansion continued to accelerate, with the consequence that the area of cultivated land nearly doubled in the region according to N.I.E.S. (However, the FAO estimates that the region's croplands grew by only 30 per cent between 1961 and 1990).

Over the same 40-year period, the total population of Southeast Asia increased even faster — by a factor of 2.5 — growing from 176 million to 440 million. The average annual rate of demographic growth reached some 2.3 per cent during this period. Fortunately, overall food *production*, particularly rice, increased even faster, thanks to a substantial improvement in yields. This, of course, has been typical of agricultural growth in most of the world's regions. With the very rapid acceleration in the rate of population growth, the only way that food production has been able to keep up has been through significant increases in yields. This has particularly been the case in Southeast Asia (De Koninck and Déry 1997). However, along with increases in yields, Southeast Asian agriculture has also continued to expand territorially, at a rate apparently unmatched anywhere else, except in Brazil.

This said, from the late nineteenth century to the late twentieth, cropland expansion evolved in nature, going through two exceptional phases of acceleration. The first began in mainland Southeast Asia, with the last decades of the nineteenth century and the first decades of the twentieth witnessing massive expansion of rice cultivation, largely achieved in the deltas and lowlands of Cochinchina (Southern Vietnam), Thailand and Burma. To this first form of food crop expansion, which was predominantly fuelled by external demand, various types of commercial crop expansion — most noticeably rubber — were gradually added. These developments occurred predominantly in Malaya and Indonesia. Consequently, the second acceleration in Southeast Asian cropland expansion, which began in the 1950s, was almost exclusively attributable to further investments in the cultivation of commercial crops, particularly rubber, coffee and oil palm, with the latter having definitely taken the lead since the 1990s. As a result, in comparison with the rest of the world, the Southeast Asian ratio of cropland expansion over population growth does appear high, with perhaps only Brazil's performance being comparable.

Throughout the region, expansion of cultivated areas has occurred primarily at the expense of forestlands, including secondary, degraded and logged-over forests. Given the different scales used, a comparison between the two sets of graphs (Figures 2.3 and 2.4) is somewhat difficult. If actual numbers are taken into account, however, the correlation between cropland expansion and forest retreat appears very clear. For example, according to N.I.E.S. data, the loss of forest cover reached nearly 13 million hectares while croplands expanded by slightly more than 13 million hectares for Southeast Asia as a whole between the years 1960 and 1980. Notwithstanding some occasional minor discrepancies, the same correlation applies at the scale of both mainland and archipelagic Southeast Asia for the entire period examined.

Figure 2.3 Southeast Asia: Population growth and cropland expansion by major region, 1700–2007

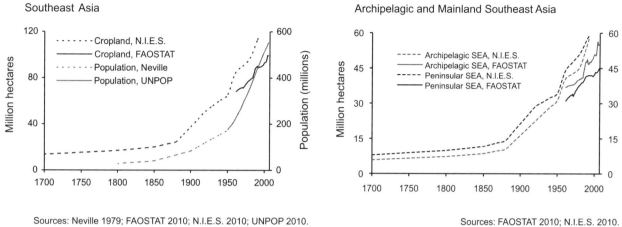

Sources: Neville 1979; FAOSTAT 2010; N.I.E.S. 2010; UNPOP 2010.

Sources: FAOSTAT 2010; N.I.E.S. 2010.

Figure 2.4 Southeast Asia: Decrease of forest cover, 1700–2007

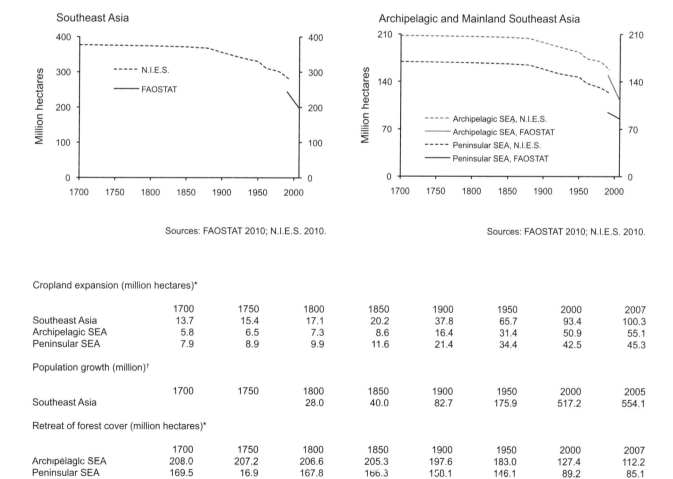

Sources: FAOSTAT 2010; N.I.E.S. 2010.

Sources: FAOSTAT 2010; N.I.E.S. 2010.

Cropland expansion (million hectares)*

	1700	1750	1800	1850	1900	1950	2000	2007
Southeast Asia	13.7	15.4	17.1	20.2	37.8	65.7	93.4	100.3
Archipelagic SEA	5.8	6.5	7.3	8.6	16.4	31.4	50.9	55.1
Peninsular SEA	7.9	8.9	9.9	11.6	21.4	34.4	42.5	45.3

Population growth (million)†

	1700	1750	1800	1850	1900	1950	2000	2005
Southeast Asia			28.0	40.0	82.7	175.9	517.2	554.1

Retreat of forest cover (million hectares)*

	1700	1750	1800	1850	1900	1950	2000	2007
Archipelagic SEA	208.0	207.2	206.6	205.3	197.6	183.0	127.4	112.2
Peninsular SEA	169.5	16.9	167.8	166.3	150.1	146.1	89.2	85.1

* Data for 1700–1950 from N.I.E.S.; data for 2000–7 from FAOSTAT
† Data for 1700–1900 from Neville (1979); data for 1950–2005 from UNPOP

Plate 3

Although overall agricultural expansion has occurred throughout Southeast Asia, the timing and intensity have been quite different not only between the two major subregions but also within them, at least from the mid-nineteenth century onwards. However, during the eighteenth century, according to the sources utilized here, expansion of cultivated land appeared more or less uniform throughout the region, or at least throughout the territories that correspond to the contemporary countries making up Southeast Asia.

Between 1700 and 1800, cultivated land increased by a total of about 25 per cent everywhere, including Burma, Thailand, Cambodia and Vietnam. For example, it grew from 2.8 million to 3.5 million hectares in Burma and from 3.1 million to 3.9 hectares in Vietnam. Then, early in the nineteenth century, the rate of expansion began to accelerate slightly in all four mainland countries. However, Burma and Vietnam broke rank during the 1880s. Over the following 40 years, under the impetus of the respective French and British colonial administrations (Adas 1974, Brocheux and Hemery 1995), the two countries witnessed an exceptional rate of agricultural expansion, with the area of cultivated land doubling in Vietnam and increasing even more in Burma — by ~215 per cent. In Thailand and Cambodia, the real take-off came later. In the case of Cambodia, rapid expansion began in the 1920s and continued until the 1960s, when it slowed down and was then abruptly reversed after the 1975 Khmer Rouge takeover. In Thailand the phase of very rapid expansion also began in the 1920s, strongly encouraged by royal policy (Feeny 1982), and it was sustained for seven decades. Between 1920 and 1990 the area of the country's croplands grew from 4.1 million to 21.7 million hectares (N.I.E.S.), an increase of 530 per cent. This was a unique achievement that was without parallel in the region or elsewhere on the planet, except in Brazil. However, during the 1980s the rate of Thailand's agricultural expansion began to slow down to such an extent that since the 1990s it has become negative — the only such case thus far in contemporary Southeast Asia.

In mainland Southeast Asia, at least until late in the twentieth century, expansion occurred predominantly in the rice sector (Figures 6.1 and 6.2) — although commercial crops, such as rubber in Vietnam (Figures 7.9–7.12), were also involved. In the archipelago countries, however, expansion took place primarily in the plantation sector, with smallholder production of cash crops also heavily involved. Indonesia played a dominant role in the expansion process, which was to be expected given its size and population. During the eighteenth century cropland expanded by some 25 per cent in Indonesia, as elsewhere in the region. Expansion accelerated moderately during the nineteenth century until the 1890s, when the pace was intensified, with a strong rate of increase being maintained until the 1950s. Then, by the 1960s and 1970s, with the transmigration programme coming into full swing, and, more importantly, commercial private plantations being given a free hand to expand, cropland grew in leaps and bounds. As a result, by 2007 Indonesia's — whose land area corresponds to 42 per cent of Southeast Asia's — share of total cropland in the region had reached 37 per cent (~37 million of ~100 million hectares), compared to 27 per cent in 1700 and still less than 30 per cent until the 1930s.

In the Philippines and Malaysia, the other two major agricultural countries of archipelagic Southeast Asia, cropland expansion has been, proportionately, nearly as significant as in Indonesia. In the Philippines, expansion began to accelerate significantly from the 1880s and remained the steadiest in the region until the 1950s. Then, it accelerated even more. However, by the turn of the twenty-first century expansion had levelled down. As for Malaysia, its colonial and postcolonial agricultural history has been closely associated with boom crop expansion, starting with rubber in the 1880s and going on primarily to oil palm by the 1960s.

Overall, cropland is still increasing in the region. As we will see further on, smaller countries, such as Cambodia and Laos, are becoming increasingly involved in the expansion.

Figure 2.5 Southeast Asia: Cropland expansion by country, 1700–2007

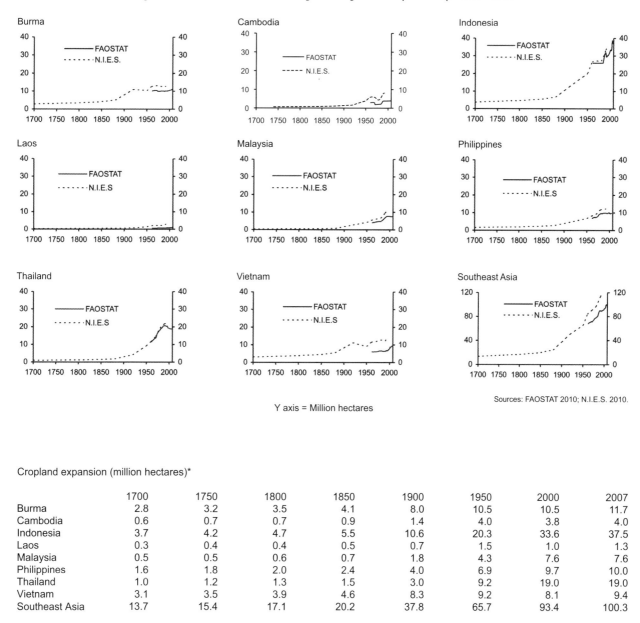

Y axis = Million hectares

Sources: FAOSTAT 2010; N.I.E.S. 2010.

Cropland expansion (million hectares)*

	1700	1750	1800	1850	1900	1950	2000	2007
Burma	2.8	3.2	3.5	4.1	8.0	10.5	10.5	11.7
Cambodia	0.6	0.7	0.7	0.9	1.4	4.0	3.8	4.0
Indonesia	3.7	4.2	4.7	5.5	10.6	20.3	33.6	37.5
Laos	0.3	0.4	0.4	0.5	0.7	1.5	1.0	1.3
Malaysia	0.5	0.5	0.6	0.7	1.8	4.3	7.6	7.6
Philippines	1.6	1.8	2.0	2.4	4.0	6.9	9.7	10.0
Thailand	1.0	1.2	1.3	1.5	3.0	9.2	19.0	19.0
Vietnam	3.1	3.5	3.9	4.6	8.3	9.2	8.1	9.4
Southeast Asia	13.7	15.4	17.1	20.2	37.8	65.7	93.4	100.3

* Data for 1700–1950 from N.I.E.S.; data for 2000 and 2007 from FAOSTAT

Plate 4

Given the different scales used, a detailed comparison of the two sets of graphs (Figures 2.5 and 2.6) is not really possible, even though the correlation between the expansion of cultivated areas and the decrease in forest cover is quite evident in just about every country examined. For example, during the eighteenth century, Burma's cultivated areas gained over 690,000 hectares while its forest cover was reduced by over 630,000 hectares. Between 1920 and 1990, Thailand's massive gain of 17.6 million hectares in cultivated land was accompanied by a loss of nearly 17.2 million hectares of forest cover. After World War II, agricultural expansion accelerated notably in several countries, as did the retreat of the forest. For example, in the Philippines, by then already the most deforested country in the region, forest cover was further reduced by some 5.4 million hectares between 1950 and 1990. This was a figure equivalent to the gain in cultivated areas. Over that 40-year period, the country lost nearly a third of its forest cover. During the same four decades, Thailand also replaced over a third of its forestland with cultivated areas. Also between 1950 and 1990, the trade-off in Malaysia was identical to the trade-off in the Philippines — a country only slightly smaller (~300,000 versus ~330,000 sq. km): an increase of 5.4 million hectares in cropland and an equivalent decrease in forestland. However, in Malaysia, this represented a loss of "only" 19 per cent of forest cover. By 1990, forests still covered ~69 per cent of Malaysia's territory versus 38 per cent of the Philippines'. Since then, the rate of forest loss has even accelerated in both countries, with Malaysia seeing extremely rapid agricultural expansion-cum-deforestation occurring in the states of Sabah and Sarawak on the island of Borneo. The same is happening in Kalimantan, on the Indonesian side of the border. For Indonesia, the loss of some 13 million hectares of forestland between 1950 and 1990 correlates clearly with a gain of 13 million hectares of cropland. Such absolute figures have no equivalent in the region. However, over that 40-year period Indonesia lost "only" 10 per cent of its forestland. Given its size, this works out to an area of ~1,900,000 sq. km, which is 3.7 times Thailand's size. Still, Indonesia's forests covered 65 per cent of the nation's territory in 1990.

Of course, forests do not always and automatically give way to agriculture. This is particularly so in Indonesia, where massive logging — whether legal or illegal — that is sometimes followed by huge forest fires is a primary cause of forest loss. However, more frequently than not — here as elsewhere — deforested areas, or forested areas under swidden cultivation, are eventually turned over to permanent agriculture. This may be due to deliberate policies of agricultural expansion over the forest domain, as with the Malaysian Federal Land Development Agency (FELDA), which was particularly active from the late 1950s until the 1990s in the establishment of pioneer fronts, primarily in the Malayan peninsula; or with the transmigration programme in Indonesia, which, although it was officially interrupted in March 2000, had from the 1950s onwards — thereby replicating a Dutch colonial policy initiated in 1905 — laid the ground for what has become a systematic transfer of agrarian and agricultural pressure from Java and Bali to the so-called outer islands, such as Sumatra and Borneo.

The recent slowdown in forest loss in Thailand and even the reforestation occurring in Vietnam (Meyfroidt and Lambin 2008) have as a corollary an increase in the pace of deforestation in neighbouring Laos and Cambodia. Between 1997 and 2007, the latter lost nearly 2 million hectares or 16 per cent of its total forest cover. Only the Philippines and Indonesia have done "better" (Figures 8.11 and 8.12). At the national scale and on an annual basis, there is no equivalent in the history of the region. The overall consequence is that as a whole, the pace of deforestation in Southeast Asia, which had definitely picked up at least twice since the end of the nineteenth century, is once again accelerating.

Figure 2.6 Southeast Asia: Decrease of forest cover by country, 1700–2007

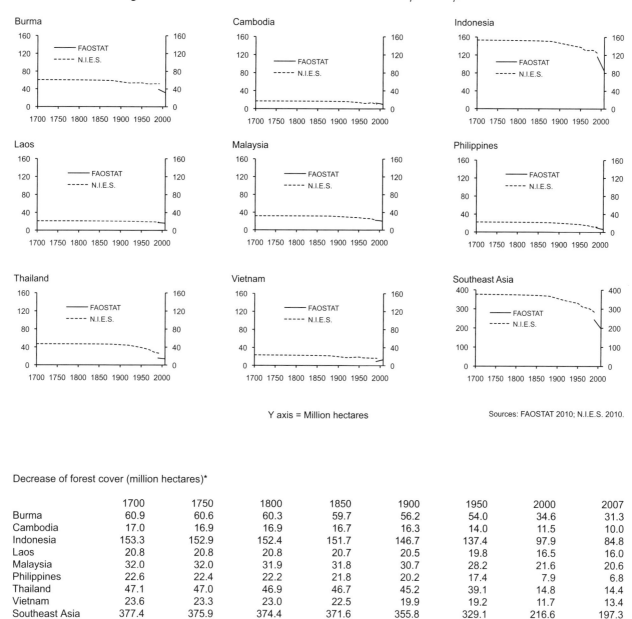

Y axis = Million hectares

Sources: FAOSTAT 2010; N.I.E.S. 2010.

Decrease of forest cover (million hectares)*

	1700	1750	1800	1850	1900	1950	2000	2007
Burma	60.9	60.6	60.3	59.7	56.2	54.0	34.6	31.3
Cambodia	17.0	16.9	16.9	16.7	16.3	14.0	11.5	10.0
Indonesia	153.3	152.9	152.4	151.7	146.7	137.4	97.9	84.8
Laos	20.8	20.8	20.8	20.7	20.5	19.8	16.5	16.0
Malaysia	32.0	32.0	31.9	31.8	30.7	28.2	21.6	20.6
Philippines	22.6	22.4	22.2	21.8	20.2	17.4	7.9	6.8
Thailand	47.1	47.0	46.9	46.7	45.2	39.1	14.8	14.4
Vietnam	23.6	23.3	23.0	22.5	19.9	19.2	11.7	13.4
Southeast Asia	377.4	375.9	374.4	371.6	355.8	329.1	216.6	197.3

* Data for 1700–1950 from N.I.E.S.; data for 2000 and 2007 from FAOSTAT

Plate 5

The list of characteristics, whether geographical, historical, cultural, political, social or economic, that set Brazil apart from Southeast Asia is certainly very long. Yet there are also a certain number of commonalities, embedded in the same realms, that justify a comparison between the largely tropical South American giant and Southeast Asia, particularly its own giant, Indonesia (De Koninck and Capataz 1992). Among these commonalities is an exceptionally dynamic agricultural sector, which is partially a tributary of colonial policies and therefore largely turned towards the export market. There is also, still with reference to the agricultural sector, an exceptional rate of territorial expansion, catering to the national as well as the world markets — to such an extent that in both cases agricultural growth has, at least over the long term, kept up with demographic growth. And, finally, again in both cases, the reduction in forest cover has been accelerating rapidly in parallel with the expansion of cultivated areas.

The evolution of population as well as of cropland and forest cover seems to have been largely similar since the eighteenth century. But, when these are examined more closely, some noticeable differences do appear, particularly since the middle of the twentieth century. Thus, between 1950 and 1990,[*] Brazil's demographic growth has been significantly more rapid, its total population having been multiplied by a factor of 2.8, while Southeast Asia's was multiplied by a factor of 2.5. During the same period, cultivated areas were multiplied respectively by 3.5 and 1.7. In other words, while in Brazil the rate of agricultural expansion overtook that of population growth, in Southeast Asia, it fell behind, at least over that 40-year period. In both cases, the expansion of cultivated areas has been achieved at the expense of forest cover. In the case of Brazil, while cropland expanded by 50 million hectares between 1950 and 1990, forest loss reached some 26 million hectares. The difference between the two figures is either attributable to a delay, in some areas, between the occurrence of deforestation and expansion or to the fact that, in Brazil, expansion was not exclusively achieved over the forest realm but also over areas of savanna land and grasslands, for example in the Matto Grosso region.

But there seems to be an additional and much more meaningful difference concerning the intensity of deforestation. During the same 40-year period, Southeast Asia's forest cover was reduced from 329 to 284 million hectares, a loss of 45 million hectares or nearly 14 per cent. In Brazil, the forest cover receded from 559 million to 533 million hectares, a loss of 26 million hectares, or less than 5 per cent of the original total. In other words, the reduction of Southeast Asia's forest cover — from the start much less extensive than Brazil's, itself nearly twice the size of Southeast Asia — is more significant in absolute terms but even more in proportionate ones. This means that more densely populated and cultivated Southeast Asia imposes a much greater pressure on its forests than Brazil does.

---

[*] As a reference date, we use 1990 rather than a more recent date such as 2000 because, as pointed out earlier, starting from the 1990s there are some significant differences concerning cropland and forest cover data between the two sources used, the Nelson Institute for Environmental Studies and the FAO (cf. figures).

Figure 2.7 Brazil: Population growth, 1700–2050

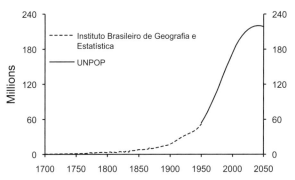

Sources: Instituto Brasileiro de Geografia e Estatística 2010; UNPOP 2010.

Figure 2.8 Brazil: Cropland expansion, 1700–2007

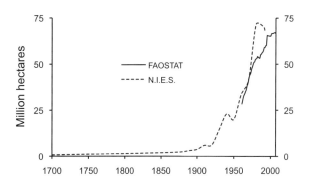

Sources: FAOSTAT 2010; N.I.E.S. 2010.

Figure 2.9 Brazil: Decrease of forest cover, 1700–2007

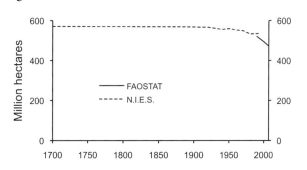

Sources: FAOSTAT 2010; N.I.E.S. 2010.

Population growth (million)*

	1700	1800	1850	1900	1950	2000	2050
Brazil	0.3	3.3	8.0	17.4	54.0	174.2	218.5

Cropland expansion (million hectares)*†

	1700	1750	1800	1850	1900	1950	2000	2007
Brazil	0.7	1.1	1.5	2.0	3.8	20.0	65.2	66.5

Decrease of forest cover (million hectares)†

	1700	1750	1800	1850	1900	1950	2000	2007
Brazil	569.9	569.7	569.4	569.2	568.1	559.2	493.2	471.5

* Data for 1700–1900 from Instituto Brasileiro de Geografia e Estatística; data for 1950–2050 from UNPOP
† Data for 1700–1950 from N.I.E.S.; data for 2000–7 from FAOSTAT

CHAPTER 3

Growth, Development, Urbanization and Globalization

"There is no longer a 'rural sector' which can be considered in splendid isolation, nor are there significant groups of people which can possibly be viewed as being contained in a mode of rural existence."

(Elson 1997: 238)

"It is acknowledged by most scholars that in the first stages of industrialization agriculture has made an important contribution in those countries which have successfully developed."

(Kay 2002: 1094)

Plate 6

If UNPOP estimates prove right, the population of Southeast Asia will total more than 760 million inhabitants by 2050, compared to a little over 175 million in 1950 and nearly 600 million by 2010. Population growth has been significant across the region, particularly in Laos, Malaysia and the Philippines. Over the last six decades, the population of these states increased by an average rate of 2.4 per cent, 2.6 per cent and 2.6 per cent per annum respectively. As elsewhere in Southeast Asia, the bulk of this growth occurred between 1950 and 1990, a period during which regional population grew at an average annual rate of 2.3 per cent. This rate has since been declining as Southeast Asians have increasingly benefited from better sanitary conditions and experienced urbanization as well as economic development. Hence, the region's average annual population growth rate was limited to 1.3 per cent during the past decade and, by the 2040s, should have fallen to a mere 0.3 per cent.

Such a tendency is, of course, consistent with that of regional fertility rates. In 1960, Southeast Asian women each gave birth to 6.2 children on average. The current average is 2.3 children per woman. It has been estimated that the rate will hit a historic low of 1.9 by 2050, well below the 2.05 "population replacement level". In a few decades and throughout the region, fertility rates should have become, once again and as in the 1950s, more homogenous than they are today. For example, Laos' rate is currently an unequalled 4.3 children per woman

while Thailand's already stands at a low 1.9. The population of Thailand is consequently the region's most rapidly ageing. The kingdom is also forecasted to be, by the 2030s, the first country to face a population decline resulting from a classic form of demographic transition. In the late 1970s and early 1980s, Cambodia's population was substantially reduced, but for completely different reasons. Those were the years of the Khmer Rouge regime and the following Vietnamese invasion.

Indonesia, Southeast Asia's most populous country, still accounts for over 40 per cent of the region's population. Having reached an estimated 240 million inhabitants in 2010, its population is still far more numerous than that of any other country in the region. It is followed by the Philippines and Vietnam, whose populations will each surpass 100 million inhabitants in the coming decade. The latter would probably have been more heavily populated had it not introduced a child birth control programme in 1988, the so-called one or two child policy. As for Burma, its fertility rate curve also shows some inconsistencies given its level of development. Although one of Southeast Asia's poorest nations, Burma has fertility rates more akin to those of Malaysia and Thailand than to those of Cambodia and Laos. Jones suggests that Burma's early fertility decline might reflect the "reaction of a formerly well educated population to hard times", while acknowledging the "failure of such an argument to hold for the Philippines" (Jones 1999: 12).[*]

---

[*] Although Singapore is not included in this study, it is worth citing that its own fertility rate is currently at a low 1.3 children/woman, and that it is expected to slowly bounce back halfway through the 2010s.

Figure 3.1 Population and fertility rate by country, 1950–2050*

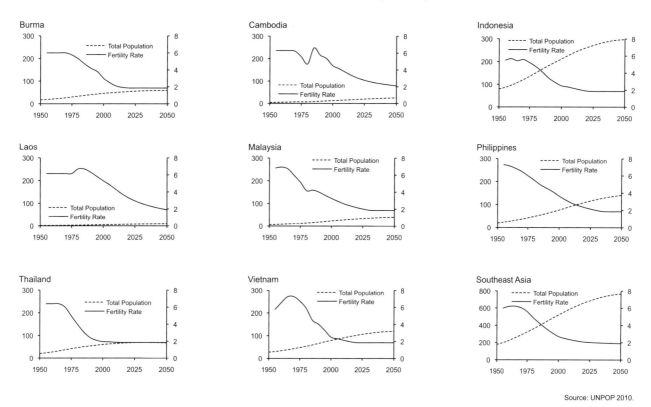

Source: UNPOP 2010.

Left Y axis = Population (million); Right Y axis = Fertility rate (children/woman)

Population (million)

	1950	1960	1970	1980	1990	2000	2005	2010	2025	2050
Burma	17.2	21.1	26.4	33.3	40.1	45.9	48.0	50.1	55.4	58.7
Cambodia	4.3	5.4	6.9	6.7	9.7	12.8	14.0	15.2	19.5	25.1
Indonesia	79.5	95.9	120.5	151.1	182.8	211.7	226.1	239.6	271.2	296.9
Laos	1.5	2.0	2.6	3.1	4.1	5.2	5.7	6.2	7.7	9.3
Malaysia	6.1	8.1	10.9	13.8	18.1	23.3	25.7	27.9	33.8	39.6
Philippines	20.0	27.1	36.6	48.1	61.2	76.2	84.6	93.0	115.9	140.5
Thailand	20.6	27.7	37.2	46.8	54.3	60.7	63.0	65.1	68.8	67.4
Vietnam	27.4	33.6	42.9	53.0	66.2	79.1	85.0	90.8	106.4	120.0
Southeast Asia	178.1	223.1	286.8	359.1	440.6	520.0	557.7	594.2	686.3	766.6

Fertility rate (children per woman)

	1950	1960	1970	1980	1990	2000	2005	2010	2025	2050
Burma		6.0	6.0	5.3	4.2	3.0	2.5	2.1	1.9	1.9
Cambodia		6.3	6.2	4.7	5.8	4.5	4.1	3.7	2.8	2.1
Indonesia		5.7	5.6	4.7	3.4	2.5	2.4	2.2	1.9	1.9
Laos		6.2	6.2	6.7	6.3	5.3	4.8	4.3	2.9	1.9
Malaysia		6.9	5.9	4.2	4.0	3.3	2.9	2.6	2.0	1.9
Philippines		7.1	6.5	5.5	4.6	3.6	3.2	2.8	2.2	1.9
Thailand		6.4	6.0	4.0	2.4	2.0	1.9	1.9	1.9	1.9
Vietnam		6.6	7.3	5.9	4.0	2.5	2.3	2.1	1.9	1.9
Southeast Asia		6.2	6.0	4.8	3.6	2.7	2.5	2.3	2.0	1.9

* Data for 2009 onwards are estimates.

Plate 7

Demographers hold that the year 2007 marked a historic turning point, as the planet's number of city dwellers then began to exceed that of rural dwellers. In Southeast Asia, such a dramatic shift is expected to occur sometime between 2010 and 2015, when the number of city dwellers will reach over 325 million, compared to some 285 million in 2010. Urbanization in the region began to accelerate significantly during the 1950s, and by the turn of the century the urban population's average annual growth rate stood at 3.5 per cent. It is expected not to drop below 2 per cent before 2020, and the region's urban population is forecasted to exceed 560 million by 2050. As for the number of rural dwellers, it has been growing until recently. It doubled between 1950 and 2000, when it peaked at 313 million. Since then, the number of Southeast Asians living in the countryside has been declining. By 2050, it is expected to return to about 200 million, the same number as in 1965.

Until 1965 the Philippines remained Southeast Asia's most urbanized country, but it still had over two-thirds of its population living in the countryside. Today, that country is home to the region's biggest megalopolis, Manila, whose population since 1950 has soared from 1.5 million to some 11 million inhabitants and is expected to reach 15 million in 2025. As for Malaysia, its urbanization ratio overtook that of the Philippines by the early 1970s, when it launched its New Economic Policy. It has since become the region's most urbanized country (excluding Singapore and Brunei), and is expected to still be so in 2050, when almost 90 per cent of its population is expected to be living in cities.

However, Indonesia was, is and will remain the country with the largest number of urban dwellers. In 2005, Indonesian cities already totalled more than 100 million inhabitants, a figure predicted to reach 235 million by 2050. Some 9 million people live in Jakarta, in the core of the much wider Jakarta-Bogor-Depok-Tangerang-Bekasi Metropolitan Area. In 2000 Jabodetabek already accounted for 21 million people, a figure expected to reach 26 million in 2020 (Asri 2005: 2309).

Along with Jabodetabek, Bangkok is considered as the region's other emerging "urban mega region" (Yusuf 2007: 2). With nearly 7 million inhabitants, the capital of Thailand is home to about one-third of that country's city dwellers. These city dwellers themselves account for a third of the population of the kingdom, the most urbanized country in mainland Southeast Asia. Thailand's urbanization ratio is growing at a slower pace than that of its neighbours, particularly Laos. However, the forecast is that Laos' own urbanization ratio will exceed that of Thailand in the coming years and reach almost 50 per cent around 2025. Vientiane, which hosted less than half a million citizens in 1990, should by then be home to some 1.5 million people. Nevertheless, in 2010, Vietnam's 26 million urban dwellers remain mainland Southeast Asia's most numerous. Some 5 million live in Ho Chi Minh City, almost 4.5 million in Hanoi and 2 million in Haiphong. As for Cambodia, its experience is unique in that it went through a traumatic experience of forced "deurbanization" under the Khmer Rouge. But since the latter's downfall, the Cambodian pace of urbanization has also been very rapid.

Figure 3.2 Urban and rural population by country, 1950–2050*

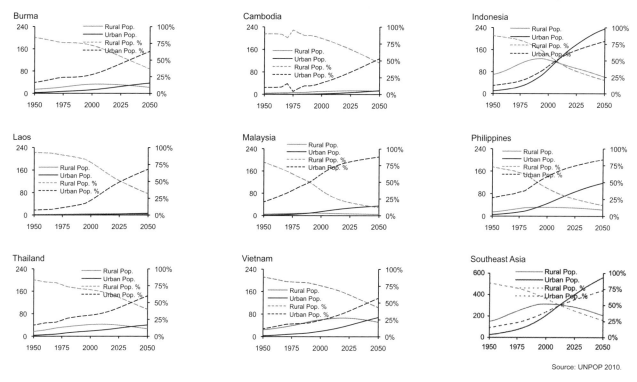

Left Y axis = Population (million); Right Y axis = Rural/urban population percentage

Source: UNPOP 2010.

Rural population (million)

	1950	1975	2000	2025	2050
Burma	14.4	22.7	33.0	30.7	21.6
Cambodia	3.9	6.8	10.6	13.0	11.7
Indonesia	69.7	109.2	122.8	92.5	61.0
Laos	1.4	2.6	4.1	3.9	3.0
Malaysia	4.9	7.6	8.8	6.6	4.8
Philippines	14.6	27.1	31.6	29.5	22.6
Thailand	17.2	32.2	41.8	39.7	27.0
Vietnam	24.2	39.0	59.9	65.9	51.6
Southeast Asia	150.6	247.8	313.3	283.1	205.0

Urban population (million)

	1950	1975	2000	2025	2050
Burma	2.8	7.1	12.9	24.7	37.1
Cambodia	0.4	0.3	2.2	6.5	13.4
Indonesia	9.9	26.2	88.9	178.7	235.9
Laos	0.1	0.3	1.1	3.8	6.3
Malaysia	1.2	4.6	14.4	27.2	34.8
Philippines	5.4	14.9	44.6	86.4	117.8
Thailand	3.4	10.0	18.9	29.1	40.4
Vietnam	3.2	9.0	19.2	40.5	68.4
Southeast Asia	15.4	23.2	39.7	58.7	73.3

Rural population (%)

	1950	1975	2000	2025	2050
Burma	84	76	72	55	37
Cambodia	90	96	83	67	47
Indonesia	88	81	58	34	21
Laos	93	89	78	51	32
Malaysia	80	62	38	19	12
Philippines	73	64	41	25	16
Thailand	84	76	69	58	40
Vietnam	88	81	76	62	43
Southeast Asia	85	77	60	41	27

Urban population (%)

	1950	1975	2000	2025	2050
Burma	16	24	28	45	63
Cambodia	10	4	17	33	53
Indonesia	12	19	42	66	79
Laos	7	11	22	49	68
Malaysia	20	38	62	81	88
Philippines	27	36	59	75	84
Thailand	16	24	31	42	60
Vietnam	12	19	24	38	57
Southeast Asia	15	23	40	59	73

* Data for 2009 onwards are estimates.

Plate 8

Since 1955, as in most of the world's regions, improved sanitary conditions and access to either basic or advanced medical care has brought about a significant improvement in life expectancy throughout Southeast Asia. This has been partly driven by a drastic reduction of the regional infant mortality rate, or the number of deaths occurring per 1,000 births. In the region, the latter stood at 166 in the early 1950s, a time when the world average was just above 150. In 2010, these values reached 28 and 43 deaths per 1,000 births respectively. Progress has, in fact, been much more important in Southeast Asia than in most regions of the world. As for the average regional life expectancy, it grew from 41 years in 1955 to about 70 in 2010 and is currently forecasted to reach 78 years by 2050. This is just below the current average life expectancy in the so-called more developed regions.

Since the 1950s, Cambodia has been the only country where the improvement in life expectancy has met with a setback. This of course occurred under the Khmer Rouge regime, during which that indicator fell from 45 years in 1970 to 31 years a decade later. It has since bounced back and is now similar to that of Laos. During the 50-year period leading to 2010, life expectancy improved the most in Indonesia, from 40 to 69 years. Such a success is attributable, at least in part, to the establishment during the 1970s and 1980s of district hospitals and subdistrict health care centres throughout the country (Kristiansen and Santoso 2006: 247). Unsurprisingly, the other regional forerunners include Thailand, the sole nation where life expectancy already surpassed 50 years in 1955. This country however copes with an important and increasing income gap, with the average per capita income having grown almost three times faster in Bangkok than in the Northeast region between 1990 and the beginning of the twenty-first century (Cornia and Court 2001: 29). Relatively widespread rural poverty explains why Thailand's average life expectancy now stands behind that of Malaysia. Currently enjoying Southeast Asia's highest life expectancy (again leaving aside Singaporeans), Malaysians born in 2010 can expect to live for 74 years. Vietnam's average life expectancy also outpaced that of Thailand, having experienced a rate of growth almost as strong as that encountered in Indonesia.

In 1980, the literacy rate was still below 70 per cent in all the region's countries except the Philippines, Thailand and Vietnam. By 2000, it was more than 85 per cent in all countries except Burma, Cambodia and Laos. Such progress is partly attributable to national policies promoting the use of national over regional and vernacular languages. However, as Kosonen (2005: 137) suggests about Cambodia, Laos and Thailand, "the present emphasis on language planning and literacy development may even widen the educational gap between the minority and majority populations".

Figure 3.3 Life expectancy and literacy rate by country, 1955–2050*

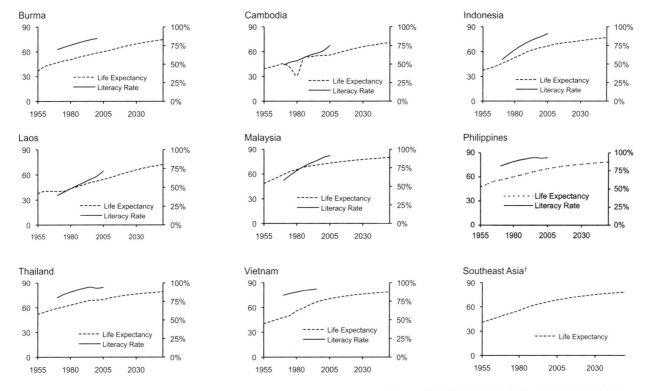

Sources: UNPOP 2010; World dataBank 2010; UNESCO 2010.

Left Y axis = Life expectancy (years); Right Y axis = Adult literacy rate

Life expectancy (years)

	1955	1975	2000	2025	2050
Burma	37	49	59	68	75
Cambodia	39	40	56	64	71
Indonesia	38	49	65	72	77
Laos	38	40	53	64	72
Malaysia	49	63	72	77	80
Philippines	48	58	69	75	79
Thailand	52	61	69	76	79
Vietnam	40	50	69	75	79
Southeast Asia	41	53	67	74	78

Literacy rate (%)

	1975	1985	1995	2005
Burma	73	78	83	
Cambodia	53	58	64	75
Indonesia	63	75	84	91
Laos	44	52	61	72
Malaysia	65	76	84	91
Philippines	85	90	94	93
Thailand	84	90	94	94
Vietnam	85	89	91	

* Data for 2009 onwards are previsions.
† Regional literacy rate data are not available.

Plate 9

According to the FAO, people whose daily dietary energy supply amounts to less than 2,200 kilocalories (kcal) have "very low levels of food consumption" (Bruinsma 2003: 5). The organization also states that malnourishment is, globally, a receding problem: 57 per cent of the world's population ingested less than 2,200kcal a day in the mid-1960s, compared to 10 per cent "of a much larger population" in the early years of the twenty-first century (Ibid.: 30). As for per capita protein intake, the UN has set its recommended minimum at 52 grams a day (Fa 2006: 120).

By 2000, Southeast Asians consumed on average more food and protein than the minimum recommended on a daily basis. Cambodia then had the most worrying food security record, as both its calorie and protein consumption levels remained similar to those recorded some 40 years earlier. Khmer Rouge agricultural policies were to blame for the chronic malnourishment of the Cambodian population during the late 1970s, when its calorie intake reached a regional low. As for Cambodia's current food problems, they are partly attributable to the remaining presence of numerous land mines. Planted by belligerent parties until 1997, these have continued to hamper agricultural production (Douglas 2006: 130). This appears particularly dramatic taking into consideration that Cambodia's average per capita calorie consumption was the region's second highest, behind Malaysia's, in the early 1960s.

On the other hand, the average Burmese and Indonesian now have access to much more appropriate food rations than they did in the early 1960s. In those days, malnourishment was particularly acute in Indonesia, where average daily per capita

protein consumption stood below 35 grams, an average value unseen in the region since. By 2007, the average per capita calorie and protein consumption in both countries was more or less equivalent to the regions'. In fact, Burma's own protein intake was among Southeast Asia's highest, standing just behind those of Malaysia and Vietnam. Also in 2007, while Laotians still got 55 per cent of their protein intake from rice, the regional average was down to some 40 per cent. This illustrates the declining preponderance of rice as Southeast Asia's staple food, as that value for the region stood at above 50 per cent in the early 1960s. Meat, fish and seafood have gained importance in the regional diet. Together, they accounted for 27 per cent of regional protein consumption in 2007, against less than 17 per cent in 1961. Over the same period, the relative contribution of maize and wheat to the region's protein intake has also been on the rise, increasing from 4 per cent to 10 per cent.

Rice is less important in the Malaysian diet, providing in 2007 the average Malaysian with only 17 per cent of his daily protein intake. Indeed, for both historical and contemporary socioeconomic reasons, sources of protein are more diversified in the Malaysian diet than in any other Southeast Asian nation. It is also in Malaysia that the proportion of either overweight or obese people (namely people with a body mass index [bmi] ≥25) is the highest. However, this does not stand comparison with what is encountered in North America, where in 2007 the average per capita daily consumption had reached over 3,700kcal and 112 grams of protein, against less than 3,000kcal and 80 grams of protein among Malaysians.

Figure 3.4 Calorie and protein consumption by country, 1961–2007

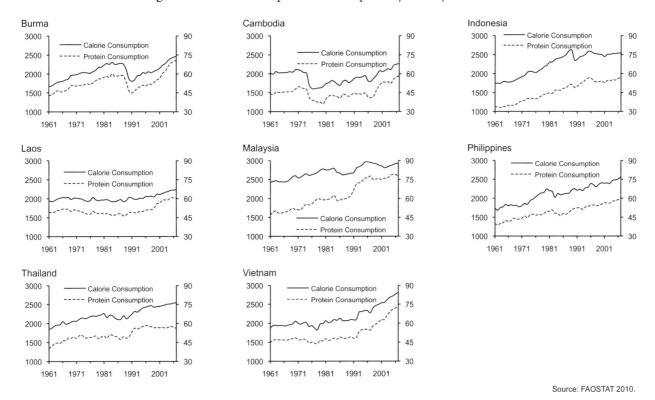

Left Y axis = Calories consumed (kcal/capita/day); Right Y axis = Protein consumed (gm/capita/day)

Calorie consumption (kcal/capita/day)

	1961–63	1971–73	1981–83	1991–93	2001–3	2007
Burma	1,697	2,011	2,254	1,867	2,216	2,465
Cambodia	2,023	2,075	1,777	1,897	2,091	2,268
Indonesia	1,745	1,969	2,327	2,429	2,487	2,538
Laos	1,939	2,003	1,964	1,995	2,138	2,240
Malaysia	2,447	2,573	2,761	2,772	2,831	2,923
Philippines	1,726	1,834	2,135	2,216	2,397	2,565
Thailand	1,885	2,107	2,212	2,286	2,469	2,539
Vietnam	1,920	1,997	2,038	2,158	2,567	2,816

Protein consumption (gm/capita/day)

	1961–63	1971–73	1981–83	1991–93	2001–3	2007
Burma	44	51	58	47	60	71
Cambodia	44	49	42	44	53	58
Indonesia	33	39	45	52	54	57
Laos	49	50	48	49	58	61
Malaysia	49	52	59	70	76	78
Philippines	40	45	50	52	56	60
Thailand	42	50	50	55	57	56
Vietnam	46	47	47	50	64	74

Source: FAOSTAT 2010.

Plate 10

Between 1970 and 2008, Southeast Asia's GDP was multiplied 43-fold, growing from $35.5 billion to $1,515 trillion. During the same period, the annual regional economic growth rate, *when calculated in current dollars*, averaged 10.4 per cent (way above the world's 8 per cent, but nonetheless inferior to China's, which stood at 10.7 per cent),[*] with a minor setback in the mid-1980s, and a major slump during the 1997–98 Asian crisis, which particularly affected Indonesia, Malaysia and Thailand, the region's three most economically extraverted economies among those examined here. Indeed, the regional GDP fell by 6.5 per cent in 1997, and lost about a third of its value the following year. The pre-1997 level of activity was only regained by 2004. Despite this, Southeast Asia's overall economic rate of growth has largely surpassed the world average, allowing the region to double its share of the global GDP from 1 per cent to 2 per cent between 1970 and 2008. Given that the region's population also grew substantially but at a much less rapid rate, the annual regional GDP per capita was multiplied by over 20, from $125 to more than $2,600.

An additional striking feature is the increase in the differentiation among Southeast Asian economies which now diverge much more than they did some four decades ago. For instance, in the early 1970s, Malaysia's GDP per capita was the most important in the region (among nations considered here), reaching almost nine times that of Laos, the lowest. In 2008, as Malaysia still held the first rank, its GDP per capita represented 9.6 times that of Laos and more than 14 times that of Burma, which overtook the $1 a day threshold only in 2007. Malaysia is also the country that experienced the most significant economic growth since the early 1970s, as its GDP was, in 2008, 50 times larger, having grown at an average rate of 10.9 per cent per year. Consequently, Malaysia's GDP represented about 15 per cent of the regional total in 2008, compared to 10 per cent in 1970. It has grown much faster than Thailand's, the region's second most important economy, whose relative share in Southeast Asia's GDP had fallen back to 19 per cent in 2008, where it stood in the early 1970s.

Indonesia is not only Southeast Asia's most populated country; it also constitutes the regional economic powerhouse. Since 1970, its GDP has always represented more than 25 per cent of the regional total. In 2008, it amounted to nearly 34 per cent. During the same period the Indonesian GDP was multiplied 48-fold — thanks to an average 10.7 per cent annual rate of growth — in spite of the country having been the hardest hit during the Asian crisis: in 1998 alone, Indonesia's GDP fell by a record 66 per cent.

Vietnam was the least affected by the Asian crisis, during which its GDP actually kept on growing, although at a slower pace. This is partly explained by its control over its non-convertible currency, and by the fact that "the failure to liberalize the capital account had, in retrospect, protected Vietnam from contracting the East Asian contagion" (Sepehri and Akram-Lodhi 2005: 558). Vietnam had however experienced its own crisis in the early 1980s, when socialist style reforms initiated after the 1975 reunification had led to a two-year (1980–81) slump in the GDP. It took the Vietnamese economy more than ten years to recover, thanks largely to the reforms (*Doi Moi*) which began in 1986.

---

[*] When calculated in constant 2005 dollars, Southeast Asia's average economic growth rate reached 5.8 per cent over the same period, compared to the world's 3.2 per cent and China's 9 per cent.

Figure 3.5 GDP and GDP per capita by country, 1970–2008

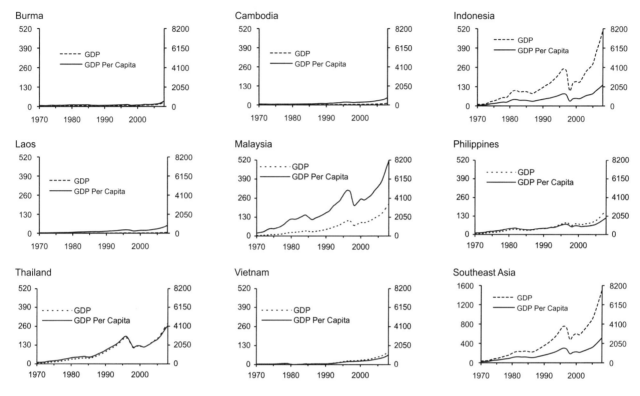

Left Y axis = GDP (billion $); Right Y axis = GDP per capita ($)

Source: UNSTATS 2010.

Gross domestic product (billion $)

	1970–72	1980–82	1990–92	2000–2	2008
Burma	2.7	6.0	5.5	8.4	28.7
Cambodia	0.6	0.6	1.7	4.0	11.2
Indonesia	10.7	94.8	139.8	173.7	510.8
Laos	0.1	0.4	1.0	1.7	5.3
Malaysia	4.4	26.4	52.7	95.8	221.4
Philippines	7.4	35.1	47.6	74.6	168.6
Thailand	7.6	34.6	98.4	121.7	282.2
Vietnam	3.0	2.2	8.0	33.0	90.6
Southeast Asia	39.1	218.8	401.8	608.0	1,515.8

Gross domestic product per capita ($)

	1970–72	1980–82	1990–92	2000–2	2008
Burma	99	174	132	179	578
Cambodia	89	93	174	306	769
Indonesia	89	630	772	834	2,247
Laos	45	119	232	307	858
Malaysia	395	1,871	2,829	4,031	8,197
Philippines	196	709	743	942	1,866
Thailand	199	715	1,711	1,931	4,187
Vietnam	69	40	118	413	1,041
Southeast Asia	135	601	896	1,159	2,633

Plate 11

The agricultural sector remains the first job provider in Southeast Asia (Figure 4.7), but its contribution to the region's GDP is relatively much less important. Since the 1960s, the share of agriculture in most countries has been dropping rapidly as those of industry and services have grown correspondingly. The only exception is Burma. Agricultural value added represented a third of its national GDP in the early 1960s; by the early 1990s it had reached nearly 60 per cent. That agriculture's relative contribution to Burma's economy has continued to increase is closely linked to the country's overall economic stagnation. In fact, as will be shown later, several subsectors of Burma's agriculture have themselves stagnated since the early 1960s. Agriculture contributed over 50 per cent of Laos' GDP until 2002 but this share has since been declining rapidly, reaching about 35 per cent 2008. At the other end of the spectrum, Malaysia's and Thailand's agricultural outputs are the least important in relative terms. Since 1960, the contribution of agriculture to GDP has evolved similarly in the two countries: it represented a third of their economic activity in the early 1960s, receded during the next 40 years, and has stabilized at about 10 per cent since the early years of the twenty-first century.

Indonesia has experienced the most rapid industrialization of all Southeast Asian states. This transition was exceptionally rapid between the mid-1960s and mid-1970s. From 12.6 per cent in 1965, industrial production's contribution to the archipelago nation's GDP had climbed to about 35 per cent some ten years later. During the same period, the relative economic importance of the country's agriculture declined correspondingly. By 2008, Indonesia's industrial output provided nearly 50 per cent of its GDP. The same threshold was reached even earlier in Vietnam, in 2003, the result of an accelerating industrialization since the advent of *Doi Moi*. In the Philippines however, industrial production provided only 31.7 per cent of the GDP in 2008, almost the same as in the early 1960s.

The Philippines is the country with the largest service sector. In 2008, services accounted for nearly 55 per cent of the national GDP. The service sector is also the most important contributor to Thailand's and Malaysia's GDP, accounting for about half of their economic activity since 2000. Malaysia, the Philippines and Thailand also stand out as the most literate nations in Southeast Asia (Figure 3.3).

The literacy rate remains significantly lower in Laos and Cambodia, where, in 2008, services nevertheless constituted a more significant component of the national economy than either agriculture or industry. In Cambodia, this is largely linked to the exceptional weight of external assistance which in 1998 still accounted for 14 per cent of the country's GDP or 167 per cent of government revenues (Godfrey *et al.* 2002: 359).

Figure 3.6 GDP structure by country, 1960–2008

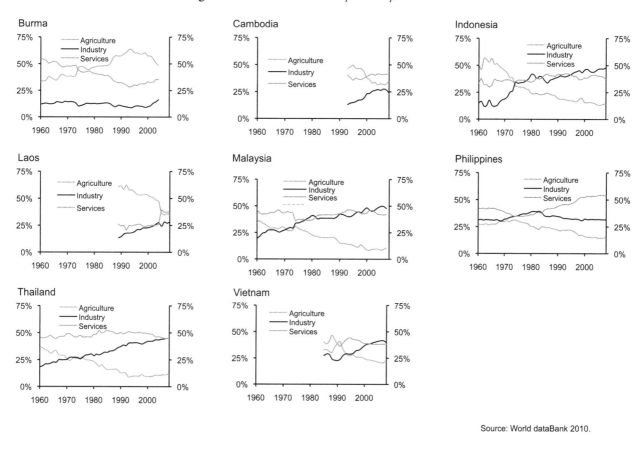

Source: World dataBank 2010.

Agriculture (%)

	1960–62	1970–72	1980–82	1990–92	2000–2	2008
Burma	34	38	47	59	56	
Cambodia					36	35
Indonesia	51	42	24	19	15	14
Laos				60	51	35
Malaysia	35	28	22	15	9	
Philippines	27	30	24	22	15	15
Thailand	35	25	21	12	9	12
Vietnam				38	24	22

Industry (%)

	1960–62	1970–72	1980–82	1990–92	2000–2	2008
Burma	12	14	13	10	11	
Cambodia					24	24
Indonesia	14	22	40	40	46	48
Laos				16	24	28
Malaysia	22	29	40	42	47	
Philippines	31	33	39	34	32	32
Thailand	20	27	29	38	42	44
Vietnam				25	38	40

Services (%)

	1960–62	1970–72	1980–82	1990–92	2000–2	2008
Burma	50	48	40	31	33	
Cambodia					40	41
Indonesia	34	36	36	41	39	37
Laos	42		23	25	37	
Malaysia	45	44	39	43	45	
Philippines		38	37	45	53	53
Thailand		48	50	50	49	44
Vietnam				38	39	38

Plate 12

Southeast Asian nations' trade has soared since the end of World War II. In 1950, the sum of imports and exports for the eight states covered in this study amounted to less than $10 billion. Fifty-eight years later, total regional trade value had reached nearly $2 trillion and the trade surplus over $50 billion, or some 3 per cent of the total. Southeast Asian economies and economic growth rely increasingly on exports, a feature also illustrated by the rapid growth of the regional export/GDP ratio, which stood at 18 per cent in 1970 and over 60 per cent four decades later. An important and growing share of this trade occurred between the countries of Southeast Asia themselves, reversing the trend that had prevailed until the late 1970s. Since the 1950s, the region's extraregional trade had been growing faster than intraregional trade (De Koninck and Comtois 1980). In 1977, the region's internal trade represented 17 per cent of the region's total trade. By 2005, this proportion had increased to 25 per cent (Lindberg and Alvstam 2007: 269).

After Singapore, Malaysia is Southeast Asia's greatest trading nation, its exports totalling nearly $210 billion in 2008. This amounted to about a fifth of all Southeast Asian exports and accounted for 95 per cent of the Malaysian GDP. Malaysia's trade surplus then reached some $45 billion. Thailand trades goods and services for an amount similar to that of the regional leader, although its commerce is much more balanced than Malaysia's, the kingdom's surplus being much more modest. As the third most important trading nation in the region, Indonesia distinguishes itself from its neighbours as it recorded trade surpluses in all but two years

between 1950 and 2008, something even Malaysia had not achieved. The Indonesian economy is also, proportionately, one of the least extraverted in Southeast Asia, with an export/GDP ratio amounting to 28.8 per cent in 2008. The sole countries with lower ratios then were Laos and Burma, with 20.3 per cent and 24.4 per cent respectively.

In the Philippines, external trade also took off in the early 1970s, as it did in Malaysia, Thailand and Indonesia. More often than not, however, the Philippines has run annual trade deficits. The financial and monetary impacts of this apparently structural problem could turn out to be very damaging were the country not benefiting from its expatriate workers' massive remittance inflows (Lim 2000: 1288). These inbound money transfers are among the most important in the world and amounted to more than $18 billion in 2008 (UNCTAD 2010). The same year, the Philippines recorded an $11.3 billion trade deficit.

Except in Thailand, trade expansion began much later among mainland states. In spite of this, Vietnam's external trade is now greater than that of the Philippines, as it became the fourth most important trading nation in Southeast Asia in 2007. Vietnam is also the country having to cope with the most important trade deficit: in 2008, it had reached $17.5 billion. In relative terms, only Cambodia did as poorly. As for Burma, the total value of its trade was equivalent to that of Cambodia, although the two countries were following opposite paths. Profiting from high energy prices, Burma in 2008 recorded a surplus of $2.7 billion, equivalent to nearly a quarter its total trade value.

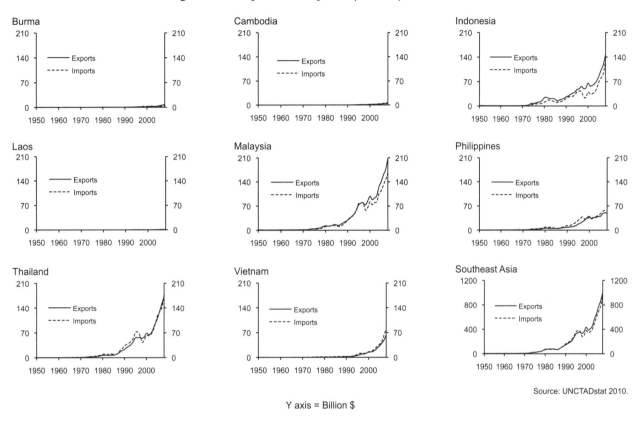

Figure 3.7 Imports and exports by country, 1950–2008

Y axis = Billion $

Source: UNCTADstat 2010.

Exports (billion $)

	1950–52	1960–62	1970–72	1980–82	1990–92	2000–2	2008
Burma	0.2	0.2	0.1	0.4	0.4	2.4	7.0
Cambodia	0.0	0.1	0.0	0.0	0.2	1.6	4.3
Indonesia	1.0	0.8	1.4	23.8	29.9	60.6	147.6
Laos	0.0	0.0	0.1	0.0	0.1	0.3	1.1
Malaysia	1.1	1.1	1.7	12.2	34.9	93.2	209.7
Philippines	0.4	0.6	1.1	5.5	8.9	36.3	49.0
Thailand	0.3	0.4	0.9	6.8	28.0	67.3	172.9
Vietnam	0.1	0.1	0.0	0.4	2.4	15.4	62.9
Southeast Asia	4.4	4.5	7.2	73.8	165.6	409.1	1,003.8

Imports (billion $)

	1950–52	1960–62	1970–72	1980–82	1990–92	2000–2	2008
Burma	0.1	0.2	0.2	0.4	0.5	2.5	4.3
Cambodia	0.0	0.1	0.1	0.2	0.3	2.1	6.4
Indonesia	0.8	0.7	1.2	13.7	25.0	36.9	129.8
Laos	0.0	0.0	0.1	0.1	0.2	0.5	1.4
Malaysia	0.7	0.9	1.5	11.6	35.3	78.6	164.4
Philippines	0.5	0.8	1.3	8.3	13.8	36.4	60.3
Thailand	0.3	0.5	1.4	9.2	37.1	62.8	178.8
Vietnam	0.3	0.2	0.6	1.4	2.5	17.2	80.4
Southeast Asia	4.0	4.8	9.3	72.1	182.3	360.7	948.4

Plate 13

Unfortunately, export data provided by the World Bank are sparse and inconsistent. In addition, the "other" category appears too broad, as it includes anything from natural resources to services. Another inconsistency concerns the Philippines' exports of manufactured products, which allegedly "jumped" from 41.5 per cent to 83.7 per cent of overall exports between 1995 and 1996, on the eve of the Asian crisis. Accordingly, its "other" exports followed an opposite path. Chances are that these somewhat awkward data hide methodological changes in the Philippines' accounting standards. In addition, data are often scanty for the four less developed mainland countries. There is also some correlation between trade data availability and WTO membership. For instance, Cambodia and Vietnam both recently joined the organization (in 2004 and 2007 respectively), and this might explain why more information about their exports has been rendered public since the mid-1990s. However, the same logic does not hold for Burma. Although it joined the then newly created WTO in 1995, the country has since remained completely mute about the structure of its exports, as it had mostly done since the mid-1970s. The sole exception to this occurred in the early 1990s, in the midst of the negotiations surrounding Burma's admission to the organization.

Among the countries for which data are more readily available, namely Indonesia, Malaysia, the Philippines and Thailand, Indonesia is the one where industrial products constitute the smallest share of overall exports. Since 2000, manufactured goods have contributed an average 52 per cent of the archipelagic country's exports, a level far below that of the two other archipelagic nations as well as Thailand. While Indonesia's economy is the largest in the region, it is also the one where manufactured exports' relative importance started increasing the latest. For instance, industrial goods only accounted for a quarter of Indonesian exports in the late 1980s, a level Thailand had reached at the beginning of the same decade. Concurrently, out of the same four countries, Indonesia is where foodstuff (agricultural raw materials + food) constitutes the greatest share of exports, still accounting for almost a quarter of total overseas sales in 2008.

In Thailand, the relative importance of manufactured exports was the earliest to grow significantly. That indicator first exceeded 25 per cent in 1980, reached the 50 per cent threshold in 1987 and averaged 75 per cent between 2000 and 2008. Malaysia has followed a similar path, although its transition was confirmed a few years later and occurred a little more rapidly. Also, driven by its overseas rice sales, Thailand's food exports still accounted for over 13 per cent of all its exports in 2008, or twice as much as those of the Philippines. Among the two archipelago nations and Thailand, the Philippines is indeed the country where the share of food exports decreased the most, starting from above 50 per cent in the mid-1970s and reaching a low 4.6 per cent two decades later. Among factors explaining this are the trade liberalization measures initiated following the end of the Marcos regime, from the mid-1980s onwards (Lim 2000: 1287–9), including the lowering of import taxes on overseas foodstuff — a "gift" to the United States, then its leading trading partner — which badly hurt the country's agriculture.

Figure 3.8 Export structure by country, 1962–2008

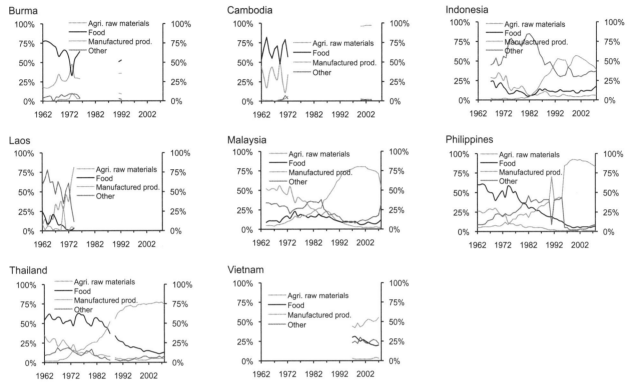

Source: World dataBank 2010.

Agricultural raw materials (%)

	1965	1975	1985	1995	2008
Burma	19	30			
Cambodia	36				
Indonesia		12	6	7	6
Laos	20				
Malaysia	50	34	18	6	2
Philippines	25	10	5	1	1
Thailand	30	12	9	5	5
Vietnam (2007)					3

Food (%)

	1965	1975	1985	1995	
Burma	75	59			
Cambodia	63				
Indonesia		8	10	11	
Laos	12				
Malaysia	11	23	17	10	
Philippines	59	57	27	13	
Thailand	56	63	46	19	
Vietnam (2007)					

Manufactured products (%)

	1965	1975	1985	1995	2008
Burma		3			
Cambodia	1				
Indonesia		1	13	51	39
Laos	6				
Malaysia	5	17	27	75	54
Philippines	6	12	27	42	83
Thailand	2	15	38	73	74
Vietnam (2007)					55

Other (%)

	1965	1975	1985	1995	
Burma	6	8			
Cambodia					
Indonesia		79	71	31	
Laos	62				
Malaysia	34	26	38	9	
Philippines	10	21	41	44	
Thailand	12	10	7	3	
Vietnam (2007)					

CHAPTER 4

The Relative Decline of Agricultural Employment

"The point, however, is that the rural producers of today are productive and enduring only insofar as they have moved from being peasants into new and different worlds of production and, consequently, of social and economic life."

(Elson 1997: 241)

"… any program that robs rural people of their foothold on the land must be firmly rejected".

(Murray Li 2011: 281)

Plate 14

Since the 1950s, the number of Southeast Asians still depending on agriculture for their livelihood, wholly or partially, has continued to increase across the region, except in Malaysia. This increase is largely attributable to demographic growth, which, although it has been slowing down, has remained relatively strong everywhere (Figure 3.2), even in Malaysia, the most urbanized and industrialized of the eight countries examined here. However, percentage wise, reliance on agriculture has been systematically receding everywhere, with the evolution in numbers and percentages following very different rhythms in the two major regions and the countries that make them up.

Significant differences appear between the mainland and archipelagic countries. On the mainland, agricultural population more than doubled from 1950 to 2010, while in the archipelago it rose by less than 60 per cent. In terms of percentage of overall population, the relative importance of agricultural population dropped from over 80 per cent to below 60 per cent among mainland countries and from almost 75 per cent to less than 35 per cent among the archipelago ones. In other words, the deagrarianization process is more advanced and proceeding more rapidly in the latter region. But, within each of the two large regions, there also exist substantial differences.

Among mainland countries, Thailand stands out. Not only has its dependence on agriculture dropped to levels approaching those that prevail in Indonesia and the Philippines, but since the 1970s that drop has been particularly significant, even more so than in those two countries. As for Vietnam, Burma and Cambodia, their evolution has been more or less parallel, their ratio of agricultural population currently being nearly equivalent. However, Laotians are still the ones that have the least livelihood options outside of agriculture. As a result, the country's agricultural population more than tripled over the 60-year period and still accounted in 2010 for nearly 75 per cent of the national total.

Within Southeast Asia, Malaysia stands out in several ways. First, as mentioned above, it is the only country where agricultural population has actually declined in absolute numbers since 1950. Second, percentage wise, the acceleration in the reduction of that population began in the 1960s, earlier than in any of the other seven countries. Third, it has by now and by far reached the lowest ratio of agricultural population to non-agricultural population. Amounting to less than 12 per cent in 2010, this ratio is way below what prevails in all the other countries and also significantly below the overall Southeast Asian average, which stands at just below 45 per cent. In itself, the latter figure appears striking. Notwithstanding the region's very rapid urbanization and industrialization since the 1950s, nearly half of its population still relies wholly or partially on agriculture for its livelihood.

Figure 4.1 Agricultural population by country, 1950–2010*

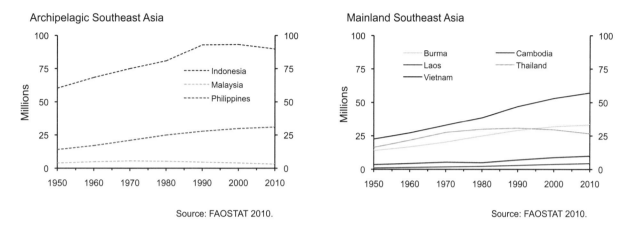

Source: FAOSTAT 2010.

Source: FAOSTAT 2010.

Figure 4.2 Percentage of agricultural population in total population by country, 1950–2010

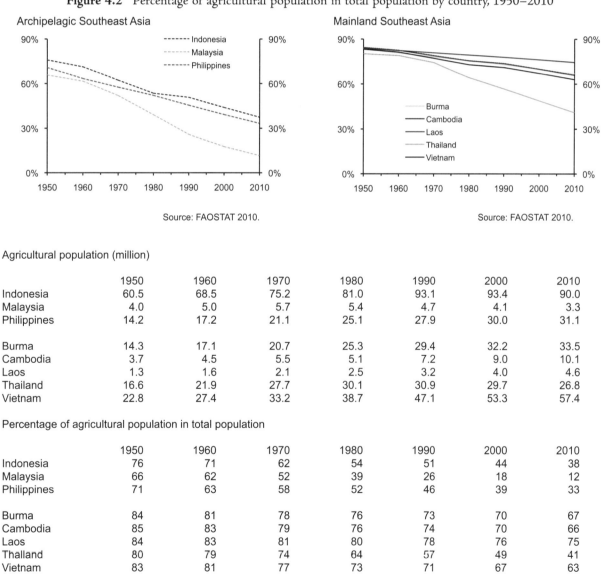

Source: FAOSTAT 2010.

Source: FAOSTAT 2010.

Agricultural population (million)

	1950	1960	1970	1980	1990	2000	2010
Indonesia	60.5	68.5	75.2	81.0	93.1	93.4	90.0
Malaysia	4.0	5.0	5.7	5.4	4.7	4.1	3.3
Philippines	14.2	17.2	21.1	25.1	27.9	30.0	31.1
Burma	14.3	17.1	20.7	25.3	29.4	32.2	33.5
Cambodia	3.7	4.5	5.5	5.1	7.2	9.0	10.1
Laos	1.3	1.6	2.1	2.5	3.2	4.0	4.6
Thailand	16.6	21.9	27.7	30.1	30.9	29.7	26.8
Vietnam	22.8	27.4	33.2	38.7	47.1	53.3	57.4

Percentage of agricultural population in total population

	1950	1960	1970	1980	1990	2000	2010
Indonesia	76	71	62	54	51	44	38
Malaysia	66	62	52	39	26	18	12
Philippines	71	63	58	52	46	39	33
Burma	84	81	78	76	73	70	67
Cambodia	85	83	79	76	74	70	66
Laos	84	83	81	80	78	76	75
Thailand	80	79	74	64	57	49	41
Vietnam	83	81	77	73	71	67	63

---

* "Agricultural population is defined as all persons depending for their livelihood on agriculture, hunting, fishing and forestry. It comprises all persons economically active in agriculture *as well as their non-working dependents*" (FAOSTAT) (our emphasis).

Plate 15

In broad terms, in every country in the region, the evolution in the number of persons and in the percentage of the population economically active in agriculture is comparable to that of the agricultural population. Relating the two sets of figures, i.e., dividing the agricultural population (Figures 4.1 and 4.2) by the number of persons economically active in agriculture (Figure 4.3), provides what could be called the agricultural dependency ratio. Generally speaking this ratio was on the rise in all Southeast Asian countries during the 1950s and 1960s. But by the 1970s, as the agrarian transition really picked up, this ratio began to decrease, with families becoming smaller and labour-induced migration out of rural areas increasing.

The agrarian transition did not affect all countries in an equal manner, and while they did fluctuate over the last 50 years, Burma's and Laos' agricultural dependency ratios ended up being similar in 2010 to where they stood in 1950: 1.7 and 1.8 respectively. During the same period, Cambodia's agricultural dependency ratio declined from 1.9 to 1.7 while Vietnamese peasants supported more household members in 2010 (1.8) than they used to in 1950 (1.6). Along with the fact that life expectancy has increased faster in Vietnam than anywhere else in the region between 1955 and 2010 (Figure 3.3), the exceptionally rapid growth of the country's agricultural sector since the mid-1980s has most likely contributed to this unusual process. In Thailand, the agricultural dependency ratio has been reduced from 1.7 to 1.4. This indicates, not surprisingly, that dependency on farming among Thailand's *agricultural* households has been reduced more significantly than in any other Southeast Asian country (Rigg 2005; Poupon 2010).

These figures take on added meaning when compared with those concerning archipelagic coun-

tries, where, in 1950, agricultural dependency ratios were significantly higher than on the mainland and where this indicator has since then remained higher, generally speaking. Indonesia's, Malaysia's and the Philippines' agricultural dependency ratios respectively stood at 2.4, 2.6 and 2.6 in 1950. They have since dropped substantially, particularly in Indonesia where, by 2010, the ratio had come down to 1.7, much lower than in the other two countries where it had been reduced to 2.0 and 2.3 respectively. Archipelagic countries' high agricultural dependency ratios exist along with the relatively limited contribution of agriculture to their employment and GDP structures (Figures 3.6 and 4.7). This may be attributable to the following reasons: in Malaysia, thanks to heavy state subsidies and generally widespread agricultural prosperity, the capacity of the average farm to support a relatively larger number of persons is more significant than elsewhere. In the Philippines, a somewhat more complex interpretation could be suggested: the attractiveness of the non-farming sectors' for agricultural populations might not be as convincing as elsewhere as overseas remittances contribute to the survival of an unparalleled number of family farms (Côté 2010).

In terms of percentage, the population that is economically active in agriculture varies tremendously among the eight countries. And while percentages have been decreasing everywhere, the gap has increased between the extremes. In 1950, these were represented by Vietnam and Malaysia, where, respectively, about 50 per cent and 25 per cent of the population were economically active in agriculture. By 2010 the extremes were in Laos, with just over 40 per cent, and in Malaysia, with less than 6 per cent.

Figure 4.3 Number of persons economically active in agriculture by country, 1950–2010*

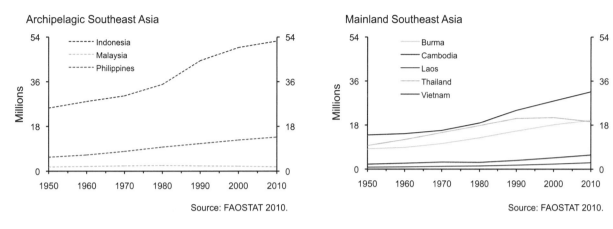

Figure 4.4 Percentage of population economically active in agriculture by country, 1950–2010

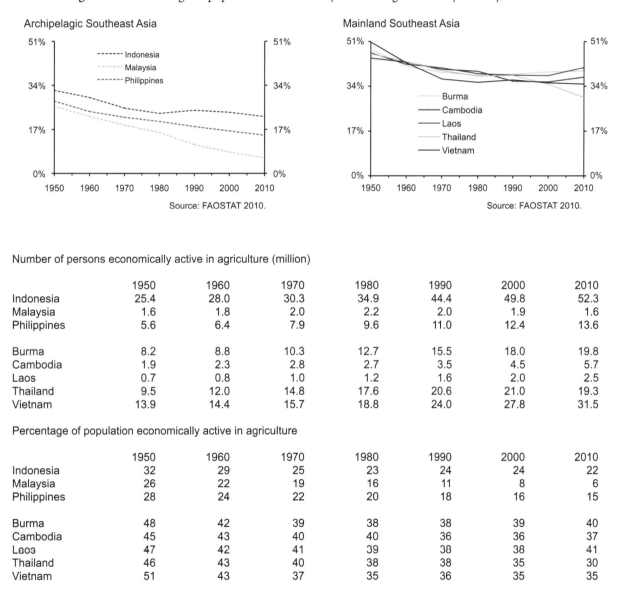

Number of persons economically active in agriculture (million)

	1950	1960	1970	1980	1990	2000	2010
Indonesia	25.4	28.0	30.3	34.9	44.4	49.8	52.3
Malaysia	1.6	1.8	2.0	2.2	2.0	1.9	1.6
Philippines	5.6	6.4	7.9	9.6	11.0	12.4	13.6
Burma	8.2	8.8	10.3	12.7	15.5	18.0	19.8
Cambodia	1.9	2.3	2.8	2.7	3.5	4.5	5.7
Laos	0.7	0.8	1.0	1.2	1.6	2.0	2.5
Thailand	9.5	12.0	14.8	17.6	20.6	21.0	19.3
Vietnam	13.9	14.4	15.7	18.8	24.0	27.8	31.5

Percentage of population economically active in agriculture

	1950	1960	1970	1980	1990	2000	2010
Indonesia	32	29	25	23	24	24	22
Malaysia	26	22	19	16	11	8	6
Philippines	28	24	22	20	18	16	15
Burma	48	42	39	38	38	39	40
Cambodia	45	43	40	40	36	36	37
Laos	47	42	41	39	38	38	41
Thailand	46	43	40	38	38	35	30
Vietnam	51	43	37	35	36	35	35

---

* "Economically active population in agriculture (agricultural labour force) is that part of the economically active population engaged in or seeking work in agriculture, hunting, fishing or forestry" (FAOSTAT).

Plate 16

Figures 4.5 and 4.6 do contribute to an improvement in our understanding of the evolution of agricultural employment and dependency. Thus, concerning the agricultural dependency ratio, the data in Figure 4.5 actually corroborates the interpretation suggested in the preceding figures (4.3 and 4.4): there is an inverse relationship between the percentage of agricultural population economically active in agriculture and the agricultural dependency ratio. In other words, the closer the number of persons economically active in agriculture gets to the number of persons making up the agricultural population (Figure 4.5), the lower the number of those whose livelihoods depend on each and every agricultural labourer. In 2010, an unequalled proportion of Thailand's agricultural population was economically active in agriculture. Hence, it is no surprise that, as mentioned earlier, Thailand has the lowest agricultural dependency ratio in the region. In a similar manner, substantial proportions of Malaysia's and the Philippines' agricultural populations are not involved in farming, which results in these countries' higher agriculture dependency ratios.

Throughout Southeast Asia, the percentage of rural population economically active in agriculture (Figure 4.6) is clearly evolving in two very opposite directions, depending on which countries are concerned. In Malaysia, Thailand and Vietnam, this percentage has been substantially reduced, meaning that, even within rural areas, the relative importance of agriculture as a source of employment has declined, although not in a uniform way. In Malaysia, where the reduction has been the strongest, it has

largely taken place between 1950 and 1990; since then, the share of agriculture as a source of employment among rural residents has remained essentially stable. In Vietnam, although the percentage also declined very markedly between 1950 and 1970, it has since levelled off and even increased somewhat since 1990. In Thailand it fluctuated down and up until the 1990s and has since been declining rapidly.

In four of the other five countries, namely Indonesia, Laos, the Philippines and Burma, the tendency has been for the share of agricultural employment in the rural areas to actually increase, which would mean that deagrarianization of the countryside is not actually taking place. Put differently, in rural areas, particularly those of Indonesia and Laos, agriculture more than holds its ground as a source of employment. Here again, the process has not been uniform nor steady, although one feature stands out. In all four countries, the "revenge", so to speak, of agriculture as a source of rural employment clearly began in the 1990s, even earlier in the case of the Philippines and Indonesia, where, following the 1997 financial crisis it increased even further (De Koninck and McGee 2001). In Cambodia, the same pattern is also noticeable, with the consequence that, after having begun to drop during the 1970s and 1980s, the share of agriculture as a source of employment in the rural areas had, by 2010, returned to its level in 1950. This suggests that, throughout much of the region, farming remains an activity many people turn to when fearing for their subsistence security. Southeast Asians still bet on the land.

Figure 4.5 Percentage of agricultural population economically active in agriculture by country, 1950–2010

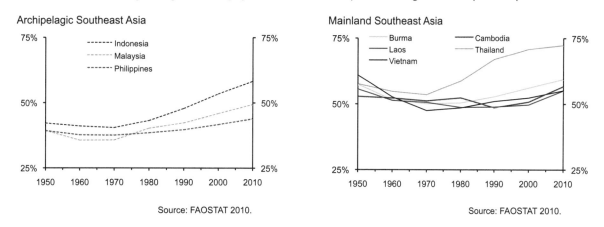

Archipelagic Southeast Asia

Mainland Southeast Asia

Source: FAOSTAT 2010.

Source: FAOSTAT 2010.

Figure 4.6 Percentage of rural population economically active in agriculture by country, 1950–2010*

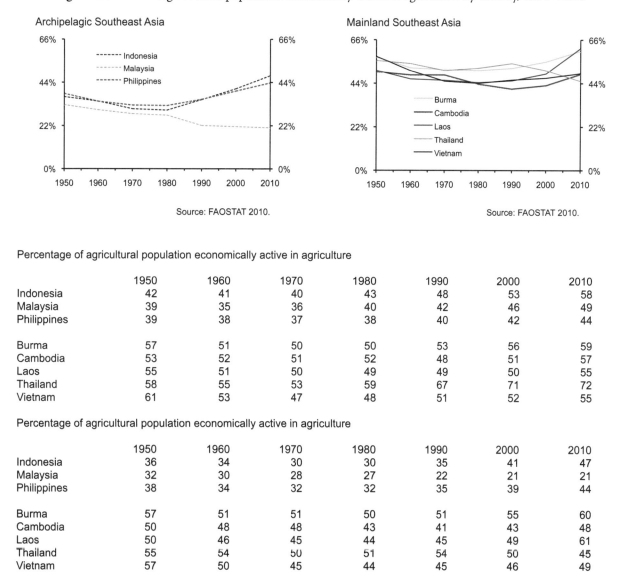

Archipelagic Southeast Asia

Mainland Southeast Asia

Source: FAOSTAT 2010.

Source: FAOSTAT 2010.

Percentage of agricultural population economically active in agriculture

	1950	1960	1970	1980	1990	2000	2010
Indonesia	42	41	40	43	48	53	58
Malaysia	39	35	36	40	42	46	49
Philippines	39	38	37	38	40	42	44
Burma	57	51	50	50	53	56	59
Cambodia	53	52	51	52	48	51	57
Laos	55	51	50	49	49	50	55
Thailand	58	55	53	59	67	71	72
Vietnam	61	53	47	48	51	52	55

Percentage of agricultural population economically active in agriculture

	1950	1960	1970	1980	1990	2000	2010
Indonesia	36	34	30	30	35	41	47
Malaysia	32	30	28	27	22	21	21
Philippines	38	34	32	32	35	39	44
Burma	57	51	51	50	51	55	60
Cambodia	50	48	48	43	41	43	48
Laos	50	46	45	44	45	49	61
Thailand	55	54	50	51	54	50	45
Vietnam	57	50	45	44	45	46	49

---

* Rural population is the "Residual population after subtracting urban population from total population". Urban population "Refers to the population residing in urban areas. Usually the urban areas and hence the urban population are defined according to national census definitions (...)" (FAOSTAT).

Plate 17

Data made available by the World Bank on the percentage of the workforce employed in, respectively, agriculture, industry and services are particularly scanty about Cambodia, Laos and Vietnam, the three countries having emerged from former French Indochina. As for Burma, information does not go beyond 1990. However scarce, these data do confirm, unsurprisingly, that in Burma, Cambodia, Laos and Vietnam, agriculture employs a greater share of the workforce than it does in other countries. It also tallies with our interpretation of the evolution in the percentage of population economically active in agriculture (Figure 4.4). Finally, and most importantly, it reinforces our assumption that data about the contribution of agriculture to Southeast Asian countries' GDP (Figure 3.6) does not properly illustrate the importance this activity holds for the population of the region. That said, more data are available concerning the four countries where the agrarian transition actually "began" earlier and where agriculture employs a smaller proportion of the active population.

Over the 27-year period examined here, the proportion of the Philippines' workforce employed in industry has remained basically the same, hovering around 15 per cent, while in Thailand it has grown from 10 per cent to 20 per cent. In the latter country, the share of the agricultural workforce has declined by nearly 30 per cent (from close to 71 per cent to 42 per cent), while in the Philippines the drop has been much less significant, from 52 per cent to 36 per cent. As a result, in this archipelago country the service sector appears exceptionally well developed when compared with other Southeast Asian countries. This is less the case with Indonesia, where the share of the agricultural workforce has been declining more slowly, still accounting for more than 40 per cent of the total workforce in 2007, and where the service sector appears proportionately less inflated than in the Philippines, particularly when its relative importance as an employer is compared with that of industry.

Not surprisingly, Malaysia, which by the mid-1980s was already the most industrialized country in the region besides Singapore, still has the highest proportion of its workforce employed in industry. This proportion, which had reached 32 per cent in 2000, has however begun to decline, having come down to 29 per cent by 2007, while the share of the service sector has been growing quite rapidly, having then reached 57 per cent. Hence, Malaysia seems to be proceeding according to plan in its official quest to become an industrial country by the year 2020 — at least as measured by employment structure. The deagrarianization process seems to evolve in a much less classic way in the Philippines, particularly, but also in Indonesia and in Thailand, where services rather than industry relay an agricultural sector that employs, in proportionate terms, fewer and fewer people, but still well over a third of the entire workforce. As far as the other four mainland countries are concerned, and regarding the same deagrarianization process, trends appear more difficult to interpret. Nevertheless, their economic structure is also undergoing rapid transformation, with, however and here again, the share of agriculture apparently showing strong resilience as a source of employment.

Figure 4.7 Percentage of workforce employed in agriculture, industry and services by country, 1980–2007

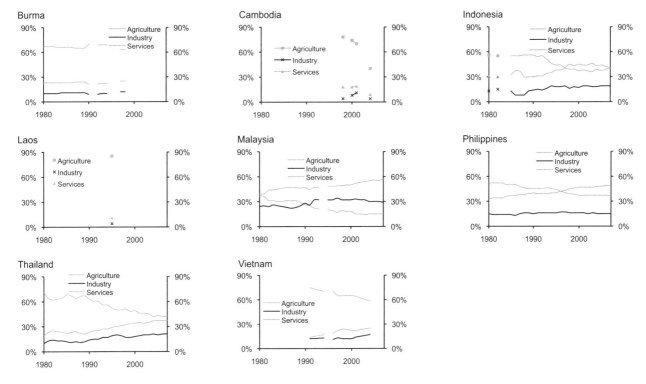

Source: World dataBank 2010.

Agriculture (%)

	1980	1985	1990	1995	2000	2007
Burma	67	66	70			
Cambodia					74	
Indonesia	56	55	56	44	45	41
Laos				85		
Malaysia	37	30	26	20	18	15
Philippines	52	50	45	44	37	36
Thailand	71	68	64	52	49	42
Vietnam					65	

Industry (%)

	1980	1985	1990	1995	2000	2007
Burma	10	11	9			
Cambodia					8	
Indonesia	13	13	14	18	18	19
Laos				4		
Malaysia	24	24	28	32	32	29
Philippines	15	14	15	16	16	15
Thailand	10	12	14	20	19	21
Vietnam					12	

Services (%)

	1980	1985	1990	1995	2000	2007
Burma	23	23	21			
Cambodia					18	
Indonesia	30	32	30	38	37	40
Laos				11		
Malaysia	39	46	47	48	50	57
Philippines	33	37	40	40	47	49
Thailand	19	22	22	28	32	37
Vietnam					22	

CHAPTER 5

Agricultural Growth, Diversification, Intensification and Expansion

"It is thus incorrect to associate economic development at all times with declining labour intensity of agricultural cultivation."

(Booth 1988: 14)

"The possibilities for increasing employment and income and for generating wealth lie not so much in maximising the production of rice as in using intensive rice cultivation as a basis for economic diversification."

(Bray 1986: 131–2)

Plate 18

Economic indicators often provide a distorted picture of the relative importance of agriculture in Southeast Asia. In this particular case, the fact that, in almost all countries, agricultural value added per worker is not as important as GDP per capita could lead to the conclusion that agricultural workers cause the economies of Southeast Asia more harm than good. This is of course in contradiction to the fact that agriculture remains the leading employer in the region. In addition, agricultural value added is an insufficient indicator of the role of agricultural workers within Southeast Asia's economy. This is because, as noted by Rigg (2005: 175), "farming is now one activity among several for many households."

As expected, agricultural value added per worker is highest in Malaysia. This may be explained by three factors. First, Malaysia is characterised by high investment in agricultural R&D, rural infrastructure, rural education and the subsidised provision of farm inputs. Second, almost half of the country's agricultural area is covered with palm tree plantations. In comparison with most crops, oil palm cultivation employs very few workers per hectare and is financially very rewarding as an agricultural commodity whose price has increased the most during recent years. Third, official figures do not reveal the number of illegal workers, which is particularly high in Malaysian agriculture (Bernard and Bissonnette 2011). Consequently, Malaysia's GDP per capita and agricultural value added per worker appears exactly the same, $5,378 in 2005.

Unsurprisingly, Indonesia is the leading agricultural producer in Southeast Asia. In 2006, it was responsible for 40 per cent of the regional agricultural value added, a proportion corresponding to its relative demographic importance in the region. Indonesian agricultural value added was hit the hardest during the Asian crisis: in 1998, it had dropped to a mere 46 per cent of its 1996 value. As a comparison, the regional average value had fallen to 62 per cent of its precrisis level. Indonesian agriculture rebounded well after the late 1990s crisis: in 2008, agricultural value added in the country had almost tripled since 2000. Thailand is the sole country that did better during the same period, as its agricultural value added did grow more than threefold. Also in the early years of the twenty-first century, Thailand's agricultural value added gradually overtook that of the Philippines, apparently bringing an end to decades of exchanging with it the title of Southeast Asia's second most important agricultural power, at least according to that indicator. As in Malaysia, agriculture is not the most important job provider in the Philippines. This is compensated by the demographic importance of that country (Figure 3.1), and by the above-mentioned high average agricultural value added per worker: Filipino agricultural workers are the second most productive in the region after Malaysian workers.

Vietnam has the lowest agricultural value added per worker, $313 in 2005, or some $16 below the figure recorded in Cambodia for the same year. Actually, Vietnam's total agricultural value added, which was only the fifth in importance in 2008, could have been much higher had it not been for the late 1980s slump. That period was marked by the introduction of a reform package known as the General Adjustment of Price, Wage and Money (Hung 1999: 6). As one would expect, that monetary shock treatment induced skyrocketing inflation and currency devaluation, which explains why the country's total agricultural value added fell by more than 80 per cent between 1987 and 1989 alone.

Figure 5.1 Value added in agriculture, in total and per worker by country, 1960–2008*

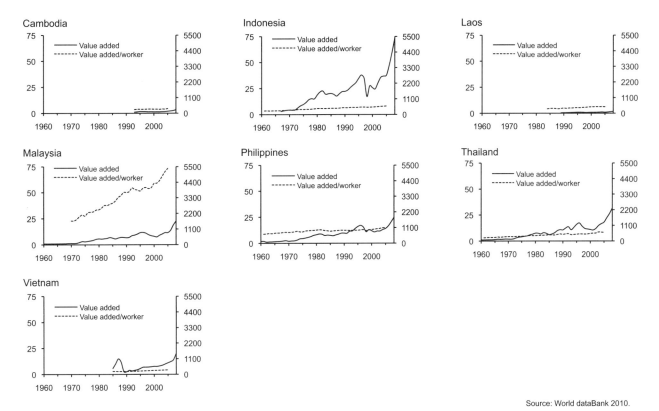

Source: World dataBank 2010.

Left Y axis = Value added (billion $); Right Y axis = Value added per worker ($)

Value added in agriculture, total (billion $)

	1960–62	1970–72	1980–82	1990–92	2000–2	2008
Cambodia					1.3	3.4
Indonesia		4.3	21.0	23.9	26.8	73.5
Laos				0.6	0.9	1.8
Malaysia	0.9	1.3	5.6	7.5	8.2	22.6
Philippines	1.6	2.2	8.6	10.3	11.4	24.8
Thailand	1.1	1.9	7.2	12.3	11.2	31.7
Vietnam				3.2	7.8	20.0

Value added in agriculture, per worker ($)

	1961–63	1971–73	1981–83	1991–93	2001–3	2005
Cambodia				264	289	329
Indonesia	260	336	429	490	553	596
Laos				362	458	456
Malaysia		1,814	2,704	3,878	4,569	5,378
Philippines	661	807	926	904	1,015	1,098
Thailand	240	313	399	489	582	607
Vietnam				219	289	313

* No data available for Burma.

Plate 19

In 2007, Southeast Asian agricultures' overall net agricultural production index* stood at 133, compared to 27 in 1961. The increase of the global net agricultural production index was somewhat less significant, growing only from 40 to 116 over the same period. In other words, Southeast Asia's "aggregate volume of agricultural production" quadrupled between 1961 and 2007, while the global figure nearly tripled. Food production indices followed almost identical trends. In other words, food remains a component of overall agricultural production as important today as it was some 50 years ago, both worldwide and in Southeast Asia.

Both these indices have grown particularly rapidly in Southeast Asia since the dawn of the twenty-first century. It has even been the case in Cambodia, where agricultural and food production indices have increased by no less than two-thirds between 1999 and 2007. This signals an important shift from the situation that prevailed in that country during the second half of the twentieth century. As Cambodia went through turbulent times in the 1970s and 1980s, agricultural and food production indices plunged and then stagnated. Only in 1995 did these values climb back to their 1970 level. Although it has performed better than its neighbours on those scores in recent years, Cambodia has not yet been able to overcome all the negative impacts of the "wasted decades".

Over the last half century, both agricultural and food production indices have increased the most in Malaysia. The country's agricultural index grew from 17 to 131 between 1961 and 2007, an eightfold increase. During the same time interval, the Malaysian food production index was multiplied by an even more impressive factor of 11. Foodstuff thus makes a much greater proportion of Malaysia's agricultural production today than it did some 50 years ago. This is largely attributable to the phenomenal expansion in Malaysian oil palm cultivation over recent decades, which has come partly at the expense of rubber cultivation (Figures 7.1–7.14). Palm oil is classified as a food crop by FAOSTAT, even if increasing proportions of it are sold to the cosmetics industry and transformed (or are expected to be) into agrofuels. This transition has occurred even though Malaysian indices were, along with those of the Philippines, the hardest hit by the 1997–98 Asian crisis.

Although its economic development trajectory does not share much with Malaysia's, Laos is the regional runner-up when it comes to the growth of agricultural and food production indices. Since 1961, both were multiplied sixfold in the PDR. Growth was particularly important during the few years prior to 2000. Burma, Indonesia and Vietnam have also done well, as their agricultural production indices were multiplied more or less fivefold between 1961 and 2007. However, the times when that growth took off are quite different. It first began in Indonesia, around 1970. Vietnam followed in the early 1980s, and then came Burma's turn, some 15 years later.

---

* Production indices "show the relative level of the aggregate volume of agricultural production for each year in comparison with the base period 1999–2001" (FAOSTAT 2010) (hence 1999–2001 = 100).

Figure 5.2 Net agricultural production index by country, 1961–2007

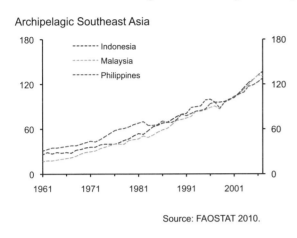

Source: FAOSTAT 2010.

Figure 5.3 Net food production index by country, 1961–2007

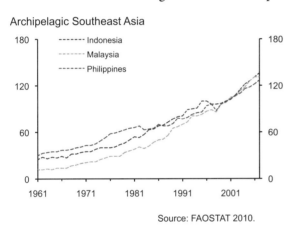

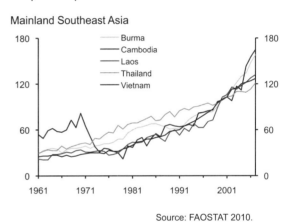

Source: FAOSTAT 2010.

Net agricultural production index (Y2000=100)

	1961–63	1971–73	1981–83	1991–93	2001–3	2007
Indonesia	27	37	55	87	108	137
Malaysia	18	32	49	79	108	131
Philippines	33	44	68	81	106	128
Burma	33	39	63	67	114	157
Cambodia	56	52	44	66	106	164
Laos	22	34	45	61	110	132
Thailand	30	43	67	86	106	121
Vietnam	25	28	41	62	110	128

Net food production index (Y2000=100)

	1961–63	1971–73	1981–83	1991–93	2001–3	2007
Indonesia	26	36	55	87	108	136
Malaysia	12	22	39	75	108	131
Philippines	32	44	66	80	107	127
Burma	32	38	62	67	114	158
Cambodia	54	51	45	65	106	165
Laos	21	31	44	58	112	132
Thailand	32	44	70	86	106	121
Vietnam	26	30	43	64	110	127

Plate 20

Between 1961 and 2007, Southeast Asian net agricultural and food production indices per capita outpaced global trends. Global net food production index per capita totalled 79 in 1961 and 106 in 2007. Over the same period, Southeast Asian values almost doubled, with the region's per capita agricultural production index increasing from 62 to 121. This occurred despite the fact that Southeast Asia's population grew about 15 per cent faster than the world's population. On top of this, the region produces ever increasing surpluses of agricultural and food products and it has become an increasingly significant exporter of such commodities,[*] another testimony to the dynamism of the region's agriculture.

The difficulties Cambodia's own agriculture went through during the last half century are illustrated here again. In 1970, agricultural and food production per capita indices stood at 150. By 2007, per capita agricultural product and foodstuff availability had not gone back to that level, with the country still having not fully regained its vitality following the Khmer Rouge era. Vietnam indices also stagnated during the 1960s and 1970s. That period corresponds not only to that of the Vietnam War, but also to the time when Vietnamese fertility rates were the region's highest. However, Vietnam managed to double both its indices from ~50 to 100 between the late 1970s and 2000. Per capita agricultural and food production indices made little progress in the Philippines, where these indicators

pretty much stagnated between 1975 and 2000. The Philippines is also the country where these indices have made the least progress since then, as their value totalled 110 and 111 respectively in 2007. This raises questions about the extent to which the 19 structural adjustment loans allocated to the Philippines between 1980 and 1999 (Easterly 2005: 5) were beneficial; as well as whether the reforms the nation undertook to join the WTO (in 1995) have had a positive impact on its agriculture (Pascual and Glipo 2002).

Malaysia distinguishes itself as the country whose indices have increased the most between 1961 and 2007. During that period, its per capita agricultural and food production indices were multiplied by factors of 2.4 and 3.5 respectively. Such a gap between those two values is unique in the region; in all other Southeast Asian nations, those two indices have grown at a similar pace. This should be understood as a consequence of that country's choice to give prominence to oil palm cultivation (Figures 5.2, 5.3 and 7.1–7.14). Burma has also managed since 1961 to significantly increase its per capita agricultural and food production indices. This is especially true for the 2000–7 period, as Burmese per capita indices both stood above 145 in 2007. Among the reasons explaining this is that Burma's population is currently increasing at a slower pace than that of all the other countries in the region, except Thailand.

---

[*] We hold that food should not be treated on par with other tradable goods (De Koninck 2009: 161–7).

Figure 5.4 Net agricultural production index per capita by country, 1961–2007

Archipelagic Southeast Asia

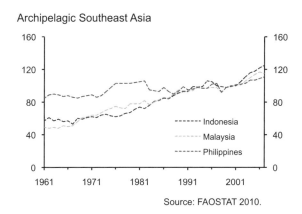

Source: FAOSTAT 2010.

Mainland Southeast Asia

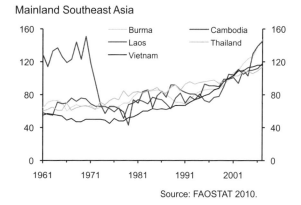

Source: FAOSTAT 2010.

Figure 5.5 Net food production index per capita by country, 1961–2007

Archipelagic Southeast Asia

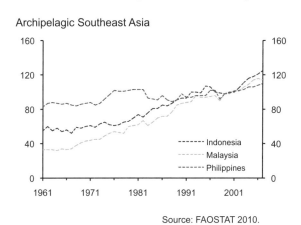

Source: FAOSTAT 2010.

Mainland Southeast Asia

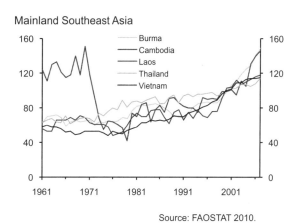

Source: FAOSTAT 2010.

Net agricultural production index per capita (Y2000=100)

	1961–63	1971–73	1981–83	1991–93	2001–3	2007
Indonesia	58	62	74	97	105	125
Malaysia	49	65	79	96	103	115
Philippines	88	88	102	96	102	111
Burma	69	65	84	75	112	147
Cambodia	125	94	80	82	102	145
Laos	56	67	72	74	107	118
Thailand	62	66	84	94	105	114
Vietnam	56	50	59	71	107	116

Net food production index per capita (Y2000=100)

	1961–63	1971–73	1981–83	1991–93	2001–3	2007
Indonesia	57	61	74	98	105	125
Malaysia	33	45	63	91	103	114
Philippines	86	87	100	95	102	110
Burma	68	63	83	74	112	149
Cambodia	122	93	80	81	102	146
Laos	54	62	71	70	108	118
Thailand	66	69	88	94	104	114
Vietnam	59	53	61	73	107	115

Plate 21

This index is less influenced by fluctuations in local currencies' exchange rates than the agricultural value added indicator (Figure 5.1). It explains, among other things, why the impacts of the 1997–98 Asian crisis appear much less important here (Figure 5.6) than according to the previously examined indicators (Figure 5.1).

According to the FAO, our planet's agricultural production was valued at 1.5 trillion international dollars (I$) in 2007, compared to some I$530 billion in 1961 (as a comparison, the WDI estimates 2007 global agricultural value added at 1.95 trillion current US dollars).* Southeast Asia's own production totalled I$22.5 billion in 1961, and I$110 billion 46 years later. The region's production value thus increased almost twice as fast as the world's. As a consequence, Southeast Asian agricultural output amounted to 7.3 per cent of the global total in 2007, compared to 4.2 per cent in the early 1960s, while its share of global population actually increased from 7.3 per cent in 1960 to 8.5 per cent in 2005. It is also worth nothing that in 2005, North America provided 8.5 per cent of global agricultural production, although its population equalled less than two-thirds that of Southeast Asia.

Since 1961, Indonesian agricultural output value has always amounted to about a third of Southeast Asia's, a proportion somewhat inferior to that of its relative regional demographic weight. Still, Indonesian agricultural output totalled almost I$37 billion in 2007, the result of an average 3.6 per cent annual growth rate since 1961. Unsurprisingly,

it is Malaysia's production that has increased the most during that period: in 2007 it reached I$8.6 billion, having expanded at an average annual growth rate of 4.4 per cent since 1961. Contributing to some 5 per cent of regional agricultural production in the early 1960s, Malaysia now accounts for some 8 per cent of the regional market, or 0.56 per cent of global value. More surprising, since the early 1960s, the growth of Laos' agricultural production has been the second fastest in Southeast Asia. The agricultural production value of the landlocked country totalled less than I$200 million in 1961, compared to I$1.1 billion today. Laos' agricultural production however remains the least important in the region (it is also, by far, the least populated country among those examined here): in 2007, it contributed to only 1 per cent of the Southeast Asian total, and less than 0.07 per cent of the global figure. Cambodia's agricultural production index is about twice as important, although its growth rate was the lowest between 1961 and 2007. During that period, Cambodia's index grew at an average annual rate of 2.8 per cent, a pace almost identical to its population growth. Neighbouring Thailand's agricultural index is the second most important in the region, almost reaching I$18.2 billion, or 1.2 per cent of the world total in 2007. However, its index is growing at a much slower pace than Vietnam's, and it is only a matter of a few years before the value of its agricultural production is overtaken by Vietnam's.

---

* Prices in international dollars (I$) "result from the iterative comparison, through mathematical methods, of the production value of all commodities in all countries, obtained from the producer prices of each commodity/country, with the corresponding value of production in the United States obtained in a similar manner" (FAOSTAT 2010).

Figure 5.6 Net agricultural production index in international dollars by country, 1961–2007*

Archipelagic Southeast Asia

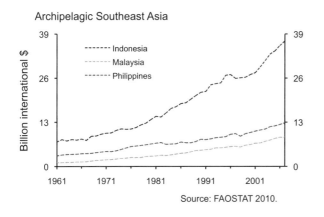

Source: FAOSTAT 2010.

Mainland Southeast Asia

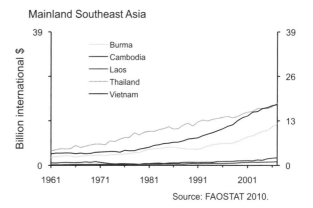

Source: FAOSTAT 2010.

Figure 5.7 Share of Southeast Asian countries in global agricultural production, 1961–2007

Archipelagic Southeast Asia

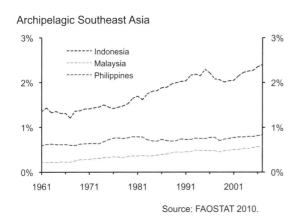

Source: FAOSTAT 2010.

Mainland Southeast Asia

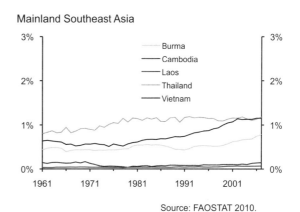

Source: FAOSTAT 2010.

Net agricultural production index (billion international $)

	1961–63	1971–73	1981–83	1991–93	2001–3	2007
Indonesia	7.5	10.1	15.0	23.5	29.4	37.0
Malaysia	1.2	2.1	3.2	5.2	7.1	8.6
Philippines	3.4	4.5	6.8	8.1	10.7	12.8
Burma	2.6	3.0	4.9	5.2	8.8	12.1
Cambodia	0.8	0.7	0.6	0.9	1.5	2.3
Laos	0.2	0.3	0.4	0.5	0.9	1.1
Thailand	4.6	6.5	10.1	13.0	16.0	18.2
Vietnam	3.5	4.0	5.7	8.6	15.3	17.8

Share of Southeast Asian countries in global agricultural production (%)

	1961–63	1971–73	1981–83	1991–93	2001–3	2007
Indonesia	1	1	2	2	2	2
Malaysia	0	0	0	0	1	1
Philippines	1	1	1	1	1	1
Burma	0	0	1	0	1	1
Cambodia	0	0	0	0	0	0
Laos	0	0	0	0	0	0
Thailand	1	1	1	1	1	1
Vietnam	1	1	1	1	1	1

* Calculated from FAOSTAT production indices in international $ values.

Plate 22

Southeast Asia's cereal production grew from 51 million to 216 million tonnes between 1961 and 2007. These values represented 5.8 per cent and 9.2 per cent of the global cereal harvest respectively for the corresponding years. Rice is of course in a class of its own when it comes to Southeast Asian cereal production. In the early 1960s, the regional staple crop harvest accounted for over 90 per cent of Southeast Asia's total cereal production, but this ratio was slightly reduced to just under 86 per cent in 2007. However, the relative importance of the Southeast Asian rice harvest over global rice production has followed the opposite direction. In 1961, 21.3 per cent of all rice produced in the world was grown in Southeast Asian fields. In 2007, the proportion had increased to over 28 per cent. This also points to the relative decline of the global rice harvest over that of other cereals as well as to the maintenance of a strong prevalence of the production of cereals, mainly rice, within Southeast Asia agricultures. The region's net cereal production index (in international dollars) equalled 44.6 per cent of its overall agricultural index in 1961, and 38.5 per cent in 2007 (Figure 5.8). Worldwide, the corresponding figures stood just below 23 per cent in both years, fluctuating up to a maximum of 27 per cent during the period. On the other hand, the fact that within Southeast Asia the relative share of rice production — as measured by its contribution to overall agricultural production value — has been declining is indicative of the increase in the relative value of cash crops in the region, a trend corroborated by the latter's faster territorial expansion (Figure 7.51).

The decrease in the relative share of cereal production within Southeast Asian agricultures is particularly significant in Malaysia, which is also the country where absolute and relative growth of cereal production is the lowest. In 2007, cereals also accounted for a lesser proportion of Indonesia's agricultural production than in the past. For instance, cereals contributed to some 36 per cent of its agricultural production index in 2007, compared to over 50 per cent in the early 1980s. Apart from being Southeast Asia's most important cereal producer, Indonesia is the country whose production increased the most in absolute terms between 1961 and 2007, and the runner up in relative terms (Figure 5.9). In 2007 the archipelagic country produced 70.4 million tonnes of grain, 40 per cent of the regional harvest and almost five times more than what it had produced in 1961.

When it comes to the relative importance of cereal production, there is a striking difference between archipelago and mainland states. On the mainland, cereals have constituted a much more important proportion of the agricultural production index throughout the period studied. They accounted for more than 50 per cent of agricultural output in the five mainland states during the early 1960s, and in 2007 this still prevailed in Burma, Cambodia and Laos. The latter country recorded the most important harvest increases, as it produced almost eight times more cereals in 2007 than it did in 1961. Burma has also made great progress during that time interval. As a result, its cereal harvest is now nearly equal to that of Thailand, the mainland's number one producer until the 1990s. Thailand's cereal production has remained ahead of Vietnam's for most of the time interval we focus on here. However, Vietnam's total grain output (essentially rice) overtook that of the Thai Kingdom in the mid-1990s, thanks largely to massive intensification undertaken from the mid-1980s onwards. Thailand nonetheless remains the region's as well as the world's leading rice exporter (Figures 6.5 and 6.6).

Figure 5.8 Share of cereal production in overall agricultural production value by country, 1961–2007*

Archipelagic Southeast Asia

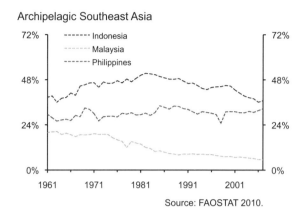

Source: FAOSTAT 2010.

Mainland Southeast Asia

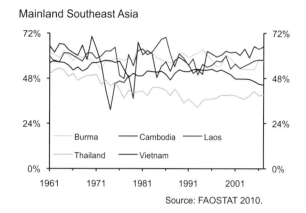

Source: FAOSTAT 2010.

Figure 5.9 Total cereal production by country, 1961–2007

Archipelagic Southeast Asia

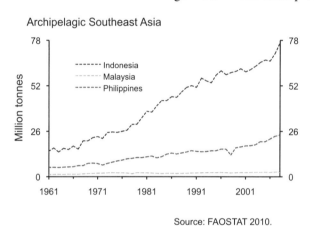

Source: FAOSTAT 2010.

Mainland Southeast Asia

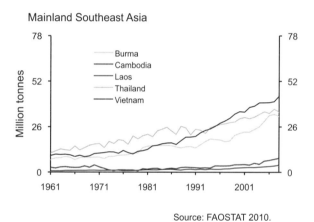

Source: FAOSTAT 2010.

Share of cereal production in overall agricultural production (%)

	1961–63	1971–73	1981–83	1991–93	2001–3	2007
Indonesia	38	46	51	46	41	37
Malaysia	20	19	12	8	7	6
Philippines	28	28	30	31	31	33
Burma	60	55	62	60	54	57
Cambodia	64	54	61	53	62	65
Laos	58	60	62	54	54	57
Thailand	52	47	41	35	38	39
Vietnam	57	57	51	52	48	44

Total cereal production (million tonnes)

	1961–63	1971–73	1981–83	1991–93	2001–3	2008
Indonesia	14.9	23.2	38.2	53.9	61.3	76.6
Malaysia	1.1	1.9	1.9	2.1	2.3	2.5
Philippines	5.2	7.1	11.2	14.2	17.7	23.7
Burma	7.6	8.2	14.8	15.4	23.2	32.0
Cambodia	2.5	2.0	1.9	2.4	4.4	7.8
Laos	0.5	0.9	1.1	1.4	2.5	3.8
Thailand	11.9	15.8	21.7	23.4	31.1	34.4
Vietnam	9.7	11.0	14.3	22.1	36.3	43.3

* Calculated from FAOSTAT production indices in international $ values.

Gambling with the Land

Plate 23

According to the FAO lexicon, crops include all agricultural products harvested either in fields, plantations, gardens or orchards. As for livestock production, it refers to all products coming from live or slaughtered animals. Consequently, not only does this category include meat, milk and eggs, but it also comprises products such as wool, honey, and so on.

The sum of a country's crop and livestock production values in I$ should equal that of its agricultural production index. However, according to FAOSTAT data, that sum is more often than not higher than that for a country's overall agricultural production. We felt it necessary to avoid perpetuating such inconsistencies and to make sure that the total corresponding values included in Figures 5.10 and 5.11 equal 100 per cent. Consequently, we are representing here the relative importance of crop and livestock production indices in I$ over the total of these two indicators rather than crop or livestock production indices in I$ over agricultural production ratio.

Considering, first, that cereals are the most important component of Southeast Asia's agricultural production (Figure 5.8) and, second, the increasing extent of commercial crops such as rubber, oil palm and coffee (Figure 7.51), it is no surprise that crops make the bulk of the regional agricultural output. Crops accounted for 87 per cent of Southeast Asia's agricultural production index in 1961, and 83 per cent in 2007, whereas the world average steadily remained around 62 per cent during that time interval. However, over the last 50 years, the relative importance of Southeast Asia's livestock production has increased faster than it has globally, although it does remain far below global averages. This has been particularly true in Cambodia where the relative importance of livestock production increased the most over that of crop production between 1961 and 2007. Indeed, the share of the country's agricultural output value represented by livestock production nearly doubled, from 7.8 per cent to 15 per cent.

In the Philippines and Malaysia, livestock production also accounts for a rapidly increasing proportion of total agricultural output. This is especially true of the Philippines, where the livestock production index amounted to more than a quarter of overall agricultural output in 2007, against less than 15 per cent in the early 1960s. This is partly due to the growth of the country's pig meat production, which is one of the region's most important, but owes more to chicken meat production (Figure 6.19), while in Malaysia only the latter has been growing significantly. Indonesia is the country where crops make for the greatest share of overall agricultural production. In 2007, the value of the archipelago country's crop harvests stood at almost $33 billion, or 87 per cent of total agricultural production. Nonetheless, as in nearly all Southeast Asian countries, livestock represents an ever-increasing proportion of Indonesia's agricultural output. Thailand is the sole country that experienced the opposite trend between 1961 and 2007. During the early 1960s, some 20 per cent of the kingdom's agricultural output value came from the livestock industry, then a unique situation. By 2007, that value had gone down to 17.4 per cent. Among the reasons explaining this downward trend is that Thailand's poultry industry was the region's most affected by the avian flu episode of the early twenty-first century (Figures 6.19–6.21). Whatever the case, among nearly all communities in the region (Table A3), overall protein intake increases appear to be strongly related to the generalized expansion of regional livestock production.

Figure 5.10 Share of crop production in overall agricultural production value by country, 1961–2007*

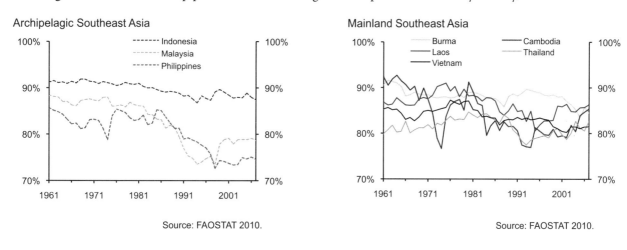

Archipelagic Southeast Asia

Mainland Southeast Asia

Source: FAOSTAT 2010.

Source: FAOSTAT 2010.

Figure 5.11 Share of livestock production in overall agricultural production value by country, 1961–2007*

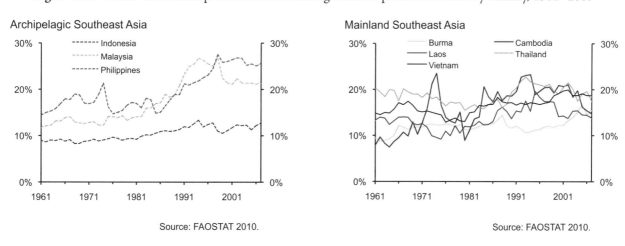

Archipelagic Southeast Asia

Mainland Southeast Asia

Source: FAOSTAT 2010.

Source: FAOSTAT 2010.

Share of crop production in overall agricultural production value (%)

	1961–63	1971–73	1981–83	1991–93	2001–3	2007
Indonesia	91	91	90	88	88	87
Malaysia	88	87	85	76	79	79
Philippines	85	82	83	79	73	74
Burma	91	88	89	89	87	84
Cambodia	91	83	87	78	80	85
Laos	86	89	88	84	86	86
Thailand	81	82	84	78	79	83
Vietnam	85	85	85	83	81	81

Share of livestock production in overall agricultural production value (%)

	1961–63	1971–73	1981–83	1991–93	2001–3	2007
Indonesia	9	9	10	12	12	13
Malaysia	12	13	15	24	21	21
Philippines	15	18	17	21	27	26
Burma	9	12	11	11	13	16
Cambodia	9	17	13	22	20	15
Laos	14	11	12	16	14	14
Thailand	19	18	16	22	21	17
Vietnam	15	15	15	17	19	19

* Calculated from FAOSTAT production indices in international $ values.

Plate 24

For unknown reasons, the inconsistencies encountered among the FAO statistics used to construct the preceding figures (5.10 and 5.11) were absent from the FAO statistics used for the present one! In other words, in this case, the sum of a country's food and non-food production indices precisely equals that of its agricultural production index.

In Southeast Asia, the importance of rubber and other non-food commercial crops explains that food production contributes slightly less to the regional agricultural production index than is the world average. Between 1961 and 2007, the global food production index's share of the global agricultural production one increased slightly, from 93.6 per cent to 95.3 per cent in 2007. In Southeast Asia, it increased from 92 per cent to 93.4 per cent. In fact, food would account for an even lower proportion of regional agricultural production if those palm oil products which are classified as foodstuffs were included instead among non-food products (Figures 5.3 and 5.5).

This is especially the case with Malaysia, where the relative importance of so-called non-food production experienced the greatest decline between 1961 and 2007. Indeed, non-food production accounted for an unequalled third of the country's agricultural production index throughout most of the 1960s and 1970s. Since then, the country's rubber production has stalled (Figure 7.12) while its palm fruit production has soared (Figure 7.4). Malaysia's food production index followed suit and reached Southeast Asia's average level in the late 1990s. Laotian food and non-food production indices have also followed distinctive trajectories when compared with those of other Southeast Asian nations. Rubber was introduced in northern Laos only in the 1980s, and its production really took off only in the first decade of the twenty-first century (Cohen 2009: 426). Thus, either available data is erroneous, or another major non-food product has long constituted an important proportion of Laos' agricultural production, especially from the early 1960s to the early 1990s. This product could of course have been opium, although one would expect that the 3,800 tonnes of opium that Laos produced in 1989 (Ibid.: 425) did not appear in that country's official agricultural statistics.

Thailand's and Vietnam's rapid rubber production increases, since the 1980s for the former and the 1990s for the latter, have pulled up both countries' non-food production indices. Thailand's value, about 6 per cent in 1980, has been maintained at some 10 per cent since 2000. In Vietnam, nearly 98 per cent of agricultural production was considered as food in 1990, compared with just over 92 per cent in 2007. The structure of agricultural production has evolved differently in Burma, Cambodia and the Philippines, with the relative importance of food production indices having increased since the early 1960s. The most important rise occurred in Cambodia, where the food production index equalled less than 95 per cent of overall agricultural production throughout the 1960s except for the year 1963. Since 2000, the index has remained above 97 per cent. Unfortunately, it appears that this has so far remained insufficient to solve that country's food security problem (Figure 3.4).

Figure 5.12 Share of food production in overall agricultural production value by country, 1961–2007[*]

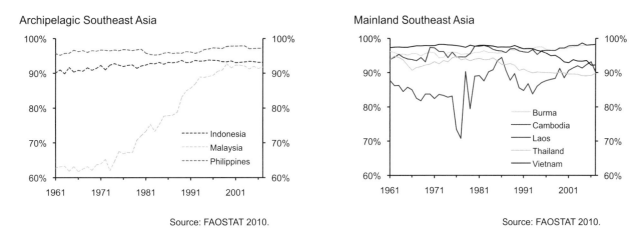

Archipelagic Southeast Asia

Mainland Southeast Asia

Source: FAOSTAT 2010.

Source: FAOSTAT 2010.

Figure 5.13 Share of non-food production in overall agricultural production value by country, 1961–2007[*]

Archipelagic Southeast Asia

Mainland Southeast Asia

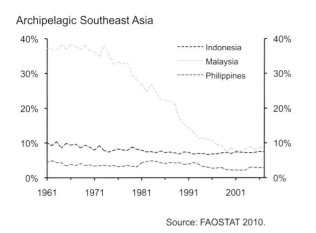
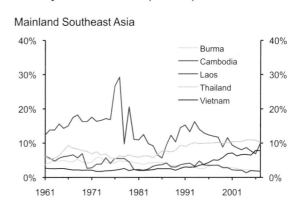

Source: FAOSTAT 2010.

Source: FAOSTAT 2010.

Share of food production in overall agricultural production value (%)

	1961–63	1971–73	1981–83	1991–93	2001–3	2007
Indonesia	90	92	93	93	93	93
Malaysia	63	64	74	87	92	92
Philippines	95	97	95	96	98	97
Burma	96	95	96	97	97	98
Cambodia	95	97	98	96	98	98
Laos	87	83	89	85	91	90
Thailand	94	93	94	90	90	90
Vietnam	97	98	98	97	93	92

Share of non-food production in overall agricultural production value (%)

	1961–63	1971–73	1981–83	1991–93	2001–3	2007
Indonesia	10	8	8	7	7	7
Malaysia	37	36	26	13	8	8
Philippines	5	3	5	4	2	3
Burma	4	5	4	3	3	2
Cambodia	5	3	2	4	2	2
Laos	13	17	11	15	9	10
Thailand	6	7	6	10	10	10
Vietnam	3	2	2	3	7	8

[*] Calculated from FAOSTAT production indices in international $ values.

Plate 25

While roundwood consists of untransformed raw wood, sawnwood has gone through some industrial transformation, making it a higher value added product. Since the early 1960s, wood exports have been much more important in archipelagic than in mainland Southeast Asia. The sizes of these regions have of course to be taken into account, the archipelagic countries being about 30 per cent more extensive than the mainland ones. Illegal logging, notoriously practised throughout the region, is also an important factor, difficult to assess. Finally, timber contraband probably accounts for a greater share of forestry activities than average in Burma, Cambodia and Laos, whose governments rank as the region's most corrupt according to Transparency International's 2009 *Global Corruption Perceptions Index* (Transparency International 2010).

Southeast Asia's roundwood exports peaked in 1978 when they amounted to nearly 40 million cubic metres, or 40 per cent of the volume traded globally. By 2008, they had fallen to just above 6 million cubic metres, about 5 per cent of global trade volumes. As for the region's sawnwood exports, they also peaked in 1979, representing over 10 per cent of globally traded volumes. Export volumes have since been reduced by half, amounting to 3 per cent of global trade volumes in 2008. Notwithstanding the issue of illegal timber trade, these downward trends do result from the implementation of export restriction on forestry products, on environmental, economic or nationalistic grounds (Tachibana 2000: 52), with the decrease in supplies becoming increasingly apparent.

Tachibana also explains that the Philippines was the first Southeast Asian country to thoroughly exploit its forest. He attributes this to both its timber product quality and its geographic proximity to Japanese markets, the two countries having ratified a free trade agreement over timber products as early as the 1960s (Ibid.). Although the Philippines' roundwood exports benefited from a head start in the region, they were rapidly overtaken by Malaysia's, by far the region's biggest roundwood and sawnwood exporter throughout most of the 1961–2008 period. Apart from the Philippines in the early 1960s, Indonesia is the sole country whose timber exports ever competed with those of Malaysia. Indonesia's roundwood exports remained above those of Malaysia during most of the 1970s, and its sawnwood exports became once again competitive after their debacle during the 1990s.

Although dwarfed by those of Malaysia and Indonesia, Thailand's forestry industry is the most important among mainland countries, its sawnwood exports having become more significant since the beginning of the twenty-first century. On the other hand, the kingdom's roundwood exports ceased in 1982. In addition, since the implementation of the 1989 logging ban, forest conservation has been particularly high on the agendas of both Thailand's state forest agency and civil society (Leblond 2008: 8). Also noteworthy are Laos' increasing exports as well as the fact that Burma has only officially exported a mere 600 cubic metres of roundwood altogether since 2000. This seems particularly questionable, given that the forests of its big neighbour, China, have been protected by a logging ban since 1998 while the country's demand for wood and most other natural resources has been soaring (Xu and Wilkes 2004: 962).

Figure 5.14 Roundwood exports by country, 1961–2008

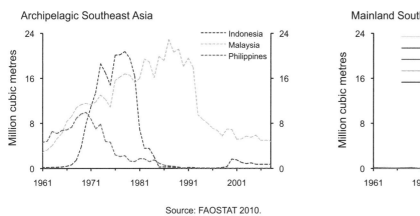

Archipelagic Southeast Asia

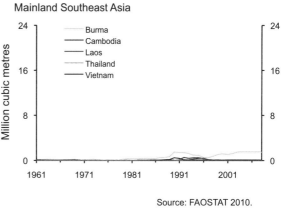

Mainland Southeast Asia

Source: FAOSTAT 2010.

Source: FAOSTAT 2010.

Figure 5.15 Sawnwood exports by country, 1961–2008

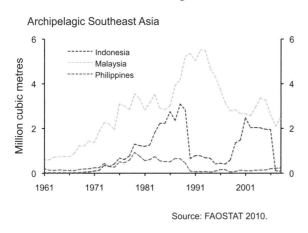

Archipelagic Southeast Asia

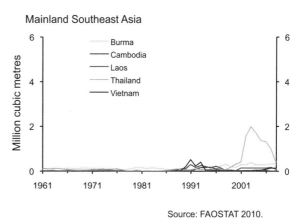

Mainland Southeast Asia

Source: FAOSTAT 2010.

Source: FAOSTAT 2010.

Roundwood exports (million cubic metres)

	1961–63	1971–73	1981–83	1991–93	2001–3	2008
Indonesia	0.1	14.3	4.7	0.1	1.1	0.7
Malaysia	3.3	12.0	18.0	15.6	5.3	4.8
Philippines	5.3	7.8	1.5	0.0	0.0	0.0
Burma	0.1	0.1	0.2	1.3	1.2	1.5
Cambodia	0.1	0.0	0.0	0.3	0.0	0.0
Laos	0.0	0.0	0.0	0.1	0.1	0.0
Thailand	0.0	0.1	0.0	0.0	0.0	0.0
Vietnam	0.0	0.0	0.0	0.1	0.0	0.0

Sawnwood exports (million cubic metres)

	1961–63	1971–73	1981–83	1991–93	2001–3	2008
Indonesia	0.0	0.2	1.4	0.7	2.2	0.1
Malaysia	0.6	1.8	3.1	5.3	2.7	2.5
Philippines	0.1	0.3	0.6	0.1	0.1	0.2
Burma	0.1	0.1	0.1	0.2	0.3	0.3
Cambodia	0.0	0.0	0.0	0.1	0.0	0.0
Laos	0.0	0.0	0.0	0.2	0.1	0.1
Thailand	0.1	0.1	0.0	0.1	1.3	0.4
Vietnam	0.0	0.0	0.0	0.4	0.0	0.1

Plate 26

Southeast Asian agricultural output amounted to 7.3 per cent of the global total in 2008, compared to 4.2 per cent in the early 1960s (Figure 5.7). In 2007, the total value of the region's agricultural exports reached some $95 billion (not to be confused with I$), 40 times higher than their early 1960s value. These 2007 exports represented a record 9 per cent of the global figure, a significant increase over the low of 4.2 per cent to which they had dropped in the early 1970s.

The role of Southeast Asia as a supplier of agricultural commodities to the global market has a long history, dating from prior to the colonial era. But during the colonial period that role was strongly enhanced by European powers, whose policy was to massively develop the cultivation of plantation crops, such as rubber, tea and sugar. Although largely a colonial legacy, crop plantations have been further developed since the waning of European control in the region and still represent some of the region's most significant agricultural achievements (Gregor 1965, Courtenay 1979).

Nowadays, dry natural rubber, copra oil and palm oil represent three of the region's key exports, each of them prominent on the world market. For example, since the early 1960s Southeast Asia *hevea* tree plantations have continued to steadily generate over three quarters of the world's natural rubber harvest. The only relapse occurred in the late 1990s, when for a few years that proportion was slightly reduced, to 73 per cent or 74 per cent. Since the 1960s, Southeast Asian natural rubber exports have always totalled more than 85 per cent of the worldwide traded volumes, often surpassing 90 per cent. Also since the early 1960s, more than half of the global coconut production has been harvested in Southeast Asia. Correspondingly, the region's copra oil exports have accounted for a dominant and steadily climbing share of the global total, from some 45 per cent in the early 1960s to over 85 per cent by the early twenty-first century. The fruits of the oil palm tree constitute the crop for which Southeast Asia's role as a global producer/exporter has increased the most since the 1960s. In 1961, the region's palm fruit production accounted for 10.6 per cent of the global total, a meagre contribution when compared with the 85 per cent reached by 2008, overshadowing in the process African countries — mainly Nigeria and D.R. Congo — that were formerly the leading producers. The same can be said about palm oil exports, for which Southeast Asia's preponderance is even more significant.

The region's role as a food crop producer/exporter is less impressive in comparison to global averages. However, it remains in a class of its own when it comes to rice, its staple crop. As mentioned earlier, the relative importance of Southeast Asia's rice harvest, which generated less than 20 per cent of the global rice production during most of the 1960s, has been increasing. By 2008, it had reached 27.6 per cent. And although the relative importance of the region's rice exports has never equalled the 1961 peak, when Southeast Asia provided 57 per cent of global rice exports, it has remained the leading contributor to the global rice market. Moreover, the reappearance in the late 1980s of Vietnam as a major exporter (Figures 6.5 and 6.6) has contributed to a new and quite significant rise in the relative importance of the region's shipments.

Figure 5.16 Southeast Asia's share of production and exports of selected crops, 1961–2008*

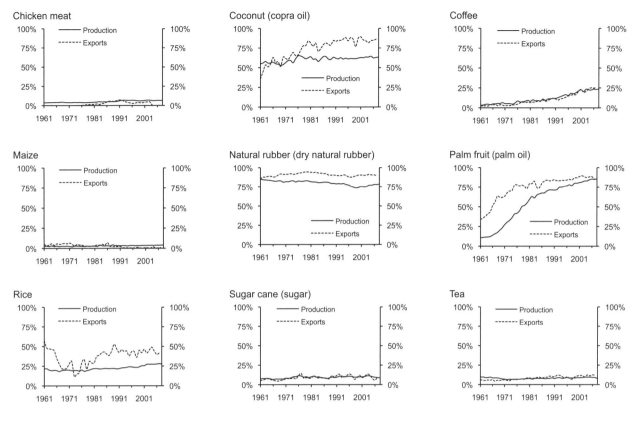

Source: FAOSTAT 2010.

Southeast Asia's share of production and export of selected crops (%)

	1961–63	1971–73	1981–83	1991–93	2001–3	2007 (2008)†
Chicken meat production	4	4	5	7	7	7
Chicken meat exports	0	0	2	6	4	0
Coconut production	56	58	62	62	63	63
Copra oil exports	45	62	80	84	86	86
Coffee production	4	5	9	13	22	24
Coffee exports	2	3	7	11	21	26
Maize production	2	2	3	3	4	4
Maize exports	4	5	4	1	1	1
Natural rubber production	85	82	81	79	75	79
Dry natural rubber exports	87	92	94	90	90	90
Palm fruit production	11	30	61	73	82	86
Palm oil exports	36	67	81	84	89	85
Rice production	21	20	22	22	27	28
Rice exports	51	24	35	44	44	42
Sugar cane production	8	8	10	10	11	9
Sugar exports	6	8	10	12	11	10
Tea production	9	7	8	8	9	8
Tea exports	6	6	8	11	11	12

* For some cash crops, export values refer to transformed products, cited in parentheses.
† Production data = 1961–2008 / Export data = 2007

Plate 27

As pointed out earlier (Figure 2.5), since the eighteenth century Southeast Asian cropland expansion* has gone through a number of phases, including two exceptional periods of acceleration. The first began in the 1880s, largely under colonial impetus, and lasted well into the twentieth century. The second and more widespread phase began around the 1950s, even earlier in some cases, and is still ongoing in most countries. However, during the last half century individual countries' trajectories have been far from identical, whether in timing, consistency or intensity.

In Thailand, a strong rate of growth in agriculture began in the 1920s, accelerated during the 1950s and was maintained until the early 1990s; but since then, the size of the country's agricultural area has been declining. In Indonesia, cropland expansion, which had also been quite significant since the late nineteenth century, seemed to stop completely in the 1960s but picked up again in the 1980s — quite spectacularly — only to slow down once again. The consequence was that between 1984 and 2004, cultivated land in Indonesia — admittedly by far the most extensive country in the region, some three times the size of Burma, the second largest — increased by nearly 13 million hectares, a huge area, more extensive than all the land currently cultivated in Burma or in the Philippines.

Although in absolute terms agricultural expansion in Indonesia has dwarfed that of other countries in Southeast Asia, in relative terms it has been strong everywhere and in most cases even more significant than in the large archipelago country, at least between 1961 and 2007 (Figure 5.18). Over the 46-year period, Malaysia, the least "agricultural" of the countries examined here — at least in terms of agriculture's relative contribution to employment and GDP — saw its agricultural area nearly double

in size. Most of that expansion was achieved over a 12-year period: from 1981 to 1993 the country's agricultural area grew by more than 3.7 million hectares, or 66 per cent. Expansion has almost stalled since then, largely because ongoing expansion in the Borneo states has barely compensated for cropland reduction in the peninsula. This increase in agricultural land on the "big island" is partly due to the conversion of forest fallow land to permanent crops. As pointed out by Cramb (2011), it represents a form of agricultural intensification rather than expansion. In Thailand, over the 30-year period from 1961 to 1991, when expansion levelled off, agricultural area expanded by some 8.1 million hectares or nearly 85 per cent, an equally impressive rate of growth.

For a number of essentially political reasons, the take-off was somewhat delayed in Vietnam, Cambodia and Laos; but it was launched by the late 1980s and early 1990s. In Vietnam, for example, new agricultural policies adopted after *Doi Moi* (1986) have favoured agricultural expansion to such an extent that between 1991 and 2007, cultivated area increased by 3.3 million hectares or some 50 per cent. Cambodia, once again because of the Khmer Rouge regime, is the only country that has experienced a spectacular decline in agricultural area — in 1971–72. Although by the late 1970s expansion had resumed, the real boom began in the mid-1980s. Between 1984 and 2007 the country's agricultural area more than doubled, largely at the expense of its forest cover, significantly depleted through illegal logging (Le Billon 2002). Overall, most modest agricultural expansion has occurred in Burma. But, since the turn of the twenty-first century and after a long stagnation period with no equivalent in the region, the pace of Burmese expansion has begun to accelerate.

---

* Croplands increased faster than "permanent meadows and pasture" between 1961 and 2007. Totalling about 80 per cent of Southeast Asia's agricultural area in 1961, their relative importance had grown to over 85 per cent by 2007.

Figure 5.17 Agricultural area by country, 1961–2007*

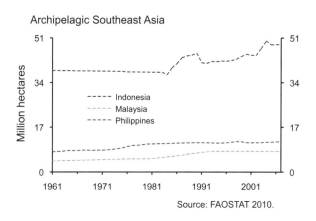
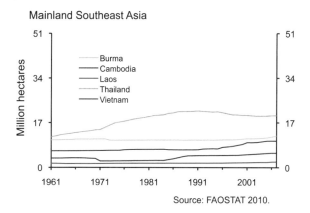

Figure 5.18 Relative growth of agricultural area by country, 1961–2007*

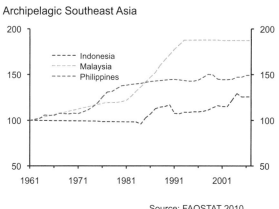
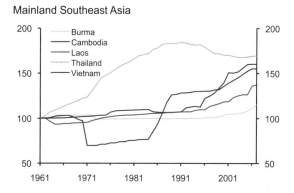

Agricultural area by country (million hectares)

	1961–63	1971–73	1981–83	1991–93	2001–3	2007
Indonesia	38.6	38.3	37.9	41.6	45.3	48.5
Malaysia	4.3	4.8	5.3	7.7	7.9	7.9
Philippines	7.8	8.4	10.7	11.1	11.1	11.5
Burma	10.5	10.6	10.4	10.4	10.9	12.0
Cambodia	3.5	2.5	2.7	4.5	5.0	5.5
Laos	1.5	1.5	1.6	1.7	1.9	2.1
Thailand	12.0	15.2	19.7	21.4	19.7	19.8
Vietnam	6.3	6.5	6.9	7.0	9.5	10.1

Relative growth of agricultural area (1961=100)

	1962–64	1972–74	1982–84	1992–94	2002–4	2007
Indonesia	100	99	97	108	122	126
Malaysia	103	115	132	186	187	187
Philippines	103	112	140	143	145	149
Burma	101	101	100	100	105	115
Cambodia	101	70	76	129	145	155
Laos	97	99	105	108	125	137
Thailand	106	138	171	182	168	169
Vietnam	100	103	110	113	153	160

---

* "Agricultural area" refers to the sum of two indicators, "arable land and permanent crops" (referred to as cropland in Figure 2.1 and following) and "permanent meadows and pastures" (FAOSTAT 2010).

Plate 28

Along with Europe, particularly so-called Central Europe, and South Asia, particularly India and Bangladesh, Southeast Asia has become one of the most densely cultivated regions in the world. Of course, in percentage terms the area devoted to agriculture remains limited in Burma and Laos, where in 2007 it amounted to only about 18 per cent and 9 per cent of these countries' respective land areas. In addition, within most countries there are still some regions with relatively low population densities and less widespread agriculture. But it is precisely those regions, such as Borneo and the Vietnamese Central Highlands, which have become the main target of agricultural expansion and the main agricultural frontiers (De Koninck 2006), especially since the 1980s. Consequently, between 1961 and 2007 the percentage of agricultural area in Southeast Asia as a whole had grown from 19 per cent to nearly 27 per cent. The region is obviously evolving well beyond the image suggested in the classical geographical literature (Gourou 1953, Robequain 1958, Fisher 1966), whereby the region was described as insufficiently cultivated and relatively empty in relation to its East and South Asian neighbours.

With nearly 40 per cent of their national territories devoted to agriculture in 2007, Thailand and the Philippines are by far the countries with the most important agricultural domains in the region. In Thailand, from the mid-1980s until 1991, the cultivated proportion reached nearly 42 per cent. But while in Thailand that proportion has since been declining, in the Philippines expansion seems to have remained on the agenda. As clearly illustrated earlier (Figure 5.18), the same can be said

of all the other countries, particularly on the mainland, where, for example, Vietnam's and Cambodia's "terroirs" occupied more than 30 per cent of their respective land areas by 2007. But such a figure does not tell all, as there remain very important differences between these two countries in several respects, including demographic size and density. In 2007, Vietnam's total population of about 86 million inhabitants was six times that of Cambodia's, which had by then reached some 14 million inhabitants; and its population density was more than three times higher: 260 versus 77 inhabitants per square kilometre. In addition, when the areas of land under cultivation per person economically active in agriculture are compared (Figure 5.20), the difference in the resulting numbers is equally revealing. In 2006, that area was three times larger in Cambodia: about one hectare versus one-third of a hectare in Vietnam. This underlines the much higher intensity of Vietnam's agriculture as well as reveals the current boom in Cambodia's plantation agriculture. An even more extended boom is behind the exceptionally high ratio found in Malaysia — nearly five hectares per capita in 2006 — by far the highest in the region. The exceptional nature of that figure is underlined by the fact that, in relative terms, Malaysia is the least "agricultural" country in the region, as has already been mentioned (Figures 5.17 and 5.18). It is the only one where land availability per agricultural worker kept on rising between the early 1980s and 2006 and, by far, the country where this indicator increased the most. In fact, over the same period, agricultural land availability per agricultural worker declined everywhere else except in Cambodia.

Figure 5.19 Percentage of agricultural area by country, 1961–2007

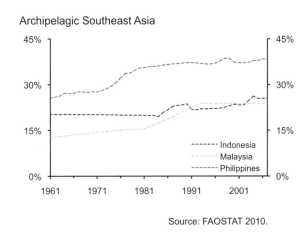

Archipelagic Southeast Asia

Mainland Southeast Asia

Source: FAOSTAT 2010.

Source: FAOSTAT 2010.

Figure 5.20 Agricultural area per person economically active in agriculture by country, 1961–2007

Archipelagic Southeast Asia

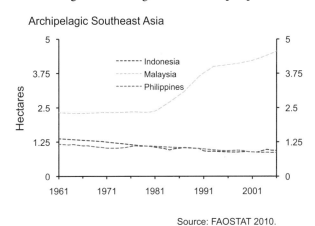

Mainland Southeast Asia

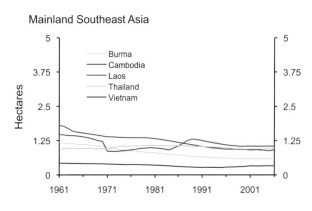

Source: FAOSTAT 2010.

Source: FAOSTAT 2010.

Percentage of agricultural area in total area

	1961–63	1971–73	1981–83	1991–93	2001–3	2007
Indonesia	20	20	20	22	24	25
Malaysia	13	14	16	23	24	24
Philippines	26	28	36	37	37	38
Burma	15	16	15	15	16	18
Cambodia	20	14	15	25	28	30
Laos	6	6	7	7	8	9
Thailand	23	30	38	42	38	38
Vietnam	19	19	21	21	29	31

Agricultural area per person economically active in agriculture (hectares)

	1961–63	1971–73	1981–83	1991–93	2001–3	2006
Indonesia	1.4	1.2	1.0	0.9	0.9	0.9
Malaysia	2.3	2.3	2.5	3.9	4.3	4.6
Philippines	1.2	1.0	1.1	1.0	0.9	0.9
Burma	1.2	1.0	0.8	0.7	0.6	0.6
Cambodia	1.5	0.9	1.0	1.2	1.0	1.0
Laos	1.7	1.4	1.3	1.0	0.9	0.9
Thailand	1.0	1.0	1.1	1.0	0.9	1.0
Vietnam	0.4	0.4	0.4	0.3	0.3	0.3

Plate 29

In the writings of classical authors, such as Dumont (1935) and Gourou (1947, 1984), as well as those of more contemporary scholars, such as Barker *et al.* (1985), Bray (1986) and Barker and Rosegrant (2007), the provision of irrigation has been advocated as the key component in Asian agricultural policies. Without surprise, throughout Southeast Asia, expansion and improvement in irrigation infrastructure have been essential factors in the intensification of agriculture, particularly peasant agriculture. Without it, there would have been no green revolution, which concerned primarily rice agriculture.

Investing in irrigation is extremely costly, yet all countries in the region made that choice, although following different agendas and with different degrees of intensity, reflecting priorities as well as means available (Mukherji *et al.* 2009). It should be added that what these figures (5.21 and 5.22) represent is an increase in the actual size of irrigated area. They do not reflect improvement in the quality of irrigation. This is crucial to remember, considering that in some instances, such as in Indonesia during the initial years of the implementation of the intensification programmes, essentially the late 1960s and early 1970s, the focus was on improving the existing irrigation infrastructure. This was particularly true in densely cultivated Java, where the *sawah* was already widespread but in need of upgrading.

Irrigation expansion has been strongest in mainland countries, particularly Thailand, Vietnam and Burma. In Thailand, the expansion picked up in the early 1960s and levelled off in the late 1990s, by which time the country had begun to drastically reduce its investments in the agricultural sector. In Vietnam, the expansion was launched in the mid-1960s and lasted until the early 1990s, by which

time the country focused on improving rice yields rather than expanding its irrigated area while becoming increasingly involved in the expansion of cash crops such as coffee, mostly in the Central Highlands on recently deforested and non-irrigated agricultural land. A consequence of this is illustrated by the striking reduction in the actual proportion of irrigated area over total agricultural area (Figure 5.22).

In Thailand, between 1961 and 1999 the size of the irrigated area more than tripled, from 1.6 million to 4.9 million hectares. In Vietnam, from 1966 to 1993, when the expansion was interrupted, it increased from 1 million to 3 million hectares. Although no other country has achieved as much expansion in absolute terms, in proportionate terms Burma, Laos and Cambodia have done even better. In the latter two countries, irrigated rice cultivation remained nearly absent until recent decades. In the case of Laos, swidden cultivation was particularly widespread, with large swiddener communities having been the object of state-sponsored massive transfers from much of the country's marginal uplands to its central lowlands and along major roads (Evrard and Goudineau 2004, Baird and Shoemaker 2007). In Cambodia rice production was insured by the cultivation of essentially non-irrigated wet rice (Delvert 1961). During colonial days, Cambodia was even producing a surplus substantial enough for the country to have become an important rice exporter. Between the early 1960s and 2007, Cambodia's irrigated area increased from some 60,000 hectares to nearly 300,000 hectares, while Laos' share of total agricultural area increased from less than 1 per cent to some 14 per cent. Finally, in Burma, the pace of irrigation expansion has been even more significant than among all other mainland countries except Laos.

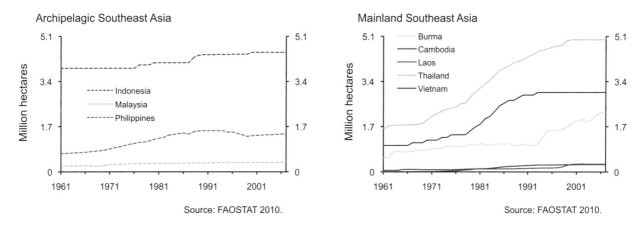

Figure 5.21 Irrigated area by country, 1961–2007*

Archipelagic Southeast Asia

Mainland Southeast Asia

Source: FAOSTAT 2010.

Source: FAOSTAT 2010.

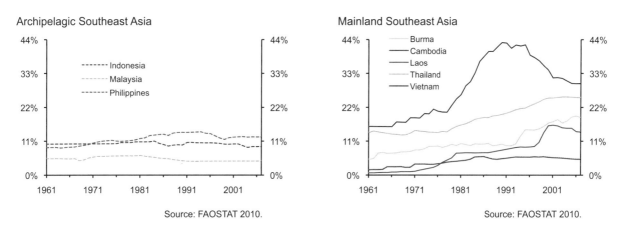

Figure 5.22 Percentage of agricultural area irrigated by country, 1961–2007*

Archipelagic Southeast Asia

Mainland Southeast Asia

Source: FAOSTAT 2010.

Source: FAOSTAT 2010.

Left Y axis = total (thousand tonnes); Right Y axis = Consumption per ha (kg)

Irrigated area (million hectares)

	1961–63	1971–73	1981–83	1991–93	2001–3	2007
Indonesia	3.9	3.9	4.1	4.4	4.5	4.5
Malaysia	0.2	0.3	0.3	0.4	0.4	0.4
Philippines	0.7	0.9	1.3	1.6	1.4	1.4
Burma	0.6	0.9	1.0	1.0	1.9	2.3
Cambodia	0.1	0.1	0.1	0.3	0.3	0.3
Laos	0.0	0.0	0.1	0.1	0.3	0.3
Thailand	1.7	2.2	3.3	4.4	5.0	5.0
Vietnam	1.0	1.2	2.0	2.9	3.0	3.0

Percentage of agricultural area irrigated

	1961–63	1971–73	1981–83	1991–93	2001–3	2007
Indonesia	10	10	11	11	10	9
Malaysia	5	6	6	5	5	5
Philippines	9	11	12	14	12	12
Burma	6	8	10	10	18	19
Cambodia	2	4	5	6	6	5
Laos	1	2	7	9	16	14
Thailand	14	14	17	21	25	25
Vietnam	16	19	29	42	32	30

* Area equipped for irrigation

Plate 30

The increase in the use of chemical fertilizers — also called inorganic or industrial fertilizers — is largely attributable to a combination of factors, themselves related to the intensification and expansion of agriculture. In the case of rice agriculture, the reliance on industrial fertilizers began to rise significantly in the 1960s, with the advent of the green revolution. As the intensification of rice cultivation became the object of major government-sponsored efforts, the increase in the reliance on inorganic fertilizers, particularly urea,[*] was closely tied to the adoption of high-yielding seed varieties and double cropping. Both of these adoptions, along with the expansion of irrigation, itself indispensable to the practice of double cropping, led to an increase in the soil's needs for nutrients.

During the 1960s, the price of industrial fertilizers followed a downward trend, which facilitated the adoption of intensification, particularly in Indonesia (Barker *et al.* 1985: 74). The sharp price increase that followed the 1973–74 oil price shock did dampen for a while the rise in the use of industrial fertilizers, but not for long, as governments increased their subsidies along with their investments in the local production of fertilizers. This was particularly the case with Indonesia, which, beginning in the early 1960s, invested in the construction of its own fertilizer plants. Over the years, Indonesia as well as Malaysia, because of their important gas resources, became self-sufficient in urea. Vietnam is also forecasted to soon become self-sufficient in nitrogenous fertilizers — particularly efficient in increasing rice yields (Ibid.: 76) — but it still has to import some of their components. More importantly, other countries, notably Thailand, have had to rely increasingly on imports to answer the growing needs of their expanding agricultures. Even Indonesia and Malaysia have had to import increasing quantities of fertilizer components, as they have massively increased their

cultivation of oil palm. This form of agriculture relies primarily on phosphorous (P) and potassium (K) fertilizers, which the local mining industry cannot supply in near sufficient quantity, particularly in Malaysia.

Not surprisingly, Indonesia, Malaysia, Thailand and Vietnam, the four major agroproducers and exporters, are by far the four major users of chemical fertilizers in the region. In Malaysia, by the early 1960s, the reliance on chemical fertilizers was already significant and rising at a quick pace that has never relented since, notwithstanding sharp fluctuations linked to those of fertilizer prices. In Indonesia, growth picked up in the mid- and late 1960s, reflecting the impact of government fertilizer subsidies to the rice cultivation sector, particularly under the BIMAS[†] programme (Gibbons *et al.* 1980), as well as cropland expansion. The pace of the latter has been such that, over a period of just over 40 years, total consumption has been multiplied by 25. The rate of growth has been nearly equivalent in Malaysia. However, while in Indonesia the extent of growth in total consumption has outpaced the increase in per hectare utilization, the opposite applies in Malaysia. Here, per hectare use has grown even faster than total use and nowadays stands way ahead of where it stands in all other countries (FAO 2004). This is largely attributable to the expansion in the cultivation of oil palm, once again, by now and by far Malaysia's dominant source of agricultural exports, but at the same time responsible for more than 75 per cent of the country's costly imports of fertilizers (Matassan 2008).

In the Philippines, total consumption is much lower than in those four countries, but the intensity of use falls within a range shared with Thailand and Indonesia, way behind Vietnam and, even more, Malaysia. As for Burma, Cambodia and Laos, their industrial fertilizer consumption still remains well behind the regional average.

---

[*] Urea is a major source, along with ammonium sulfate and ammonium chloride, of nitrogen (N), itself the major nutrient used in rice agriculture.
[†] BIMAS stands for *Bimbingan Masal* or mass guidance.

Figure 5.23 Use of chemical fertilizers by country, 1961–2005

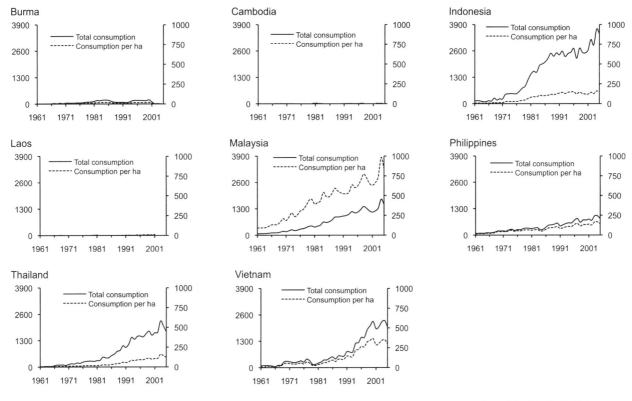

Source: World dataBank 2010.

Left Y axis = Total (thousand tonnes); Right Y axis = Consumption per ha (kg)

Total use of chemical fertilizers (thousand tonnes)

	1961–63	1971–73	1981–83	1991–93	2001–3	2005
Burma	6.5	44.5	151.2	78.8	44.6	2.1
Cambodia	2.4	2.5	11.6	10.4	17.9	
Indonesia	138.5	387.2	1,530.5	2,433.4	2,895.8	3,442.8
Laos	0.1	0.2	1.6	3.0	12.3	
Malaysia	76.9	217.5	445.0	979.0	1,215.0	1,517.8
Philippines	84.2	220.2	342.9	506.2	814.0	812.7
Thailand	24.5	146.0	371.9	1,178.3	1,884.1	1,724.0
Vietnam	96.3	264.7	289.4	767.5	2,057.3	1,984.9

Use of chemical fertilizers per hectare (kg)

	1961–63	1971–73	1981–83	1991–93	2001–3	2005
Burma	0.7	4.5	15.7	8.2	4.5	0.2
Cambodia	0.9	1.4	5.7	2.8	4.8	
Indonesia	7.7	21.5	85.0	134.4	129.7	149.7
Laos	0.1	0.3	2.1	3.7	14.0	
Malaysia	91.6	231.0	411.3	528.1	675.0	843.2
Philippines	17.3	46.8	65.4	92.1	142.8	142.6
Thailand	2.3	11.1	21.7	68.3	124.6	121.4
Vietnam	17.4	46.8	49.3	140.5	311.3	300.7

Plate 31

During the 1960s and early 1970s, a period corresponding to the early days of the green revolution in the region, agricultural mechanization was minimal and its adoption was slow. According to many, mechanization represented a "straightforward substitution of capital for labour" and, given the generally ample supply of labour then prevailing in the Southeast Asian countryside, it was "socially undesirable" (Barker *et al.* 1985: 108). Nevertheless, as the demand for production growth became increasingly pressing, particularly in the rice sector, the reliance on tractors began to spread, even if the supply of labour did not recede very rapidly. In Malaysia, where tractors were, in proportionate terms, already in the 1960s much more common than in any other country in the region, further reliance on them was strongly encouraged by the government, first through extension services. By the 1970s, tractors, including pedestrian ones, were increasingly seen in the paddy fields, fast replacing buffalos (Jegatheesan 1972). These pedestrian two-wheeled tractors have since become a common sight throughout most of the region's lowland rice-growing areas with, as a corollary, a very noticeable decline in the number of buffaloes and a reduction in grazing areas.

Throughout the region, the positive correlation between overall growth of agricultural mechanization and that of non-agricultural employment (Figure 4.7), although fairly evident over the long term, has been quite uneven among the countries — especially in their respective regions — just like the rate of adoption of tractor use. In Malaysia the latter has grown fast and steadily, more or less following the pace of its rapid industrialization. Since the mid-1990s, by which time the rice harvested area had ceased to expand (Figure 6.1), the total number of tractors in the country's agricultural countryside has levelled off.

Elsewhere in Southeast Asia, tractorization has been slower, delayed or less steady. In Burma, although expanding with a spurt in the 1960s, tractor use slowed down during the 1970s and then

wavered during the 1980s, reaching a peak in 1990. Since then it has continued to fluctuate, but with a downward trend, the total number of tractors reported in operation for 2003 being very low — 10.6 million units compared to 13 million in 1990. That is the only case of significant redution in tractor use in the region. The Philippines is another country where tractorization, although already off to a good start in the 1960s, has expanded at a slow pace, also to the point of levelling off in the early 1990s, with the consequence that the country's agriculture now seems very much undermechanized, at least in comparison to that of Malaysia, Thailand and Vietnam. In the latter two countries, and even more in Indonesia, the rapid spread of tractors is a more recent occurrence. In Vietnam, although take-off occurred even before the launching of *Doi Moi* in 1986, growth has since become quite spectacular. It levelled off at the turn of the century, by which time the density in tractor use — as measured by number of tractors per 100 sq. km of arable land — had become the highest in the region, slightly above Malaysia's and well ahead of Thailand's. In the latter country, tractorization also went through a burst during the same period as Vietnam, and peaked at the same time.

In Indonesia, where labour supply is arguably the most significant in the region, particularly in the mountainous and very intensively cultivated island of Java, reliance on tractor use began to accelerate during the mid-1980s, but more moderately. At the turn of the century, tractorization had also levelled off, by which time the intensity of tractor use was still way behind that of Vietnam, Malaysia and Thailand, and only twice that of the Philippines.

In all countries, including Laos but except Cambodia — where tractorization is still expanding but agriculture remains the least mechanized in the region — expansion of tractor use stopped or even regressed at the turn of the century. This near universal pause is obviously not a coincidence and is probably attributable to several reasons including labour issues in rice cultivation (Bray 1986).

Figure 5.24 Use of tractors per 100 sq. km of arable land by country, 1961–2003*

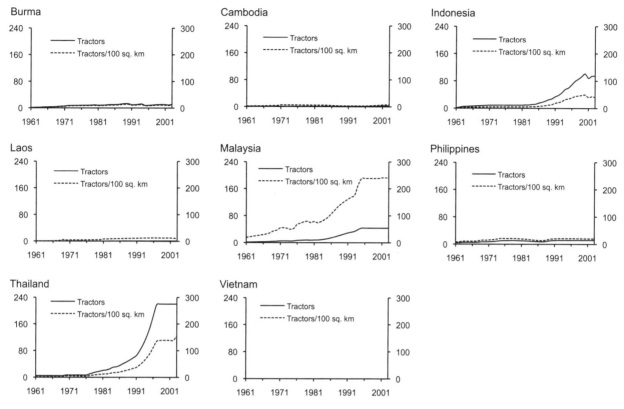

Source: World dataBank 2010.

Left Y axis = Tractors (thousand); Right Y axis = Tractors/100 sq. km of arable land

Use of tractors, total (thousand)

	1961–63	1971–73	1981–83	1991–93	2001–3
Burma	1.4	6.7	8.5	10.3	10.1
Cambodia	0.7	1.2	1.2	1.2	2.6
Indonesia	3.1	9.0	9.7	39.4	92.4
Laos	0.0	0.3	0.7	0.9	1.1
Malaysia	1.8	5.1	8.3	31.3	43.3
Philippines	4.5	7.7	9.8	11.3	11.5
Thailand	5.0	7.0	22.6	81.0	220.0
Vietnam	2.5	2.9	27.0	39.6	163.0

Tractors per 100 sq. km of arable land

	1961–63	1971–73	1981–83	1991–93	2001–3
Burma	1.4	6.9	8.9	10.8	10.1
Cambodia	2.5	6.9	6.1	3.2	7.0
Indonesia	1.7	5.0	5.4	21.8	41.4
Laos	0.5	5.0	8.8	11.8	11.6
Malaysia	21.4	54.3	76.8	168.8	240.6
Philippines	9.2	16.4	18.7	20.6	20.2
Thailand	4.7	5.3	13.2	46.9	144.3
Vietnam	4.6	5.1	45.9	72.4	246.6

---

* Tractors "… refer to wheel and crawler tractors (excluding garden tractors) in use in agriculture" (World dataBank, 2010).

CHAPTER 6

Expansion and Intensification of Food Crops and Increase in Livestock Production

"Despite the shifting fads and fancies in development paradigms on the role of the state, and despite accumulating examples of government failures in the past decades, all would agree that the public sector has crucial roles to play in the process of economic development."

(Balisacan and Fuwa 2007: 11)

81

Plate 32

Although in several regions, other cereals and tubers are widely consumed and in some cases even favoured, rice remains by far the major staple in Southeast Asia. It is also the most widely cultivated food crop and, in every country, the one which has received and continues to receive the most attention from the authorities. In fact, the green revolution in the region has primarily targeted rice cultivation. Its expansion, or rather the expansion of its harvested area,* has been substantial everywhere, largely thanks to improved and more widespread irrigation, which itself has allowed for the diffusion of the practice of double cropping (Figures 5.21 and 5.22). Also, notwithstanding the phenomenal territorial expansion over recent decades of several cash crops, notably oil palm, rubber and coffee, in terms of area cultivated, let alone harvested, rice remains the most widespread single crop in all countries except Malaysia, where oil palm dominates the landscape. Finally, it is almost exclusively a peasant crop, as nearly everywhere it is only produced on family farms.

Between the early 1960s and 2008, the entire Southeast Asian rice harvested area increased over 60 per cent, from 28 million to nearly 47 million hectares, a large yet undetermined proportion of that growth being attributable to the increasing adoption of double cropping. Every country has been involved, but to different degrees, with the largest one having taken the lead. Indonesia's rice area grew by 80 per cent, only Burma matching that rate of growth. Thailand and Vietnam have also done quite well, having both expanded their rice domain by about 60 per cent over the same 50-year period. However, in the latter three countries, the percentage of agricultural area allocated to rice cultivation remains much higher than in Indonesia, where rice land represents "only" 25 per cent of all cultivated area. In Burma, where that percentage has increased by more than half, a growth rate unequalled in the region, rice land occupied nearly 70 per cent of all agricultural land in 2008. Very high proportions are also found in Thailand and Vietnam. But in both countries, these have not changed much since the early 1960s. In fact, in Vietnam, even if it has been slightly reduced, proportion of rice land to total cultivated area is still the highest in the region, at more than 70 per cent.

Overall, rice cultivation represents by far the dominant form of agricultural land use in mainland Southeast Asia. However, in Laos and Cambodia, where it is proportionately less widespread than in the other three mainland countries, the share of rice land has been decreasing since the early 1960s. In the case of Cambodia, the decrease was particularly significant on two occasions: during the Khmer Rouge regime; and in 1984–85, when expansion of commercial crops started to boom, reducing thereby the share of rice land. Almost the opposite has been occurring in Burma, the second most rice focused country in the entire Southeast Asian region. In the archipelago, where plantation crops have been more widely cultivated since colonial days (Robequain 1958, Courtenay 1965), the share of rice land over total agricultural land is still much less significant, particularly in Malaysia, where it has also been decreasing steadily since the late 1970s.

---

* "Data refer to the area from which a crop is gathered. … If the crop under consideration is harvested more than once during the year as a consequence of successive cropping (i.e., the same crop is sown or planted more than once in the same field during the year), *the area is counted as many times as harvested*" (FAOSTAT 2010) (our emphasis).

Figure 6.1 Harvested area of rice by country, 1961–2008

Archipelagic Southeast Asia

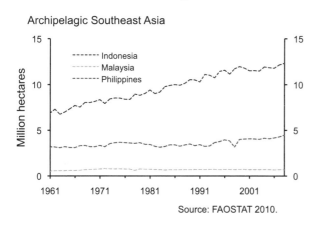

Source: FAOSTAT 2010.

Mainland Southeast Asia

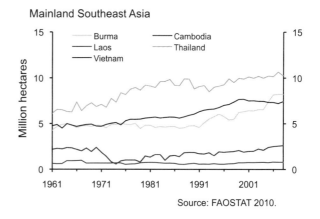

Source: FAOSTAT 2010.

Figure 6.2 Percentage of agricultural area allocated to rice production by country, 1961–2008

Archipelagic Southeast Asia

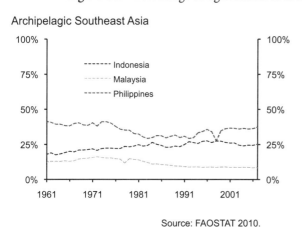

Source: FAOSTAT 2010.

Mainland Southeast Asia

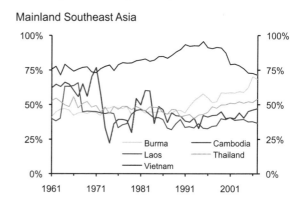

Source: FAOSTAT 2010.

Harvested area of rice (million hectares)

	1961–63	1971–73	1981–83	1991–93	2001–3	2008
Indonesia	7.0	8.2	9.2	10.8	11.5	12.3
Malaysia	0.5	0.8	0.7	0.7	0.7	0.7
Philippines	3.1	3.4	3.3	3.3	4.0	4.5
Burma	4.6	4.7	4.7	5.0	6.4	8.2
Cambodia	2.2	1.4	1.5	1.7	2.1	2.6
Laos	0.6	0.7	0.7	0.6	0.7	0.8
Thailand	6.4	7.2	9.2	8.9	10.1	10.2
Vietnam	4.7	4.9	5.7	6.4	7.5	7.4

Percentage of agricultural area allocated to rice cultivation

	1961–63	1971–73	1981–83	1991–93	2001–3	2008
Indonesia	18	21	24	26	25	25
Malaysia	13	16	13	9	9	8
Philippines	40	40	31	30	36	37
Burma	44	44	45	48	59	68
Cambodia	63	56	57	39	41	47
Laos	39	44	45	34	39	37
Thailand	53	47	47	42	51	54
Vietnam	75	76	82	93	79	71

Plate 33

Between the early 1960s and 2008, total rice area harvested in the eight countries of Southeast Asia examined here increased by 60 per cent, at an average annual rate of 1.1 per cent (Figure 6.1). At the same time, total annual rice production nearly quadrupled, growing from some 46 million tonnes in 1961 to 189 million tonnes in 2008, in this case at the average annual rate of 3.1 per cent. In other words, yield increases were the main factor behind the substantial growth in production. The latter appears particularly significant when it is compared with the growth of overall population. During the same period, population increased by a factor of 2.6 (Figure 3.1). This actually means that, as a whole, Southeast Asia has been quite successful in improving its level of self-sufficiency in its number one staple food crop.

However, here again meaningful differences do appear among the eight countries. In simple statistical terms, Laos' performance has been the most impressive, its average rice yields and total rice production having been multiplied respectively by factors of four and five between 1961 and 2008. But Indonesia's and Vietnam's achievements are equally — if not even more — significant. By the early 1960s, their rice yields were already relatively high, slightly above those obtained in Thailand and Burma and well superior to those in the Philippines, Cambodia and Laos. In Indonesia, following implementation of large-scale intensification programmes in the 1960s (Beers 1970), average rice yields began to increase steadily, reaching nearly 5 tonnes per hectare by 2008. In Vietnam, rapid productivity growth began later, in the mid-1980s, but it has since been even higher, the country's rice yields being by now the highest in the region. The 5 tonnes per hectare average yield means that double-cropped — and occasionally triple-cropped — fields produce way over 10 tonnes of rice per year, a performance nearly comparable to that of East Asian countries such as Japan, Taiwan and South Korea.

In the same two countries, overall annual production was multiplied between 1961 and 2008 by factors of nearly five for Indonesia and more than four in the case of Vietnam. In 2008, the total production of Vietnam remained well below that of Indonesia (~39 million versus ~60 million tonnes), but its population equalled only about 37 per cent of that of Southeast Asia's giant (~85 million versus ~230 million). Consequently, Vietnam has been producing much more than it needs for its internal consumption and has become a major rice exporter, although its exports still lag behind Thailand's (Figure 6.5). Vietnam's total rice production nonetheless overtook that of Thailand in the early 1990s, apparently for good. Besides internal demand factors, Thailand's capacity to generate a bigger export-oriented surplus is largely attributable to the vastness of its rice estate and not to its rice yields per se, as the latter have risen "only" by about 70 per cent in 50 years against some 260 per cent in Vietnam. Only Malaysia has achieved a comparable "mediocre" performance in terms of rice yields, but in this case we are talking of a country that has made a deliberate choice to gradually reduce its investments in the rice sector, favouring instead the cash crop sector. In the Philippines and Burma, increases in rice yields as well as total rice production appear quite significant. In the Philippines, rice yields began to rise rapidly by the late 1960s, just like in Indonesia, while the bulk of Burma's own rice yield increase occurred during the following decade. Between the early 1960s and 2008, yield increases along with territorial expansion allowed Burma to raise its rice production more than twofold and the Philippines to quadruple its rice production.

Finally, contrary to what happened with some cash crops, the very wide fluctuations in world rice prices (Figure 6.4) do not seem to have had a meaningful impact on production.

Figure 6.3 Rice yield by country, 1961–2008

Archipelagic Southeast Asia

Source: FAOSTAT 2010.

Mainland Southeast Asia

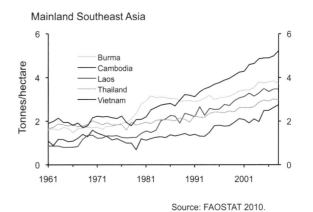

Source: FAOSTAT 2010.

Figure 6.4 Rice production by country (with prices), 1961–2008

Archipelagic Southeast Asia

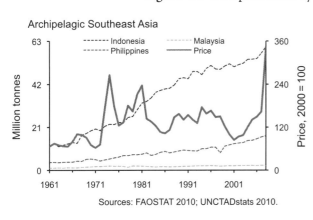

Sources: FAOSTAT 2010; UNCTADstats 2010.

Mainland Southeast Asia

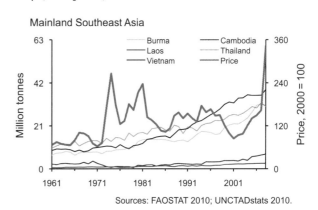

Sources: FAOSTAT 2010; UNCTADstats 2010.

Rice yield (tonnes/hectare)

	1961–63	1971–73	1981–83	1991–93	2001–3	2008
Indonesia	1.8	2.5	3.7	4.4	4.5	4.9
Malaysia	2.1	2.5	2.7	2.9	3.2	3.6
Philippines	1.2	1.5	2.4	2.9	3.3	3.8
Burma	1.6	1.7	3.1	3.0	3.5	3.7
Cambodia	1.1	1.4	1.2	1.3	2.0	2.7
Laos	0.9	1.3	1.5	2.4	3.2	3.5
Thailand	1.8	1.9	2.0	2.2	2.6	3.0
Vietnam	2.0	2.2	2.4	3.3	4.5	5.2

Rice production (million tonnes)

	1961–63	1971–73	1981–83	1991–93	2001–3	2008
Indonesia	12.2	20.4	33.9	47.0	51.4	60.3
Malaysia	1.1	1.9	1.9	2.0	2.2	2.4
Philippines	3.9	5.0	7.9	9.5	13.2	16.8
Burma	7.4	8.0	14.3	14.9	22.3	30.5
Cambodia	2.3	1.9	1.8	2.3	4.2	7.2
Laos	0.5	0.8	1.1	1.3	2.4	2.7
Thailand	11.2	13.7	18.1	19.6	26.5	30.5
Vietnam	9.5	10.8	13.8	21.3	33.7	38.7
Price (Y2000 = 100)	71	102	172	142	92	344

Plate 34

The contemporary regional distribution of rice-exporting and -importing countries is reminiscent of the situation that prevailed during the colonial period, particularly during the first decades of the twentieth century. Several mainland countries, namely Burma, Thailand and Cambodia, along with Cochinchina (which corresponds to the southernmost region of Vietnam, centering on the Mekong Delta), were rice exporters, while the archipelago countries, particularly Indonesia and Malaysia, imported rice. In general terms, the situation has not changed much, except that: 1) the trade flows have been somewhat modified, 2) Vietnam's share of the export market has increased very significantly, and 3) the Philippines' rice deficit has become even more important than Indonesia's.

Regarding trade flows, although still focused on the Southeast Asian region, they have diversified. During colonial days, surpluses were largely redistributed either within a given colonial domain or at least within the more immediate Asian realm. For example, Cochinchina's rice surpluses were predominantly destined for other French colonies, particularly Tonkin (Northern Vietnam); Burma's were in part sold to Malaya, like itself a British colony, and also to India, Pakistan and Ceylon, as well as Indonesia, while two of the major importers of Thailand's surpluses were Malaya and Indonesia (Fisher 1966: 456, 512). In 2007, Thailand's and Vietnam's total exports were over three times more substantial than the combined rice deficits of the major regional importers, the Philippines, Indonesia and Malaysia (~14 million versus some 4 million tonnes). Consequently their exports have become much more globalized.

The respective contribution of the leading rice exporters has evolved markedly. That is notably the case of Burma, which, by the mid-1950s, had regained over Thailand its rank as the world's leading rice exporter (Fisher 1966: 455) and held that position until 1962–63, when it was definitely overtaken by its neighbour to the east. Since then, its

absolute contribution, and even more its relative contribution, have declined dramatically, to such a degree that by the middle of the first decade of the twenty-first century Burma was not exporting any significant amount of rice anymore. On the other hand, Thailand's own exports have grown in leaps and bounds, notwithstanding very strong annual fluctuations* that are largely linked to international prices and market instability, which themselves are partly linked to crop harvesting hazards throughout the world. This also explains the even more noticeable fluctuations in the annual rice imports of Indonesia, Malaysia and the Philippines. These variations do not, however, hide the fact that among those three countries, the long-term trend has been one of an increase in annual rice imports. The only exception among the region's traditional rice importers is Laos, which seems to have been able to reduce its dependency, largely thanks to the very strong growth of national rice production (Figure 6.4).

The phenomenal rate of growth of Thailand's exports, more noticeable from the mid-1970s onwards, has been duplicated by Vietnam in a particularly sharp manner since 1987, which happens to be the year that followed the adoption of *Doi Moi*, the Vietnamese "New Economic Policy". In this manner, Vietnam's exports more than filled the gap left by the collapse of Burma's and, less importantly Cambodia's, own exports. Such "transfers" of crop surpluses have long been a key characteristic of the evolution of Southeast Asian agricultures, and become even more noticeable when cash crop production and exports are concerned. Rubber production and export patterns clearly exemplify this (Figures 7.9–7.14).

Along with an increase in their exports, both Thailand and Vietnam have seen their rice export ratio climb significantly, while the reverse has understandably occurred in Burma. Overall, Thailand is the country which by far devotes the largest share of its annual rice production to exports.

---

* As mentioned in the introductory chapter, these fluctuations are clearly illustrated in Figures 6.5–6.7, but not in the tables, where, because of limited printing space, only triannual averages are presented.

Figure 6.5 Rice exports in selected countries (with prices), 1961–2007

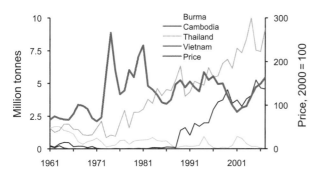

Source: FAOSTAT 2010; UNCTADstats 2010.

Figure 6.6 Rice export ratio in selected countries, 1961–2007

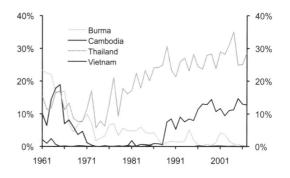

Source: FAOSTAT 2010.

Figure 6.7 Rice imports in selected countries, 1961–2007

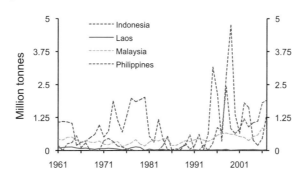

Source: FAOSTAT 2010.

Rice exports (million tonnes)

	1961–63	1971–73	1981–83	1991–93	2001–3	2007
Burma	1.7	0.5	0.7	0.2	0.7	0.0
Cambodia	0.2	0.0	0.0	0.0	0.0	0.0
Thailand	1.4	1.5	3.4	4.8	7.8	9.2
Vietnam	0.2	0.0	0.0	1.6	3.6	4.6

Rice export ratio (%)

	1961–63	1971–73	1981–83	1991–93	2001–3	2007
Burma	23	6	5	1	3	0
Cambodia	10	1	1	0	0	0
Thailand	13	11	19	25	29	29
Vietnam	2	0	0	7	11	13

Rice imports (million tonnes)

	1961–63	1971–73	1981–83	1991–93	2001–3	2007
Indonesia	1.1	1.0	0.7	0.3	1.4	1.4
Laos	0.1	0.1	0.0	0.0	0.0	0.0
Malaysia	0.4	0.2	0.4	0.4	0.5	0.8
Philippines	0.1	0.4	0.0	0.1	1.0	1.9
Price (Y2000 = 100)	71	102	172	142	92	163

Plate 35

In 2008, a total of 9.6 million hectares of maize was harvested throughout Southeast Asia, versus some 46.7 million hectares of rice. Since the 1960s, the expansion in rice and maize cultivation has proceeded at a more or less equal pace. However, in strict territorial terms, maize cultivation, spurred by the increasing demand from the local livestock industry, has expanded more rapidly. Even so, rice cultivation has continued to benefit from two types of advantages. The first is cultural in nature, rice remaining by far the more commonly preferred staple food across the region. The second is technical: thanks to improvement and expansion of irrigation, double and occasionally triple cropping of rice has become increasingly possible (Figures 5.21, 5.22 and 6.1–6.4), while maize has remained single cropped. Accordingly, while areas cultivated with rice may be counted two or even three times in rice harvested area statistics (Figure 6.1), that cannot be the case with maize harvested areas.

Even if the cultivation of corn (or maize) is much less widespread, this crop nonetheless remains of considerable importance, largely as a staple food, in Indonesia and even more so in the Philippines. In the latter country, area devoted to corn in 2008 represented nearly a quarter of total agricultural area, while rice covered slightly more than a third. Given that areas where rice is grown are often counted twice or three times in harvested area statistics, this strongly suggests that more land is actually devoted to the cultivation of maize in the Philippines. In Indonesia, the equivalent proportions stood respectively at about 7 per cent and 25 per cent. Furthermore, in each country, corn cultivation is regionally concentrated. In Indonesia it is widespread in Central and East Java as well

as on the neighbouring island of Madura and in the province of Nusa Tenggara Timur. There are also plans to expand its cultivation in Papua. In the Philippines, although some corn is cultivated on a majority of the larger islands, nearly 50 per cent of its acreage is found in Mindanao. It is also present in several of the Visayas islands, such as Bohol, Cebu and even Negros, where sugar remains nonetheless the dominant crop. However, while in Indonesia the corn harvested area has been expanding for decades, albeit with very sharp annual variations, in the Philippines it has been giving ground after having peaked in the early 1990s.

In Malaysia, Burma and Cambodia, corn has always remained a marginal crop, at least at the national scale. Such is not the case in Thailand and Vietnam, nor in Laos where, relatively speaking, corn harvested areas expanded most rapidly between 2000 and 2008. In Thailand, by the early 1960s corn cultivation had begun to expand rapidly, particularly in the Northeast region, largely to supply the country's animal feed industry and its exports to Japan. But by the mid-1980s, as Japan was reducing its own animal husbandry industry, external demand began to dwindle for Thailand, leading to a gradual and equivalent reduction in the area devoted to corn cultivation. In Vietnam, even if by 2008 corn harvested area was equivalent to only one seventh of that devoted to rice, cultivation has been expanding at an accelerating pace since the 1970s. Although it is still too early to judge, an expansion phase also seems to be in the making in Burma and Cambodia. Finally, Malaysia is the only country in the region remaining largely indifferent to corn cultivation.

Figure 6.8 Harvested area of maize by country, 1961–2008

Archipelagic Southeast Asia

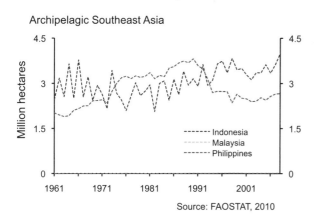

Mainland Southeast Asia

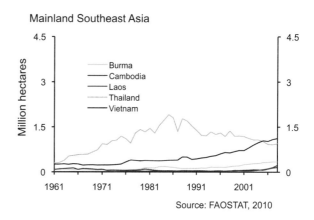

Figure 6.9 Percentage of agricultural area allocated to maize production by country, 1961–2008

Archipelagic Southeast Asia

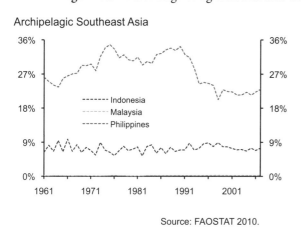

Mainland Southeast Asia

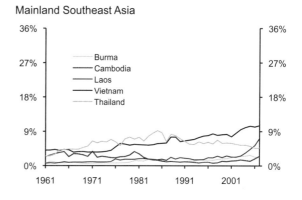

Harvested area of maize (million hectares)

	1961–63	1971–73	1981–83	1991–93	2001–3	2008
Indonesia	2.7	2.7	2.7	3.2	3.3	4.0
Malaysia	0.0	0.0	0.0	0.0	0.0	0.0
Philippines	2.0	2.5	3.3	3.4	2.4	2.7
Burma	0.1	0.1	0.2	0.1	0.3	0.4
Cambodia	0.1	0.1	0.1	0.1	0.1	0.2
Laos	0.0	0.0	0.0	0.0	0.1	0.2
Thailand	0.3	0.1	1.5	1.3	1.8	1.0
Vietnam	0.3	0.2	0.4	0.5	0.8	1.0

Percentage of agricultural area allocated to maize cultivation

	1961–63	1971–73	1981–83	1991–93	2001–3	2008
Indonesia	7	7	7	8	7	7
Malaysia	0	0	0	0	0	0
Philippines	25	30	30	31	22	23
Burma	1	1	1	1	2	2
Cambodia	3	3	2	1	1	3
Laos	1	1	2	2	2	7
Vietnam	4	4	6	7	9	11
Thailand	3	6	7	6	6	5

Plate 36

Between 1961 and 2008, maize producers did even better than rice producers in terms of yield increases, even if, by 2008, average yields of maize had still not quite reached the level of those obtained with rice. In three of the four major maize-producing countries, namely, Indonesia, Vietnam and Thailand, yields then stood at about 4 tonnes per hectare, having more or less quadrupled in the first two countries. However, Thailand's yields, which in the early 1960s were already — and by far — the highest in the region, only doubled over the nearly 50-year period. In the Philippines, where cornfields were already among Southeast Asia's least productive in the early 1960s, yields were actually the lowest by 2008, remaining well below 3 tonnes per hectare. Laotian producers then did much better, with an unequalled 4.8 tonnes per hectare. As for Burmese corn growers, they achieved the most important yield increases in the region, their land's average productivity having grown at the average annual rate of 3.4 per cent between 1961 and 2008.

Across the region, overall maize production was multiplied by a factor of 7.3, a proportionately much more important increase than the one attained in the rice sector, although total volume of production remained largely inferior (in 2008, ~34 million tonnes of maize versus 189 million tonnes of rice). In other words, harvested area expansion contributed more to rice production growth — largely thanks to double and occasionally triple cropping — than it did for corn production. This was nonetheless compensated by the fact that corn producers achieved greater yield improvements than rice farmers did.

In 2008, nearly half of the total volume of corn produced throughout Southeast Asia was contributed by Indonesia. In that country, total production over the nearly 50-year period was multiplied by more than six, a performance slightly inferior to the overall regional average. However significant that increase, it pales when compared to that achieved in Vietnam, where total production was multiplied by a factor of 15.8. Even more spectacularly high increases were achieved in Burma and Laos. Between 1961 and 2008, Burma's corn production was multiplied by a factor of 17, while Laos multiplied its production by 66 over the same period! This still ongoing and accelerating burst of corn production in Laos is largely attributable to the growth of contract farming, in which large business concerns such as the CP group — Thailand's largest multinational company specializing in food product manufacturing — are increasingly investing, in order to supply their animal feed mills. The same is occurring within Cambodia and Vietnam, where yields and production have also increased rapidly since the mid-1990s. Thailand is the only country where total production peaked and then, in the mid-1990s, started decreasing more or less steadily.

Figure 6.10 Maize yield by country, 1961–2008

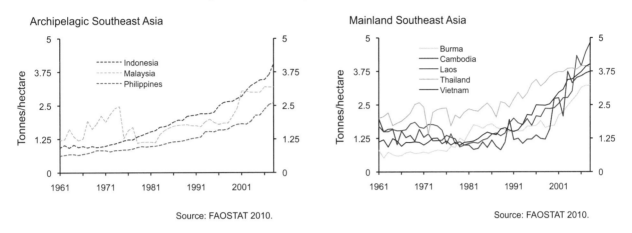

Archipelagic Southeast Asia

Source: FAOSTAT 2010.

Mainland Southeast Asia

Source: FAOSTAT 2010.

Figure 6.11 Maize production by country (with prices), 1961–2008

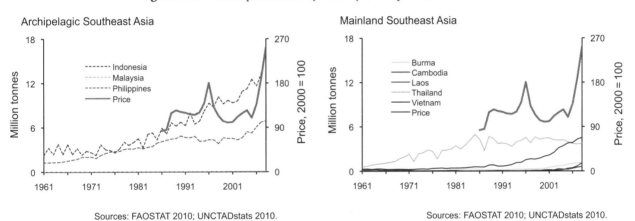

Archipelagic Southeast Asia

Sources: FAOSTAT 2010; UNCTADstats 2010.

Mainland Southeast Asia

Sources: FAOSTAT 2010; UNCTADstats 2010.

Maize yield (tonnes/hectare)

	1961–63	1971–73	1981–83	1991–93	2001–3	2008
Indonesia	1.0	1.0	1.6	2.2	3.1	4.1
Malaysia	1.4	2.2	1.2	1.8	3.0	3.2
Philippines	0.7	0.8	1.0	1.4	1.8	2.6
Burma	0.7	0.7	1.6	1.5	2.3	3.2
Cambodia	1.7	1.3	0.9	1.2	2.9	3.8
Laos	1.6	1.7	1.1	1.9	2.7	4.8
Thailand	2.1	2.0	2.3	2.8	3.8	3.9
Vietnam	1.1	1.1	1.2	1.6	3.2	4.0

Maize production (million tonnes)

	1961–63	1971–73	1981–83	1991–93	2001–3	2008
Indonesia	2.6	2.9	4.3	6.9	9.9	16.3
Malaysia	0.0	0.0	0.0	0.0	0.1	0.1
Philippines	1.3	2.0	3.3	4.7	4.5	6.9
Burma	0.1	0.1	0.3	0.2	0.6	1.1
Cambodia	0.2	0.1	0.1	0.1	0.2	0.6
Laos	0.0	0.0	0.0	0.1	0.1	1.1
Thailand	0.7	2.0	3.3	3.6	4.3	3.8
Vietnam	0.3	0.3	0.4	0.8	2.6	4.5
Price (Y2000 = 100)				118	111	253

Plate 37

Since the early 1960s, total exports of maize throughout the Southeast Asian region have remained modest. Their 2007 value was just above that of 1961. In 2007, they were equal to a small fraction (~5 per cent) of rice exports. Only Thailand appears as an important exporting country, but that status is unlikely to last for long. Beginning in the early 1960s, the country's exports — largely intended for the Japanese market — went through a period of very strong growth, which peaked then collapsed in the mid-1980s, at a time when local production had begun to slow down, while local demand, basically from the animal feed industry, particularly for chicken rearing, was growing rapidly. Consequently, its maize export ratio, exceptionally high until the mid-1980s, also collapsed. Indonesia, by far the region's most important corn producer, keeps a very low export ratio and remains a marginal source of corn exports. Burma on the other hand, whose production has been increasing significantly since the late 1980s, has maintained a relatively high ratio of exports, albeit modest in comparison to the rest of the region.

Southeast Asia's maize imports are much more important than its exports, while the reverse situation prevails in the rice sector (Figures 6.5 and 6.7). Still insignificant in the early 1960s, annual maize imports had grown substantially by 2007, from less than 100,000 to more than 4 million tonnes. Until the 1980s, Thailand supplied much of the demand.

Since then, the demand, while fast rising, has been increasingly met by producers from the Americas: the United States, Brazil and Argentina. In the region, demand for foreign corn emanates primarily from Malaysia, the country's imports accounting for two-thirds of the region's total in 2007. As already pointed out, the cultivation of maize remains quite limited in Malaysia (Figure 6.8), while local market demand from the pig rearing and particularly the chicken rearing sectors has been growing fast (Figures 6.19–6.24). Production in the latter sector keeps expanding, particularly from large-scale broiler and layer farms. Consequently, among Malaysia's cereal imports, corn tops the list, well ahead of rice and wheat (USDA 2010).

Vietnam's growing presence on the import market is revealing of its agricultural dynamism. The country's imports have risen sharply since the early years of the twenty-first century along with the even sharper expansion of the chicken and, particularly, pig rearing industries (Figures 6.19–6.24).

Throughout the region, demand for corn is likely to continue to grow, along with the expansion of the chicken and pig rearing sectors, themselves largely determined by the growth of the regional population's purchasing power and nutritional requirements. Whether this will mean an increasing reliance on corn imports from outside the region remains to be seen as the potential for increases in local corn production remains strong.

Figure 6.12 Maize exports in selected countries (with prices), 1961–2007

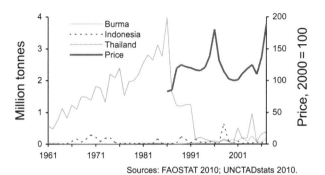

Sources: FAOSTAT 2010; UNCTADstats 2010.

Figure 6.13 Maize export ratio in selected countries, 1961–2007

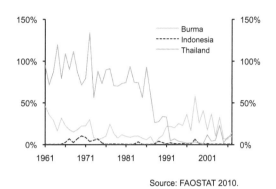

Source: FAOSTAT 2010.

Figure 6.14 Maize imports in selected countries, 1961–2007

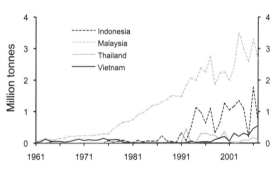

Source: FAOSTAT 2010.

Maize exports (million tonnes)

	1961–63	1971–73	1981–83	1991–93	2001–3	2007
Burma	0.0	0.0	0.0	0.0	0.1	0.2
Indonesia	0.0	0.2	0.0	0.1	0.1	0.1
Thailand	0.6	1.6	2.7	0.5	0.3	0.4

Maize export ratio (%)

	1961–63	1971–73	1981–83	1991–93	2001–3	2007
Burma	46	20	9	21	21	14
Indonesia	0	6	0	1	0	1
Thailand	95	89	80	14	7	10

Maize imports (million tonnes)

	1961–63	1971–73	1981–83	1991–93	2001–3	2007
Indonesia	0.0	0.0	0.0	0.3	1.2	0.7
Malaysia	0.1	0.2	0.9	1.8	2.6	2.7
Thailand	0.0	0.0	0.0	0.2	0.0	0.1
Vietnam	0.0	0.1	0.0	0.0	0.2	0.5

Price (Y2000 = 100)				118	111	189

Plate 38

Fruit cultivation is particularly widespread in Southeast Asia, where it has a long and well-documented history (Blench 2004 and 2008). With improvements in living standards in the region as well as a gradual increase in world demand, it has been expanding steadily over recent decades. Between 1961 and 2008, areas devoted to the production of fruits more than doubled in all countries. In absolute terms, the greatest expansion was achieved in the Philippines and Thailand, with Vietnam and Indonesia also doing quite well. In the last country, expansion seems to have been somewhat bumpy, although this might be attributable to the difficulty of compiling adequate data on a yearly basis. The term "fresh fruits" covers a wide array of products,* and it is not difficult to imagine that, given the size of the Indonesian archipelago, uneven reporting may occur. This being said, sharp declines in area harvested reported in Indonesia for the mid-1970s, the late 1990s and the middle of the first decade of the twenty-first century are hard to explain, although they might be partly attributable to climatic vagaries as well as the intensity of the 1997–98 Asian economic crisis that hit the archipelagic country particularly hard. Since the early 1960s, overall Southeast Asian fruit production has been multiplied by a factor of 4.6. Given that total fruit cultivated area has expanded by a factor of 2.2, this means that average yield per hectare has itself more than doubled, and/or that species producing a higher tonnage per hectare are gradually being favoured in the region. As for overall production growth, the greatest fruit producers in the region, Indonesia and the Philippines, are also those that achieved by far the best performances between 1961 and 2008.

The largest expanse of land devoted to fruit cultivation, both in absolute and in proportionate terms (in relation to total agricultural land), is found in the Philippines, its total harvest being more or less equal, weight wise, to that of its much larger Indonesian neighbour. The highest fruit land productivity (production/area) is also achieved in these archipelagic countries, Indonesia being well ahead of the Philippines on that count, with Vietnam and Thailand following not too far behind. This superiority cannot be attributed to the nature of fruits being cultivated as diversity seems to prevail nearly everywhere, particularly in the two archipelagic countries. Nevertheless, weight wise, bananas represent the most important fruit crop in just about every country in the region, generally accounting for ~20 per cent to ~40 per cent of total harvests, their share being exceptionally high in Cambodia, where they account for more than half of the total fruit harvest. The second most important fruit or fruit category is "mangoes, mangosteens, guavas", particularly well represented in, again, the Philippines, Indonesia, and especially Thailand. In these three countries, the three species of fruit accounted for 17 per cent, 27 per cent and 33 per cent of the total 2005 fruit harvest respectively. Among other "specialties", oranges are much more widespread in Indonesia as well as in several mainland countries.

Malaysia, Laos and Cambodia appear as the countries least involved in fruit cultivation, as measured by area cultivated and production, in absolute as well as relative terms. However, notwithstanding its relatively limited production — equivalent to one tenth that of the Philippines', whose surface area is slightly less extensive — Malaysia's fruit yields are comparable to those of its archipelagic neighbour.

---

* FAO statistics used here do not actually reveal the extent of that diversity, given the importance of the category "Fruit Tropical, NES (not elsewhere stated)", which includes a large number of well-known products, such as durian — the region's so-called king of fruits — jackfruit, dragon fruit and pineapple. The relative importance of that NES category is indicative of the imprecision of national reporting; it represents percentages as high as 82 per cent of all tropical fruits in Burma and 47 per cent in Vietnam and as "low" as 22 per cent in Thailand and 20 per cent in the Philippines.

Figure 6.15 Harvested area of fresh fruits by country, 1961–2008*

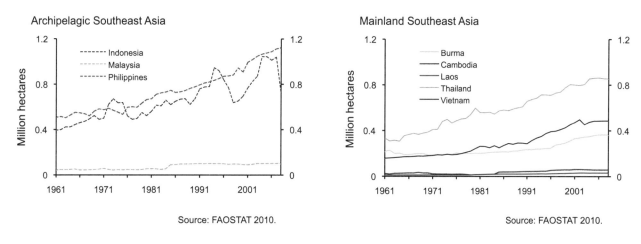

Source: FAOSTAT 2010.

Source: FAOSTAT 2010.

Figure 6.16 Fresh fruit production by country, 1961–2008*

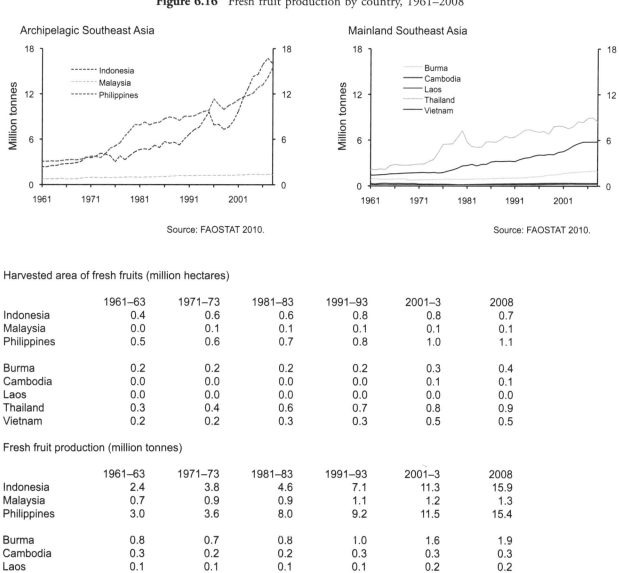

Source: FAOSTAT 2010.

Source: FAOSTAT 2010.

Harvested area of fresh fruits (million hectares)

	1961–63	1971–73	1981–83	1991–93	2001–3	2008
Indonesia	0.4	0.6	0.6	0.8	0.8	0.7
Malaysia	0.0	0.1	0.1	0.1	0.1	0.1
Philippines	0.5	0.6	0.7	0.8	1.0	1.1
Burma	0.2	0.2	0.2	0.2	0.3	0.4
Cambodia	0.0	0.0	0.0	0.0	0.1	0.1
Laos	0.0	0.0	0.0	0.0	0.0	0.0
Thailand	0.3	0.4	0.6	0.7	0.8	0.9
Vietnam	0.2	0.2	0.3	0.3	0.5	0.5

Fresh fruit production (million tonnes)

	1961–63	1971–73	1981–83	1991–93	2001–3	2008
Indonesia	2.4	3.8	4.6	7.1	11.3	15.9
Malaysia	0.7	0.9	0.9	1.1	1.2	1.3
Philippines	3.0	3.6	8.0	9.2	11.5	15.4
Burma	0.8	0.7	0.8	1.0	1.6	1.9
Cambodia	0.3	0.2	0.2	0.3	0.3	0.3
Laos	0.1	0.1	0.1	0.1	0.2	0.2
Thailand	2.1	2.9	5.3	6.8	7.7	8.4
Vietnam	1.4	1.7	2.7	3.4	4.8	5.7

* Excluding melons

Plate 39

Cultivation as well as trade of fruits and vegetables are deeply embedded in village economy throughout the region, even if the nature of the demand and of the ensuing markets is increasingly influenced by the rapid growth of urban demand (Cadilhon *et al.* 2003). By 2008, throughout the Southeast Asian region, the total area devoted to vegetable cultivation remained slightly inferior to that devoted to fruit cultivation (3.2 million versus 3.8 million hectares for fruits). During the period examined, cultivated area doubled, while total production nearly quadrupled, a performance nearly equal to that achieved by the fruit production sector. However, fruit remained more productive, at least in terms of yield per hectare. While the region's fruit lands produced nearly 50 million tonnes of fruits in 2008, Southeast Asia's gardens and vegetable plots then yielded some 31 million tonnes of vegetables.

Although all countries have been involved in the growth in area cultivated, productivity and production achievements have differed rather widely, with major performers not necessarily being the same as for the fruit sector. Among more populated countries, the more remarkable rates of increase in area cultivated have been achieved in Burma, Vietnam and Indonesia. While Burma has been characterized by a steady and increasingly strong rate of growth throughout the period, the rate of expansion has been exceptionally rapid in Vietnam since the mid-1980s. As for Indonesia, although its vegetable harvested area benefited from a level of growth similar to the regional average over the nearly 50-year period examined, expansion was punctuated by more acute fluctuations than in other countries. Somewhat surprisingly, expansion of vegetable land in both Thailand and the Philippines has proceeded less rapidly than in all other countries except Cambodia, despite having maintained a steady rate of growth. Both Laos and Malaysia have done quite well, even if their respective total area cultivated remains relatively modest in absolute figures. When average yields are calculated, Malaysia, Burma and Vietnam show the best results, while the three countries having achieved the highest rates of increase are Indonesia, the Philippines and Burma.

When evolution of production is examined, Laos appears as the leading performer, with Burma not far behind. Laos' performance is attributable to a combination of well above average rates of growth in area cultivated as well as yields. Indonesia, Malaysia and Vietnam benefited from above average production increases, something the Philippines, Thailand and Cambodia could not achieve. Overall, region wide, the average rate of growth in vegetable production surpassed that of population: while production grew more than fourfold over the 47-year period, population was multiplied by ~2.6. Over the same period, vegetable production grew much faster than population in Burma and Laos, and, to a lesser extent, in Indonesia, Malaysia and Vietnam. While both indicators grew at a similar pace in Thailand, Cambodia's and the Philippines' growth in vegetable production did not keep pace with demographic growth.

In comparison, the growth in fruit production was slightly more significant, as it was multiplied by 4.6, but national performances were somewhat differently distributed. For example, Indonesia and the Philippines, where the fruit sector benefited from the greatest production increase in both absolute and relative terms (Figures 6.15 and 6.16), were among the countries where the rate of growth was higher than that of the population.

Figure 6.17 Harvested area of fresh vegetables by country, 1961–2008

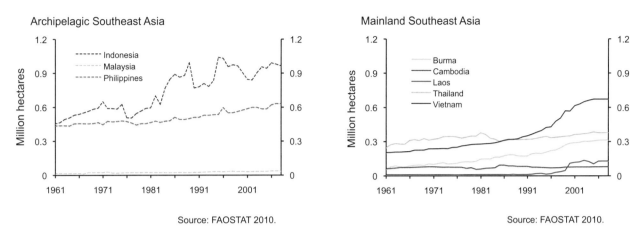

Archipelagic Southeast Asia

Source: FAOSTAT 2010.

Mainland Southeast Asia

Source: FAOSTAT 2010.

Figure 6.18 Fresh vegetable production by country, 1961–2008

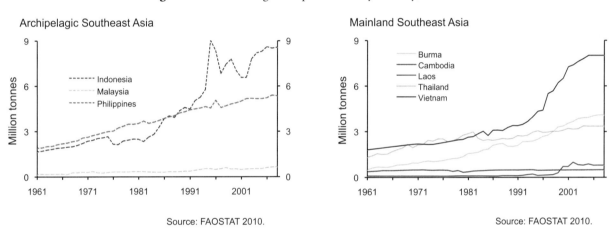

Archipelagic Southeast Asia

Source: FAOSTAT 2010.

Mainland Southeast Asia

Source: FAOSTAT 2010.

Harvested area of fresh vegetables (million hectares)

	1961–63	1971–73	1981–83	1991–93	2001–3	2008
Indonesia	0.5	0.6	0.6	0.8	0.9	1.0
Malaysia	0.0	0.0	0.0	0.0	0.0	0.0
Philippines	0.4	0.5	0.5	0.5	0.6	0.6
Burma	0.1	0.1	0.1	0.2	0.3	0.3
Cambodia	0.1	0.1	0.1	0.1	0.1	0.1
Laos	0.0	0.1	0.0	0.0	0.1	0.1
Thailand	0.3	0.3	0.4	0.3	0.4	0.4
Vietnam	0.2	0.2	0.3	0.4	0.6	0.7

Fresh vegetable production (million tonnes)

	1961–63	1971–73	1981–83	1991–93	2001–3	2008
Indonesia	1.7	2.4	2.5	4.9	7.0	8.5
Malaysia	0.1	0.3	0.3	0.4	0.5	0.6
Philippines	1.9	2.7	3.6	4.5	5.1	5.3
Burma	0.6	1.0	1.6	2.2	3.7	4.1
Cambodia	0.4	0.5	0.4	0.5	0.5	0.5
Laos	0.1	0.1	0.1	0.1	0.8	0.8
Thailand	1.4	2.2	2.8	2.7	3.2	3.4
Vietnam	1.8	2.2	2.7	3.5	7.4	8.0

Plate 40

Southeast Asian agricultures are predominantly focused on crop production, livestock being relatively marginal, at least in comparison with most other major agricultural regions of the world (Figure 5.11). However, two forms of livestock production, chickens and pigs, have become increasingly important over the last decades. Thus, since the early 1960s, chicken production has grown at a faster rate than that of any major food crop, and even of most commercial crops. However, the rate of growth remained modest until the late 1970s, when production really took off, along with the practice of raising battery chickens, particularly in four countries, namely the three archipelagic ones and Thailand. Between the early 1970s and 2008, total annual production in these four countries was multiplied by nine and, in Indonesia alone, by about 15. This is notwithstanding the major collapse which occurred during the 1997–98 Asian financial crisis and impacted Indonesia's production more badly than any other and following which 1996 production levels were regained only in 2001–2 (Bond *et al.* 2007). In Thailand, production, which had begun to expand earlier than anywhere else, underwent a spectacular boom from 1985 until 2002–3, collapsing in 2004 following an outbreak of the avian flu (Tiensin *et al.* 2005). By 2008, pre-outbreak production levels had not yet recovered.

In Malaysia and the Philippines growth rates, particularly since the late 1980s, although not quite as strong as in the other two major producing countries, have been steadier and less affected by conjuncture, as they relied more on domestic markets. In Burma and Vietnam, production has also increased significantly, with truly rapid growth having begun more recently. For example, in Burma production picked up in 1994 with a vengeance,

having since been multiplied by 8.7, thus growing at an average yearly rate of ~17 per cent. Vietnamese chicken production also began to rise significantly in the mid-1990s, though this growth stopped abruptly in 2003–4 following the rapid spread of a highly pathogenic strain of H5N1, an avian influenza that claimed victims in the region's poultry and human populations. The impact on production of the avian flu epidemic was less damaging in Vietnam than it had been in Thailand, where it had begun to spread rapidly a year earlier and brought about an almost complete interruption in the kingdom's chicken exports.

By the early 1980s, exports had started to develop significantly in Thailand, expanding at an exceptionally rapid rate until their 2004 collapse. As a percentage of national production, exports had reached nearly 30 per cent the preceding year, a unique achievement in the region, where chicken meat production is almost exclusively oriented towards the local market, as are most other forms of poultry production, particularly duck meat. This is yet another illustration of Thailand's rather special position in Southeast Asia as a very dynamic food exporter. Having recovered from the 2003–4 sanitary crisis, its chicken production sector is already eyeing new export markets, such as Russia, the world's largest chicken importer. In the region, Malaysia is the only other country to have made a foray into chicken meat export activities, a move that began in the late 1980s. However, those exports never became significant, nor were they maintained for much more than a decade.

Finally, in Laos and particularly in Cambodia, the chicken production sector seems to have grown at a much slower pace than in the other countries.

Figure 6.19 Chicken meat production by country, 1961–2008

Archipelagic Southeast Asia

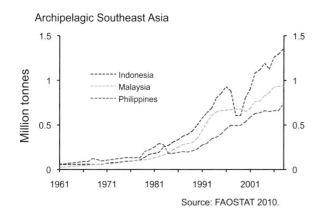

Source: FAOSTAT 2010.

Mainland Southeast Asia

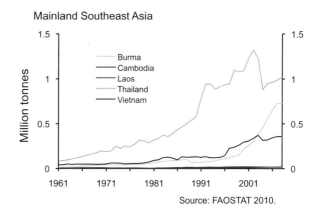

Source: FAOSTAT 2010.

Figure 6.20 Chicken meat exports in selected countries, 1961–2007

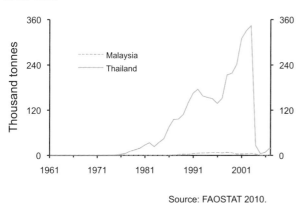

Source: FAOSTAT 2010.

Figure 6.21 Chicken meat export ratio in selected countries, 1961–2007

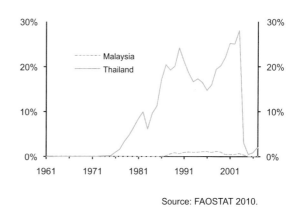

Source: FAOSTAT 2010.

Chicken meat production (million tonnes)

	1961–63	1971–73	1981–83	1991–93	2001–3	2008
Indonesia	0.1	0.1	0.2	0.6	1.0	1.4
Malaysia	0.0	0.1	0.1	0.5	0.7	0.9
Philippines	0.1	0.1	0.3	0.3	0.6	0.7
Burma	0.0	0.0	0.1	0.1	0.3	0.7
Cambodia	0.0	0.0	0.0	0.0	0.0	0.0
Laos	0.0	0.0	0.0	0.0	0.0	0.0
Thailand	0.1	0.2	0.3	0.9	1.3	1.0
Vietnam	0.0	0.1	0.1	0.1	0.3	0.4

Chicken meat exports (thousand tonnes)

	1961–63	1971–73	1981–83	1991–93	2001–3	2007
Malaysia	0.0	0.0	0.0	5.0	3.9	0.7
Thailand	0.0	0.0	27.7	165.4	327.8	19.9

Chicken meat export ratio (%)

	1961–63	1971–73	1981–83	1991–93	2001–3	2007
Malaysia	0	0	0	1	1	0
Thailand	0	0	8	19	26	2

Plate 41

Pig rearing has a long history in the region, with renowned cultural geographer Carl O. Sauer (1952) having even argued that its domestication actually began in Southeast Asia and spread from there to China. Among many minority groups, notably — but not exclusively — in upland regions, pig rearing and the hunting of wild boar are still widespread; and most cultural groups, including the Chinese, tend to include pork meat in their diet. Yet, largely for cultural reasons, including its rejection by Islam, it remains almost absent from some regions, particularly within Malaysia and Indonesia. However, in these two places, pig meat was not completely banned from the diet of Muslim populations until recently.

Whatever the case, throughout Southeast Asia pig production quadrupled over the 25-year period from 1983 to 2008. During the same quarter of a century, in absolute terms, production by far increased the most in Vietnam, where the consumption of pork meat is common among most cultural groups, including the largely dominant Kinh. Following were the Philippines, where Christianity prevails, and predominantly Buddhist Thailand. However, relatively speaking, it is in Burma that pork meat production grew the most rapidly. In a country where Buddhists also constitute a strong majority, production has leaped forward from 1990 onwards, having altogether increased more than eightfold during the following 18 years.

Indonesia took a different pathway: production nearly tripled during the 1980s and continued to increase until 1994, having since levelled off and wavered. This might be seen as a consequence of the increasing pressure exerted by radical Islamists on the majority Muslim population to abstain from consuming pork meat. The same probably explains the even more noticeable production drop — at least in proportionate terms — that has occurred in neighbouring Malaysia over the same period; at least in the sense that, in that country, the intolerance to pork rearing and consumption has been applied towards non-Muslim populations, particularly the Chinese, allegedly because of Muslim sensitivities. This has occurred in a context where the Malaysian pork rearing industry has found a partial solution to its predicament by attempting to answer to the increasing demand from its urbanized and largely Chinese neighbour, the city-state of Singapore (Taiganides 1992). Beginning in the late 1970s, the latter had begun to restructure its pig farming industry, finally phasing it out completely by 1990, largely for environmental reasons.

Regarding exports, the Vietnamese pig rearing industry behaved somewhat like the Thai chicken rearing industry had done (Figures 6.20 and 6.21). Beginning in the early 1980s, pig meat shipments increased noticeably, although not so massively, since total exports never surpassed 6 per cent of national production. And, shortly after a peak had been reached — in 1997 for the export ratio and in 2000 for gross exports — shipments collapsed in 2001–2, following an outbreak of swine fever in the region. However, and contrary to what happened with Thai chicken meat production following the avian flu outbreak of 2003, this sanitary crisis did not significantly affect the actual local production of pig meat, which kept on rising, leveling off only in 2006–8.

Figure 6.22 Pig meat production by country, 1961–2008

Archipelagic Southeast Asia

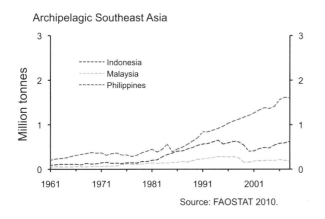

Mainland Southeast Asia

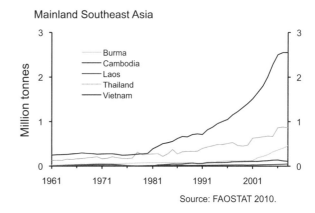

Source: FAOSTAT 2010.

Figure 6.23 Pig meat exports in selected countries, 1961–2007

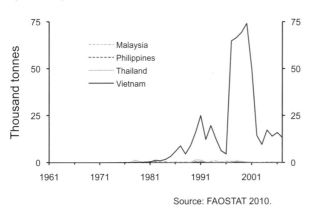

Source: FAOSTAT 2010.

Figure 6.24 Pig meat export ratio in selected countries, 1961–2007

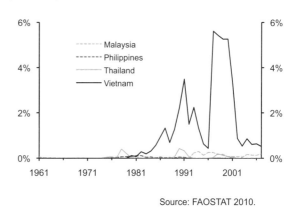

Source: FAOSTAT 2010.

Pig meat production (million tonnes)

	1961–63	1971–73	1981–83	1991–93	2001–3	2008
Indonesia	0.1	0.2	0.2	0.6	0.5	0.6
Malaysia	0.1	0.1	0.1	0.3	0.2	0.2
Philippines	0.2	0.4	0.4	0.9	1.3	1.6
Burma	0.0	0.1	0.1	0.1	0.2	0.5
Cambodia	0.0	0.0	0.0	0.1	0.1	0.1
Laos	0.0	0.0	0.0	0.0	0.0	0.1
Thailand	0.1	0.2	0.3	0.4	0.7	0.9
Vietnam	0.3	0.3	0.5	0.8	1.7	2.6

Pig meat exports (thousand tonnes)

	1961–63	1971–73	1981–83	1991–93	2001–3	2007
Malaysia	0.0	0.0	0.0	0.2	0.1	0.4
Philippines	0.0	0.0	0.4	0.1	0.0	0.0
Thailand	0.0	0.0	0.0	0.5	0.1	0.1
Vietnam	0.0	0.0	0.9	19.0	24.7	13.3

Pig meat export ratio (%)

	1961–63	1971–73	1981–83	1991–93	2001–3	2007
Malaysia	0	0	0	0	0	0
Philippines	0	0	0	0	0	0
Thailand	0	0	0	0	0	0
Vietnam	0	0	0	2	2	1

CHAPTER 7

Expansion and Intensification of Cash Crops

"An increase in agricultural productivity in lowlands, for example, reduces pressures on natural resource exploitation on marginal lands as we noted in the case of the likely effects of Green Revolution on deforestation."

(Balisacan and Fuwa 2007: 25)

Plate 42

Among major plantation crops cultivated in South-east Asia, oil palm is the one whose territorial expansion has been the most significant since the postcolonial period. In 1961 oil palm plantations covered less than 115,000 hectares, and in 2008 they covered over 9 million hectares. In absolute figures, this expansion has been exceeded only by that of rice fields, which gained some 18 million hectares over the same period (Figure 6.1).

The actual oil palm boom began in the 1970s in Malaysia and Indonesia, with Thailand joining in during the 1990s, but at a much slower pace. Thai palm tree plantations, totalling 450,000 hectares in 2008, cannot compare to those of the two archipelago giants, whose combined plantation area, i.e., almost 9 million hectares, accounted for 60 per cent of the world total. In Malaysia, the increase in the relative importance of palm tree plantations over total agricultural area has been particularly spectacular: hardly significant in the early 1960s, it had reached 47.5 per cent in 2007. Except for rice in mainland Southeast Asia, particularly in Vietnam (Figure 6.2), no other crop has dominated the agricultural landscape to such an extent. Although they account for a much smaller proportion of the country's vast agricultural lands, Indonesia's oil palm plantations have by now expanded over a greater total area, having increased fivefold since 1990. As a result, by 2008 Indonesia's palm fruit production had become more abundant than Malaysia's.

Over the years, Malaysia's predominance has been partly attributable to the higher average yields obtained on its plantations, which almost doubled between 1961 and 2003, when they reached 20 tonnes of fruit per hectare. Those high yields have been maintained since, and so has the competitiveness of the country's oil palm industry. But the latter has to increasingly rely on foreign labour, largely provided by Indonesian migrants, particularly in Sabah and Sarawak. In fact, as the expansion of the Malaysian oil palm sector overflows into Indonesian territory, much of the capital fuelling the expansion of the Indonesian oil palm industry is being provided by Malaysian multinationals (De Koninck *et al.* 2011).

As for yield increases, crucial to the growth of the industry, they have been more important in Thailand than anywhere else. Thai plantations produced less than 6 tonnes of fruit per hectare from the early 1960s until 1975, but since 1999 Thai yields have averaged well over 16 tonnes per hectare. Nevertheless, Thailand's palm fruit production still has a long way to go before it can challenge that of Indonesia's and Malaysia's, whose combined production still amounted in 2008 to more than 80 per cent of the global total, a predominance never achieved by any other crop in the region. That year marked the fifth time the palm oil price index had stood over 200 since 1961, reaching a summit of 305.8. Previous occasions were in 1974, that is, one year after the first oil shock, then in the midst of the second oil shock in 1979, as well as in 1995 and 2007.

Figure 7.1 Harvested area of palm fruit in selected countries, 1961–2008

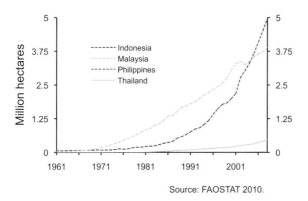

Source: FAOSTAT 2010.

Figure 7.2 Percentage of agricultural area allocated to palm fruit cultivation in selected countries, 1961–2007

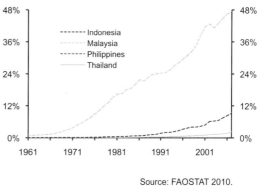

Source: FAOSTAT 2010.

Figure 7.3 Palm fruit yields in selected countries, 1961–2008

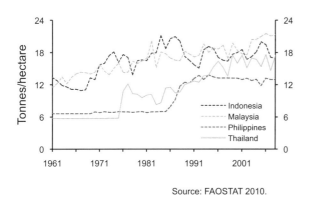

Source: FAOSTAT 2010.

Figure 7.4 Palm fruit production in selected countries (with palm oil prices), 1961–2008

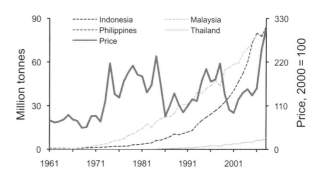

Sources: FAOSTAT 2010; UNCTADstats 2010.

Harvested area of palm fruit (million hectares)

	1961–63	1971–73	1981–83	1991–93	2001–3	2008
Indonesia	0.1	0.1	0.2	0.9	2.7	5.0
Malaysia	0.0	0.2	0.9	1.9	3.3	3.9
Philippines	0.0	0.0	0.0	0.0	0.0	0.0
Thailand	0.0	0.0	0.0	0.1	0.3	0.5

Percentage of agricultural area allocated to palm fruit cultivation

	1961–63	1971–73	1981–83	1991–93	2001–3	2007
Indonesia	0	0	1	2	6	9
Malaysia	1	5	17	25	42	48
Philippines	0	0	0	0	0	0
Thailand	0	0	0	1	1	2

Palm fruit yields (tonnes/hectare)

	1961–63	1971–73	1981–83	1991–93	2001–3	2008
Indonesia	12.7	16.4	17.5	16.5	17.6	17.0
Malaysia	12.5	14.7	17.5	18.2	18.6	21.3
Philippines	6.7	6.9	7.0	13.3	13.0	13.0
Thailand	5.8	5.8	9.6	13.0	16.6	17.5

Palm fruit production (million tonnes)

	1961–63	1971–73	1981–83	1991–93	2001–3	2008
Indonesia	0.9	1.6	4.2	14.2	46.8	85.0
Malaysia	0.6	3.4	15.9	34.8	61.8	83.0
Philippines	0.0	0.0	0.1	0.2	0.2	0.3
Thailand	0.0	0.0	0.2	1.5	4.3	7.9
Price (Y2000 = 100)	70	92	163	119	120	306

Plate 43

Although an increasing number of Southeast Asian countries are attempting to join the palm oil boom, none of their production withstands any comparison with the production of Indonesia and Malaysia, respectively the region's and the world's first and second most important producers in 2008. That year, Indonesia's production of palm oil accounted for 50 per cent of the regional total and 44 per cent of the world's. For Malaysia, the same values respectively reached 47 per cent and 41 per cent. In the early 1960s, Indonesia's palm oil production was already superior to that of its neighbour. However, as Malaysia's palm oil expansion picked up later during that decade, its production rapidly overtook Indonesia's. From the mid-1970s until the end of the 1980s, Malaysia's production remained between three and four times more important than that of Indonesia. By the 1980s, however, Indonesia's production had begun to grow faster than Malaysia's. Between 1990 and 2007, it was multiplied by seven, reaching nearly 17 million tonnes in 2008. In comparison, Malaysia's output was multiplied by a factor of 2.6 over the same period. Concurrently, Indonesia's production exceeded that of its neighbour's in 2006, in the midst of a never before seen price increase.

Since the early 1960s, Malaysia has been steadily exporting over 75 per cent of its palm oil produced, although that ratio has been somewhat reduced over the years. The outlook is different for Indonesia, whose export ratio has generally remained below that of Malaysia, largely because of much greater internal demand. Although its recent production boom has allowed for a significant rise in both its total exports and export ratio, internal demand is likely to continue to limit the latter, which will continue to lag behind its neighbour's. In addition to these internal demand issues, part of Malaysia's palm oil exports consist of re-exports, as the country's palm oil imports — largely from Indonesia — have been the most important in the region since the early years of the twenty-first century. Given the relative importance of its imports, the fact that Malaysia is a leading producer also distinguishes it from the other regional importers, whose production, if any, remains modest.

As already stated, the Philippines' and Thailand's palm oil production stand no comparison with that of the regional giants. Thailand's production reached almost 1 million tonnes in 2007, a benchmark Malaysia had attained some 30 years earlier. As for the Philippines' output, in 2008 it remained behind Indonesia's as well as Malaysia's 1961 production levels. Also, the bulk of the oil palm milled in Thailand and the Philippines serves to fulfil local needs, as both these countries' export ratios have steadily remained much lower than those of the regional leaders, notwithstanding Thailand's export peak in the mid-1970s. However, although impressive in relative terms, this has to be understood as of limited significance, Thailand's exports then being equivalent to a fraction of both Malaysia's and Indonesia's overseas sales.

Figure 7.5 Palm oil production in selected countries (with prices), 1961–2008

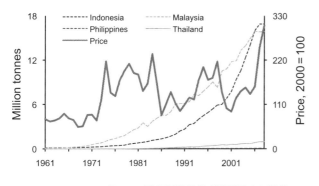

Sources: FAOSTAT 2010; UNCTADstats 2010.

Figure 7.6 Palm oil exports in selected countries (with prices), 1961–2007

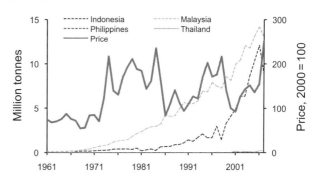

Sources: FAOSTAT 2010; UNCTADstats 2010.

Figure 7.7 Palm oil export ratio in selected countries, 1961–2007

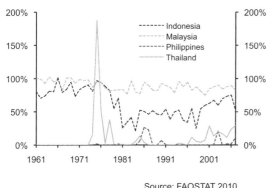

Source: FAOSTAT 2010.

Figure 7.8 Palm oil imports in selected countries, 1961–2007

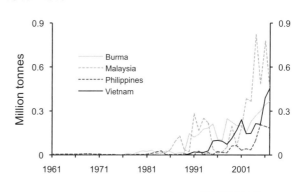

Source: FAOSTAT 2010.

Palm oil production (million tonnes)

	1961–63	1971–73	1981–83	1991–93	2001–3	2008
Indonesia	0.1	0.3	0.9	3.1	9.2	16.9
Malaysia	0.1	0.7	3.1	6.6	12.4	15.8
Philippines	0.0	0.0	0.0	0.1	0.1	0.1
Thailand	0.0	0.0	0.0	0.3	0.6	1.0

Palm oil exports (million tonnes)

	1961–63	1971–73	1981–83	1991–93	2001–3	2007
Indonesia	0.1	0.2	0.3	1.5	5.9	8.9
Malaysia	0.1	0.7	2.7	5.6	10.8	13.0
Philippines	0.0	0.0	0.0	0.0	0.0	0.0
Thailand	0.0	0.0	0.0	0.0	0.1	0.3

Palm oil export ratio (%)

	1961–63	1971–73	1981–83	1991–93	2001–3	2007
Indonesia	75	87	34	48	64	53
Malaysia	97	98	86	85	88	82
Philippines	0	0	0	0	7	11
Thailand	0	0	0	0	21	29

Palm oil imports (million tonnes)

	1961–63	1971–73	1981–83	1991–93	2001–3	2007
Burma	0.0	0.0	0.0	0.1	0.2	0.4
Malaysia	0.0	0.0	0.0	0.2	0.3	0.4
Philippines	0.0	0.0	0.0	0.0	0.0	0.2
Vietnam	0.0	0.0	0.0	0.0	0.2	0.5
Price (Y2000 = 100)	70	92	163	119	120	251

Plate 44

It could be argued that rubber tree plantations in the 1960s were then what oil palm tree plantations are now to Southeast Asia. As is the case for palm fruit nowadays, more than 85 per cent of the world's natural rubber was harvested in Southeast Asia some 50 years ago. However, contrary to its palm oil production in the 1960s, which then represented only a fraction of the global total, the region has contributed to at least three quarters of the world's natural rubber production over the entire time period examined here. The relative importance of rubber tree plantations over Malaysia's agricultural area, which has long remained the region's — and the world's — biggest natural rubber producer, was, however, less than that of palm trees nowadays. Finally, it should be remembered that prices of both commodities are linked to that of mineral oil, and have thus followed similar trends over the last 50 years, including an important rise beginning early in the first decade of the twenty-first century; to which must be added the fast-increasing demand from China's automotive industry.

As already stated, Malaysia long remained Southeast Asia's most important rubber producer, with both its production and yields outpaced by those of Thailand only by the late 1980s. Barlow understands Malaysia's production decline as a response "to very high land and labour costs accompanying its economic advance" (Barlow 1997: 1596). One could add that Malaysian rubber plantations were predominantly established in peninsular Malaysia, where such tendencies were felt the strongest. Such processes are not felt as strongly in Sarawak and Sabah, Malaysia's new agricultural frontier, where the cultivation of palm trees is favoured, as it is much less labour demanding than that of rubber trees.

Thailand's natural rubber production has followed an opposite path. This is the consequence of two factors, starting with a steady expansion of the country's rubber plantations, whose area tripled between 1960 and 1980 from 0.4 million to 1.2 million hectares, having long since overtaken Malaysia's. Thailand also undertook a major replanting programme and introduced high-yielding-variety trees. Such efforts, which lasted from the mid-1960s to the late 1980s, explain the country's unequalled yield hike (Ibid.: 1596, 1599): though still low at 0.4 tonne/hectare in 1980, Thailand's rubber yields peaked at just over 1.8 tonnes/hectare in 2004.

Like Malaysia, Indonesia has a long historical experience with the commercial cultivation of rubber trees, going back to the late nineteenth century and early twentieth. Relatively stable from the early 1960s until the mid-1980s, the area devoted to it began to expand exactly at the time when Malaysia's rubber area began to contract. Since then, Indonesia's rubber cultivation has been expanding rapidly, even faster than Thailand's. However, Thailand's unequalled yields have allowed it to remain the most prolific producer. That said, although Indonesia's yields still lag far behind those of the region's leading producer, its output has been growing far more rapidly than that of Thailand since the early years of the twenty-first century. Reaching 1.5 million tonnes in 2000, Indonesia's production stood at 2.9 million tonnes in 2008 and is forecasted to soon overtake that of Thailand. Vietnam also figures among Southeast Asia's rising producers, as its rubber output grew more than tenfold between 1990 and 2008. Over the same period, its harvested area expanded by 285 per cent, while average yields were over three times more important in 2008 than in the early 1990s.

Finally, as has so often occurred throughout the region's history, its agricultural land use map, in this case that of rubber, is undergoing various forms of redistribution, as decline of production in some countries is compensated by expansion in others. Over recent years Laos and Cambodia have both been the object of rubber expansion, largely financed by Chinese and Vietnamese concerns, resulting in a form of land grab (Manivong and Cramb 2008).

Figure 7.9 Harvested area of rubber in selected countries, 1961–2008

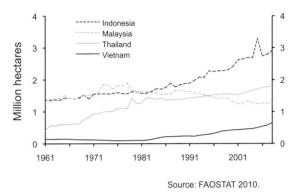

Source: FAOSTAT 2010.

Figure 7.10 Percentage of agricultural area allocated to rubber cultivation in selected countries, 1961–2007

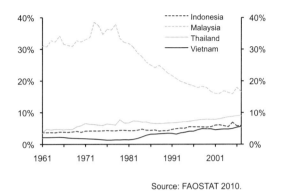

Source: FAOSTAT 2010.

Figure 7.11 Rubber yields in selected countries, 1961–2008

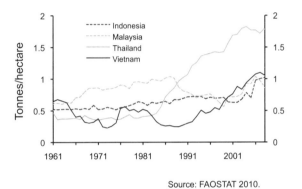

Source: FAOSTAT 2010.

Figure 7.12 Rubber production in selected countries (with prices), 1961–2008

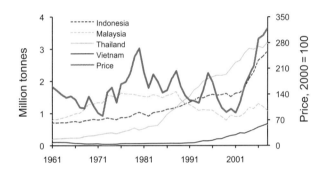

Sources: FAOSTAT 2010; UNCTADstats 2010.

Harvested area of rubber (million hectares)

	1961–63	1971–73	1981–83	1991–93	2001–3	2008
Indonesia	1.4	1.5	1.6	2.0	2.6	2.9
Malaysia	1.3	1.7	1.6	1.6	1.3	1.2
Thailand	0.5	0.9	1.4	1.4	1.6	1.8
Vietnam	0.1	0.1	0.1	0.2	0.4	0.6

Percentage of agricultural area allocated to rubber cultivation

	1961–63	1971–73	1981–83	1991–93	2001–3	2007
Indonesia	4	4	4	5	6	6
Malaysia	31	35	30	21	16	17
Thailand	4	6	7	7	8	9
Vietnam	2	2	1	3	5	5

Rubber yields (tonnes/hectare)

	1961–63	1971–73	1981–83	1991–93	2001–3	2008
Indonesia	0.5	0.5	0.6	0.7	0.6	1.0
Malaysia	0.6	0.8	0.9	0.7	0.7	0.9
Thailand	0.4	0.4	0.4	1.2	1.7	1.8
Vietnam	0.6	0.3	0.5	0.3	0.8	1.0

Rubber production (million tonnes)

	1961–63	1971–73	1981–83	1991–93	2001–3	2008
Indonesia	0.7	0.8	1.0	1.4	1.7	2.9
Malaysia	0.8	1.4	1.5	1.2	0.9	1.1
Thailand	0.2	0.3	0.6	1.7	2.7	3.2
Vietnam	0.1	0.0	0.0	0.1	0.3	0.7
Price (Y2000 = 100)	149	105	183	121	124	320

Plate 45

The FAO provides export data for three different types of products made from natural rubber, namely: gums natural, natural rubber and dry natural rubber. Southeast Asia's "natural rubber" exports grew some 30 times faster than those of dry natural rubber between 1961 and 2007. But that year, exports of natural rubber still barely reached 100,000 tonnes, most of which was from Malaysia, compared to almost 6 million tonnes of dry natural rubber. By far the most widely traded both in Southeast Asia and globally, dry natural rubber is therefore the sole commodity we are focusing on here.

Major trends in rubber exports are quite comparable to those in natural rubber production (Figure 7.12). Unsurprisingly, Southeast Asia has long been the top exporter of natural rubber, under any form, and the region's overseas sales regularly represent at least 85 per cent of global traded volumes. In fact, between 2000 and 2007, Southeast Asia's combined exports averaged 90 per cent of all overseas sales. From the late 1950s, when Malaya's production overtook the Netherlands Indies' (Fisher 1966: 320, 611), Malaya, then Malaysia (1963) became Southeast Asia's most important contributor to this export market and remained the leader for about three decades. But by the late 1980s and early 1990s, Malaysia's production and exports were in turn overtaken by those of Indonesia as well as Thailand, these two countries having since been competing for leadership. Indonesian exports in particular have increased rapidly since the beginning of the twenty-first century, growing by over three quarters between 2000 and 2007. As an ever-increasing proportion of Thailand's rubber production is locally consumed, Indonesia became the region's leading exporter once again in 2006, as it had done on two previous occasions since Malaysia ceded the top rank. Finally, although the total volume of its overseas rubber sales remains way behind those of its regional competitors, Vietnam's exports have also grown rapidly, even taking into account the setback experienced in 2005–6.

Among the reasons explaining why Malaysia remained Southeast Asia's most important rubber exporter for almost three decades is the fact that its average export ratio systematically remained above that of the three other countries. Its imports have also remained far above those of its neighbours, and equivalent to no less than an average 20 per cent of its total exports between 2000 and 2006. Thailand's situation differs, as a greater share of its rubber production is devoted to its local market, including its condom industry, a rubber-made commodity for which the kingdom was the world's biggest exporter in 2006 (Prasso 2006).

Figure 7.13 Dry natural rubber exports in selected countries (with prices), 1961–2007*

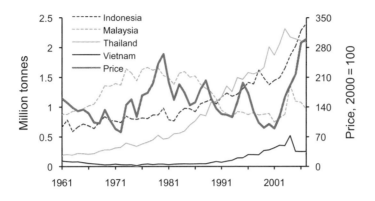

Source: FAOSTAT 2010; UNCTADstats 2010.

Figure 7.14 Dry natural rubber imports in selected countries, 1961–2007

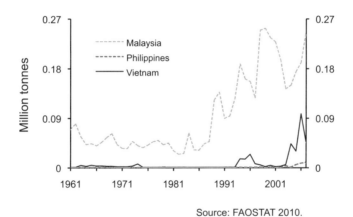

Source: FAOSTAT 2010.

Dry natural rubber exports (million tonnes)

	1961–63	1971–73	1981–83	1991–93	2001–3	2007
Indonesia	0.7	0.8	0.8	1.2	1.5	2.4
Malaysia	0.9	1.5	1.5	0.9	0.8	1.0
Thailand	0.2	0.3	0.5	1.3	2.1	2.1
Vietnam	0.1	0.0	0.0	0.1	0.3	0.2

Dry natural rubber imports (million tonnes)

	1961–63	1971–73	1981–83	1991–93	2001–3	2007
Malaysia	0.1	0.0	0.0	0.1	0.2	0.2
Philippines	0.0	0.0	0.0	0.0	0.0	0.0
Vietnam	0.0	0.0	0.0	0.0	0.0	0.0
Price (Y2000 = 100)	149	105	183	121	124	300

* Natural rubber prices

Plate 46

In the early 1960s, Indonesian coffee trees covered an area some five times more extensive than all other coffee plantations in the region. By 2008, they accounted for 1.3 million hectares, or almost two-thirds of the regional total. While coffee covered about 0.5 per cent of Indonesia's total agricultural area in the early 1960s, the proportion had reached 2 per cent in 2007. Robusta beans represent about 90 per cent of the Indonesian coffee production (Neilson 2008). By the early years of the twenty-first century, 30 per cent of all robusta beans produced in Indonesia were harvested in Southern Sumatra's Lampung District, where coffee expansion threatened the Bukit Barisan Selatan National Park (O'Brien and Kinnaird 2003). This is the result of five decades of almost uninterrupted expansion. However, the expansion peaked in the beginning of the twenty-first century, in the midst of a significant price slump (Figure 7.19).

Already cultivated during colonial days in Vietnam, coffee began its comeback just after *Doi Moi* — the official "renovation" which began in 1986 — and boomed during the 1990s. Covering only 0.9 per cent of that country's agricultural area in 1990, land planted with coffee trees had increased to 5 per cent by 2000, when the rhythm of expansion slowed down considerably. Such substantial growth resulted largely from the implementation of policies aimed at colonizing Vietnam's central and southern highlands. These policies were indeed part of *Doi Moi* and were facilitated by the wide-ranging privatization of coffee plantations. They led to massive and planned population redistribution towards so-called New Economic Zones. Initially state-led, population migrations became increasingly spontaneous, leading to massive deforestation (De Koninck 1999) and frequent displacement and marginalization of ethnic minorities (Hardy 2003)

throughout the Central Highlands. Prior to the coffee boom, the population of the Central Highlands was predominantly non-Kinh. After the boom, the Kinh population had become predominant. Coffee expansion occurred in Vietnam at a pace that finds no match in the recent history of Southeast Asia, and it does represent a classic pattern of a geopolitically motivated form of agricultural expansion and population redistribution (De Koninck 1996, De Koninck and Déry 1997). As explained by Tan (2000: 51), the "colonisation of frontier lands for agriculture is mediated by the expansion of export agrocommodity production. Coffee cultivation in particular has played this role in many parts of the world".

Coffee cultivation is present in several other countries in the region, always in upland areas, but nowhere as extensively as in Indonesia and Vietnam. In Thailand, it slowly accelerated in the 1980s but peaked during the first decade of the twenty-first century, with the extent of cultivation having since receded even more rapidly. In Malaysia, limited expansion occurred in the 1990s, but the total area cultivated — in the peninsula and in Sabah — remains the smallest in the region and is also on the decline. Steadier since the early 1980s, Laos' expansion was boosted by increasing prices towards the end of the first decade of the twenty-first century (Figure 7.19). This is especially true of the Boloven Plateau, a southern region where the crop was introduced early during the French colonial period and is now considered as the most suitable for coffee growing in Laos (Andersson *et al.* 2007: 35). In the Philippines, area wise the third most important coffee grower in the region, cultivation expanded rapidly as early as the 1970s, particularly in Northern Mindanao, but peaked before the end of the century.

Figure 7.15 Harvested area of coffee in selected countries, 1961–2008

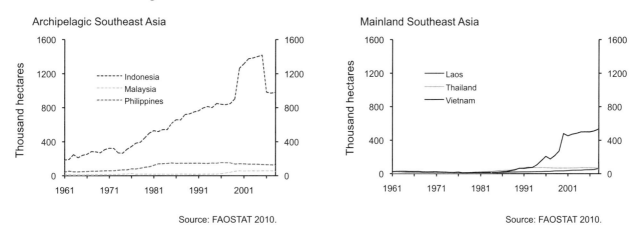

Source: FAOSTAT 2010.

Source: FAOSTAT 2010.

Figure 7.16 Percentage of agricultural area allocated to coffee cultivation in selected countries, 1961–2007

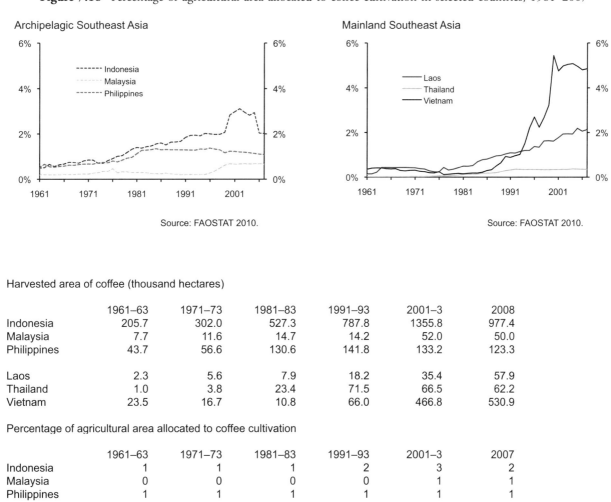

Source: FAOSTAT 2010.

Source: FAOSTAT 2010.

Harvested area of coffee (thousand hectares)

	1961–63	1971–73	1981–83	1991–93	2001–3	2008
Indonesia	205.7	302.0	527.3	787.8	1355.8	977.4
Malaysia	7.7	11.6	14.7	14.2	52.0	50.0
Philippines	43.7	56.6	130.6	141.8	133.2	123.3
Laos	2.3	5.6	7.9	18.2	35.4	57.9
Thailand	1.0	3.8	23.4	71.5	66.5	62.2
Vietnam	23.5	16.7	10.8	66.0	466.8	530.9

Percentage of agricultural area allocated to coffee cultivation

	1961–63	1971–73	1981–83	1991–93	2001–3	2007
Indonesia	1	1	1	2	3	2
Malaysia	0	0	0	0	1	1
Philippines	1	1	1	1	1	1
Laos	0	0	0	1	2	2
Thailand	0	0	0	0	0	0
Vietnam	0	0	0	1	5	5

Plate 47

In Southeast Asia, large-scale coffee plantations were first settled in Indonesia, where the crop
was first introduced in Java in 1699 (Neilson 2008).
Building on that historical head start, Indonesia
long remained the region's most important producer
by far. In 1961, its production still equalled more
than twice that of all other Southeast Asia's countries combined. Indonesian production has maintained a steady growth since, with its 2008 harvest
about six times more important than half a century
before. However, that growth has relied essentially
on the expansion of the archipelago country's coffee
area rather than on an increase in yields, which
have remained very stable throughout the years.

Significant in itself, Indonesia's production
growth has however been spectacularly eclipsed by
the rise of Vietnam's, which boomed during the
1990s.While in the early 1990s Indonesia's coffee
production was almost four times more important
than Vietnam's, by 1999 the mainland country had
taken the lead, apparently for good. Since then
Vietnam has become the world's second largest
producer, and though far behind Brazil — a country
some 26 times more extensive — it produced a
substantial 13 per cent of the world's coffee beans
by 2008. Vietnam's status as a leading coffee producer has been achieved over a very short period of
time. Massive coffee planting began only during the
late 1980s in its Central Highlands (Figures 7.15
and 7.16), where robusta beans made for most of
the harvest (Fortunel 2000). To this rapid territorial expansion must be added the yield factor.
The fact that coffee yields are the highest when
trees are aged between five and 15 years explains
why Vietnamese yields peaked to an impressive

2.4 tonnes/hectare in 1997. In 2008 they still
averaged 2 tonnes/hectare, making the coffee plantations of Vietnam among the most productive
anywhere in the world.

As one could expect, the production boom
that occurred in Vietnam had major impacts on the
global coffee market. The ensuing growth in supply
coincided with an important price decline from
which markets only began to recover a few years
ago. However, the scale of this price drop does not
stand comparison with the 15-year-long deprecia-
tion that followed the price peak of the mid-1970s.
Trying to capitalize on that upward trend, the
Philippines had then undertaken to raise its own
production. Along with yields, Philippine production peaked during the following decade but has
since been on the decline. Thailand's coffee production followed a similar trajectory, although it never
reached a level similar to that of the Philippines.
Close to nil in the 1960s, Thailand's production
took off in the early 1970s, peaked in 1995 and
has declined steadily since the beginning of the
twenty-first century. Thai yields remained above 1
tonne/hectare for a few years, a performance achieved
only by the Philippines and Vietnam. Furthermore,
Thailand is the country where the relative growth
of coffee yield was the most important since 1961.
This is mainly attributable to the fact that Thai
yields were, along with production itself, especially
low at the time. Finally, the last to take off, Laos
has seen its production grow sevenfold since the
1980s. This should not be too surprising, as Laotian
coffee is said to "enjoy a very good reputation in the
world market and is famous for its high quality"
(Andersson *et al.* 2007: 35).

Figure 7.17 Coffee yields in selected countries, 1961–2008

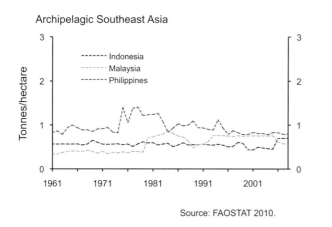

Archipelagic Southeast Asia

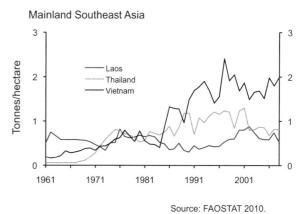

Mainland Southeast Asia

Source: FAOSTAT 2010.

Source: FAOSTAT 2010.

Figure 7.18 Coffee production in selected countries (with prices), 1961–2008

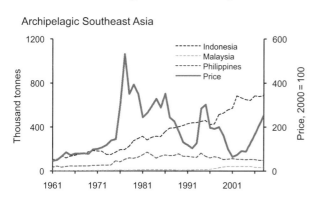

Archipelagic Southeast Asia

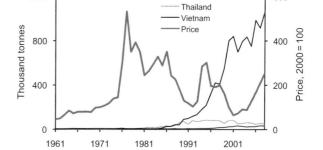

Mainland Southeast Asia

Sources: FAOSTAT 2010; UNCTADstats 2010.

Sources: FAOSTAT 2010; UNCTADstats 2010.

Coffee yields (tonnes/hectare)

	1961–63	1971–73	1981–83	1991–93	2001–3	2008
Indonesia	0.6	0.6	0.6	0.6	0.5	0.7
Malaysia	0.4	0.4	0.8	0.6	0.8	0.8
Philippines	0.8	0.9	1.2	0.9	0.8	0.8
Laos	0.6	0.4	0.7	0.4	0.8	0.7
Thailand	0.1	0.4	0.7	0.9	1.0	0.8
Vietnam	0.2	0.4	0.5	1.8	1.7	2.0

Coffee production (thousand tonnes)

	1961–63	1971–73	1981–83	1991–93	2001–3	2008
Indonesia	116.5	169.9	300.6	434.7	638.3	682.9
Malaysia	2.7	4.4	11.2	9.2	39.2	28.7
Philippines	36.1	50.7	155.0	128.3	108.6	97.4
Laos	1.5	2.3	5.2	7.4	28.6	31.1
Thailand	0.1	1.7	16.2	66.0	64.3	50.4
Vietnam	4.2	6.7	5.4	118.4	777.9	1,055.8
Price (Y2000 = 100)	54	109	268	116	76	252

Plate 48

Coffee trees can grow only in the tropics. However, coffee beans are roasted mostly in Western countries, whose inhabitants remain by far the most addicted to their morning caffeine. Coffee is thus grown in the South but largely financed by Northern stakeholders and predominantly for a Northern market. Consequently, as in all coffee growing countries, export ratios are high in Southeast Asia while coffee imports have always remained particularly low. The region's most important importers are the archipelago countries, led by Malaysia, which imported almost as much coffee as it produced in 2006. This situation is unique in Southeast Asia, as coffee imports are equivalent to only a tiny fraction of the other producers' own output.

On the export side, from the 1960s until the mid-1990s, Indonesian overseas sales of coffee remained more important than the combined total for all the other regional exporters. They climbed to over 420,000 tonnes in 1990, a peak that the archipelago nation did not reach again until 2005. But this did not prevent Vietnam's exports from overtaking those of Indonesia by 1995, and by 2007 being almost four times more substantial, even though Indonesia had briefly claimed back its regional number one spot in 1996. Vietnam's exports also overtook those of Colombia several years ago, making the Indochinese country the world's second most significant exporter after Brazil. Furthermore,

Vietnam's exports totalled over 1 million tonnes for the first time in 2007, when they reached 1.2 million tonnes, 25 per cent higher than the previous year. Such a performance relies not only on the country's overseas sales of its own coffee production, but also on re-exports, Vietnam's export ratio having remained above 100 per cent from 2001 to 2007.

As mentioned earlier (Figure 7.18), Vietnam's soaring production contributed to the downward trend in the 1990s coffee prices. That conjuncture probably convinced Thailand growers to devote their energies to other crops. In 1991–93 the kingdom exported an average 54,000 tonnes of coffee a year, but the figure had dropped to only half of this amount a decade later. Laotian coffee exports were also affected by the price drop but to a more modest degree, as they stagnated throughout most of the last decade. Both of these countries' export ratios have also declined significantly from their late 1980s and early 1990s peak, an evolution partly attributable to the rapid growth of local consumption.

Finally, all this explains that Southeast Asia's contribution to world coffee exports grew significantly between the early 1960s and 2007, a period during which the region's share of global coffee exports rose from 3 per cent to 25 per cent (Figure 5.16). The fact that this was accompanied by a rapid rise in regional coffee consumption makes this achievement even more significant.

Figure 7.19 Coffee exports in selected countries (with prices), 1961–2007

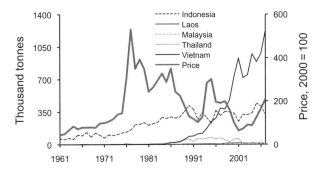

Source: FAOSTAT 2010; UNCTADstats 2010.

Figure 7.20 Coffee export ratio in selected countries, 1961–2007

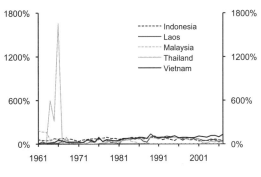

Source: FAOSTAT 2010.

Figure 7.21 Coffee export ratio in selected countries, 1961–2007 (without Thailand's 1964–66 upsurge)

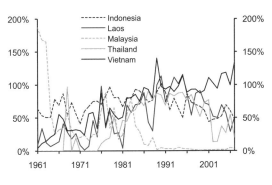

Source: FAOSTAT 2010.

Figure 7.22 Coffee imports in selected countries, 1961–2007

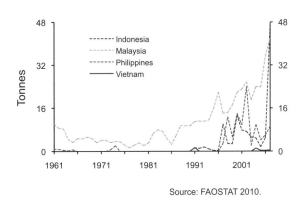

Source: FAOSTAT 2010.

Coffee exports (thousand tonnes)

	1961–63	1971–73	1981–83	1991–93	2001–3	2007
Indonesia	64.5	94.0	226.3	332.8	297.7	320.6
Laos	0.3	0.1	2.3	6.8	16.2	16.9
Malaysia	4.7	0.9	6.1	0.3	0.6	1.0
Thailand	0.0	0.0	8.2	53.5	26.7	11.1
Vietnam	0.4	2.5	3.8	110.6	799.7	1,229.0

Coffee export ratio (%)

	1961–63	1971–73	1981–83	1991–93	2001–3	2007
Indonesia	56	56	76	77	47	47
Laos	19	6	44	93	57	51
Malaysia	174	20	53	3	1	3
Thailand	0	0	50	79	35	20
Vietnam	10	37	70	94	103	134

Coffee imports (tonnes)

	1961–63	1971–73	1981–83	1991–93	2001–3	2007
Indonesia	0.0	0.0	0.0	1.3	6.8	47.9
Malaysia	8.9	3.8	5.9	11.1	22.6	42.2
Philippines	0.7	0.2	0.0	0.0	12.0	9.2
Vietnam	0.0	0.0	0.0	0.5	0.0	0.5
Price (Y2000 = 100)	54	109	268	116	76	210

Plate 49

Also an upland crop, tea is made from the dried leaves of the evergreen shrub *Camellia sinensis*. Depending on the extent to which these leaves have fermented, tea can either be green (unfermented and heated), oolong (partially fermented) or black (made from withered and then fermented leaves [Wickizer 1951: 172]). Most of the tea produced in Southeast Asia is black tea, although Indonesia is also among the major and less numerous green tea producers (Banerjee and Chaudhuri 2005: 11). Of all the Southeast Asian crops covered by this research, tea is by far the one cultivated over the smallest area. It is also the least important in terms of tonnage. In addition, gains in productivity have remained modest. Although tea yields of over 1.5 tonnes/hectare are not uncommon in the world, such a level of productivity has rarely been attained on Southeast Asia's estates. Southeast Asia is nonetheless located at the convergence of the two most important tea cultures, China and India, whose combined production accounted for more than half of the global total in 2008. It is therefore no surprise that Burma and Vietnam are among Southeast Asia's leading producers, as their history is closely linked with that of both India and China. Vietnam's historical and cultural links with the latter are particularly significant.

Vietnam's overall agricultural intensification and expansion programmes from the early 1980s onwards have also impacted its tea production. Areas allocated to tea plantations in Vietnam increased from less than 35,000 hectares in 1980 to nearly 130,000 hectares in 2008. A few years earlier, the country's tea plantations had become more extensive than Indonesia's, until recently the region's leader on that count. Although initially slow to improve, Vietnam's achievements in terms of yield increases have been strong, particularly since the 1990s. Its plantations' yields averaged 1.4 tonnes/hectare in 2008, a more than threefold increase over their 1961 level. While Vietnamese yields surged, those of Indonesia levelled off. As a result, Vietnam has become Southeast Asia's leading tea producer and the world's sixth.

As in the case of coffee, Indonesia's tea production, coming primarily from Java, benefited from a head start over its neighbours. The Dutch introduced tea in their colonial domain first in West Java, then in northeast Sumatra. By 1940, Indonesian plantations extended over more than 213,000 hectares (Etherington 1974: 85). But following the post-independence nationalization of previously Dutch-owned estates and a drop in prices, area cultivated decreased rapidly. By 1961 it had come down to some 100,000 hectares. Though it climbed back to a still modest total of 107,000 hectares by 2008, the price of tea remained very unfavourable for producers. In Indonesia producers can be state or private estates as well as smallholdings. With a 2008 production of 151,000 tonnes, the country ranked seventh in the world, behind Vietnam.

In Burma also, tea cultivation represents a colonial legacy. In 2008, the country's modest production of nearly 26,500 tonnes of tea leaves was nevertheless five times that of 1961. Comparable to Thailand's yields over many decades, Burmese yields benefited from a nearly threefold increase between the early 1960s and 2000. As for Thai yields, they skyrocketed, reaching an unequalled 3.4 tonnes/hectare in 2008. Although Thailand's tea areas have remained stable in the meantime, its total tea production has grown accordingly, while remaining relatively modest.

Figure 7.23 Harvested area of tea in selected countries, 1961–2008

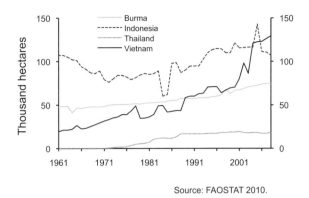

Source: FAOSTAT 2010.

Figure 7.24 Percentage of agricultural area allocated to tea cultivation in selected countries, 1961–2007

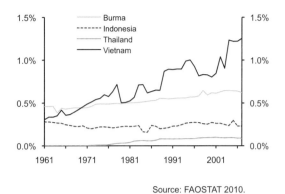

Source: FAOSTAT 2010.

Figure 7.25 Tea yields in selected countries, 1961–2008

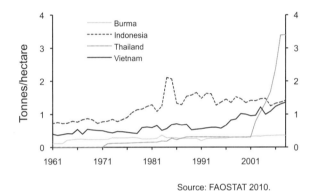

Source: FAOSTAT 2010.

Figure 7.26 Tea production in selected countries (with prices), 1961–2008

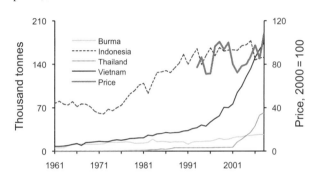

Sources: FAOSTAT 2010; UNCTADstats 2010.

Harvested area of tea (thousand hectares)

	1961–63	1971–73	1981–83	1991–93	2001–3	2008
Burma	48.3	49.4	52.6	57.9	68.9	74.5
Indonesia	106.3	78.3	86.7	97.3	115.8	106.9
Thailand	0.0	0.5	9.5	16.5	18.2	18.1
Vietnam	20.4	33.1	41.3	62.1	88.0	129.3

Percentage of agricultural area allocated to tea cultivation

	1961–63	1971–73	1981–83	1991–93	2001–3	2007
Burma	0	0	1	1	1	1
Indonesia	0	0	0	0	0	0
Thailand	0	0	0	0	0	0
Vietnam	0	1	1	1	1	1

Tea yields (tonnes/hectare)

	1961–63	1971–73	1981–83	1991–93	2001–3	2008
Burma	0.1	0.2	0.3	0.2	0.3	0.4
Indonesia	0.7	0.8	1.2	1.6	1.4	1.4
Thailand	0.0	0.1	0.2	0.3	0.7	3.4
Vietnam	0.4	0.5	0.6	0.6	1.0	1.4

Tea production (thousand tonnes)

	1961–63	1971–73	1981–83	1991–93	2001–3	2008
Burma	5.2	12.2	15.2	13.5	22.3	26.5
Indonesia	77.7	62.8	104.1	152.7	165.0	150.9
Thailand	0.0	0.1	1.5	5.0	12.7	61.6
Vietnam	7.7	15.2	23.7	35.7	91.4	174.9
Price (Y2000 = 100)				77	77	109

Plate 50

The evolution of Vietnam's tea exports shows similarities with that of its tea production. Tea exports remained relatively limited until the early 1990s, when they began to rise rapidly, reaching some 114,000 tonnes in 2007. Such a performance relied on a series of institutional measures, beginning with the halving of the country's export tax. The latter was reduced from 10 per cent to 5 per cent in 1989, and actually cancelled a few years later (Nguyen and Grote 2004: 27). In 1991 the export monopoly of the state-owned Union of Tea Enterprises was abolished (Ibid.: 18), as were tea export quotas in 1995. Quotas on all other agricultural commodities were cancelled as well, except the one on rice, which lasted until 2001 (Ibid.: 27).

As Vietnam overtook Indonesia as Southeast Asia's leading tea exporter in 2006, its overseas sales then accounted for about 6 per cent of global exports. Unsurprisingly, Vietnam's export ratio, although fluctuating wildly, had overtaken that of Indonesia, Southeast Asia's only other significant tea exporter. As for Burmese overseas sales of tea, they were minimal during the 1960s and then disappeared almost totally from the world market until the early 1990s. Since then they have been making a comeback, still modest, as exports and export ratio remain far behind those of the two regional leaders. Thailand's exports have followed a similar pattern, and although they have grown faster than Burma's since the mid-1990s, they still account for only a tiny fraction of those of the two regional leaders.

Having benefited from a long period of growth that started in the early 1960s, Indonesian exports began to drop in the early 1990s. In 1961, at more than 32,000 tonnes of tea, they represented over ten times the combined overseas sales of Vietnam

and Burma, although still only 5 per cent of the world's total. In 1993 they peaked at nearly 125,000 tonnes, but began to crumble in 1994, falling back to their early 1980s level (~67,000 tonnes) in the midst of the 1997–98 Asian financial crisis. They have since stabilized at around 100,000 tonnes per year. From the 1970s onwards, and notwithstanding the generally fluctuating and unfavourable prices fetched by Indonesian tea — whose quality does not always meet the best standards — on the world market, the country's export ratio has remained relatively high and stable, never dropping much below 50 per cent. The very sharp drop in harvested areas in the early 1980s, concurrent with an equally noticeable hike in yields, was attributable to the introduction of new clones.

While its coffee imports have recently been overtaken by Indonesia's (Figure 7.22), Malaysia remains the region's leading importer of tea. In 2007, Malaysian tea drinkers chose mostly foreign products, as the country's yearly domestic production, largely coming from the Cameron Highlands and always relatively modest, peaked at 6,200 tonnes in 2007 (hence not appearing on Figures 7.23–7.26). That year, its most important suppliers were Indonesia and Vietnam. The former is also Southeast Asia's second most important tea importer, its purchases however being equivalent to only a small fraction of its own production (~5 per cent in 2007). The same can be said about Burma's imports, equivalent, for that same year, to about 4 per cent of its production. Finally, Thailand's tea imports reached some 1,700 tonnes in 2007, or, again, the equivalent of just a small fraction of its fast-increasing national production. Its most important suppliers were its Burmese neighbour and Vietnam.

Figure 7.27 Tea exports in selected countries (with prices), 1961–2007

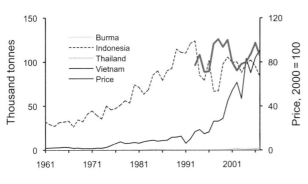

Sources: FAOSTAT 2010; UNCTADstats 2010.

Figure 7.28 Tea export ratio in selected countries, 1961–2007

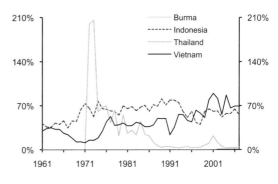

Source: FAOSTAT 2010.

Figure 7.29 Tea imports in selected countries, 1961–2007

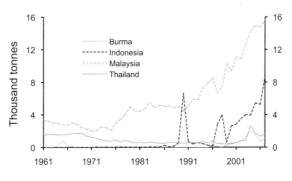

Source: FAOSTAT 2010.

Tea exports (thousand tonnes)

	1961–63	1971–73	1981–83	1991–93	2001–3	2007
Burma	0.0	0.0	0.0	0.0	0.3	0.7
Indonesia	29.6	40.0	67.8	118.5	96.1	83.7
Thailand	0.1	0.1	0.4	0.2	1.3	2.7
Vietnam	2.5	2.1	9.6	14.0	67.8	114.0

Tea export ratio (%)

	1961–63	1971–73	1981–83	1991–93	2001–3	2007
Burma	0	0	0	0	1	3
Indonesia	38	64	65	78	58	56
Thailand		203	27	4	13	5
Vietnam	33	14	40	39	76	70

Tea imports (thousand tonnes)

	1961–63	1971–73	1981–83	1991–93	2001–3	2007
Burma	0.0	0.0	0.0	0.0	0.9	1.1
Indonesia	0.0	0.0	0.1	0.6	3.5	8.7
Malaysia	3.2	2.2	4.9	5.7	11.6	15.7
Thailand	1.6	1.1	0.6	0.6	0.7	1.6

| Price (Y2000 = 100) | | | | 77 | 77 | 85 |

Plate 51

Since the mid-1970s, Southeast Asia has accounted for anywhere between 60 per cent and 66 per cent of the world's coconut harvested area. Within the region itself, most of that area has been located in the two large island countries, with the Philippines holding the largest share. Significant coconut expansion in the Philippines goes back to the early decades of the twentieth century, when coconut trees were massively planted on areas previously allocated to *abaca* (Manila hemp) (Borja 1927: 386). Writing on the eve of the Great Depression, Borja explained that, thanks to the archipelago's favourable geographic and climatic conditions, "prolific coconut plantations are found on many different kinds of soils and it is quite usual to find a thriving coconut grove on the sandy seashore" (Ibid.: 384). Building on such assets, the Philippines rapidly became the world's leading coconut tree grower. In 1961, the country's plantations covered some 1.2 million hectares, or 23 per cent of the world total, with major production zones located in Southern Luzon, Western Mindanao and Southern Mindanao. By 2008, the size of the country's coconut harvested area had almost tripled, reaching 3.4 million hectares, almost a third of the global total. The bulk of this growth occurred from 1960 to 1980, after which coconut expansion stalled. Although the Philippines' agricultural model is often associated with large estates, coconut has predominantly been a smallholder crop. Indeed, in 1970, 75 per cent of the ~500,000 coconut farms in the Philippines covered less than 5 hectares, the average size standing at only 2.4 hectares (Clarete and Roumasset 1983: 3–4). By the late 1990s, their number had increased to over 1.5 million, with an estimated 71 per cent covering less than 5 hectares, while plantations of more than 50 hectares

represented only 3 per cent of all coconut farms/plantations (Arancon 1997: 4).

In terms of the extent of coconut cultivation, Indonesia has never been very far behind the Philippines, though the Philippines did gain a good lead from the 1960s to the mid-1990s. Since then, however, coconut hectarage has increased much faster in Indonesia, to such a point that by now it is nearly as extensive as that in the Philippines. However, in the Philippines, land devoted to the cultivation of coconut represents an exceptionally high proportion of all agricultural area, nearly 30 per cent since the late 1970s as against 6 per cent in Indonesia in 2007. Six per cent was also the approximate proportion that coconut land represented in Malaysia, at least until the early 1980s. Since then it has been decreasing rapidly, which is not surprising considering the acceleration in the deagrarianization of the country. In fact, even in the Philippines and in Indonesia, few smallholders can draw sufficient revenue from coconut cultivation, which remains a "poor man's crop". More often than not, it does not even account for a significant proportion of peasant families' revenue. Many do, however, draw some income from raising a variety of farm animals, whether cattle, goats or fowl, under the coconut trees' canopy, or from working for wages on coconut plantations. But coconut plantation workers are generally very poorly paid, particularly in the Philippines, where wages are insufficient to sustain a decent livelihood. Finally, throughout most of mainland Southeast Asia, for a number of reasons — essentially ecological and cultural — coconut cultivation remains marginal, although not among a certain number of coastal communities, notably in southern Thailand.

Figure 7.30 Harvested area of coconut in selected countries, 1961–2008

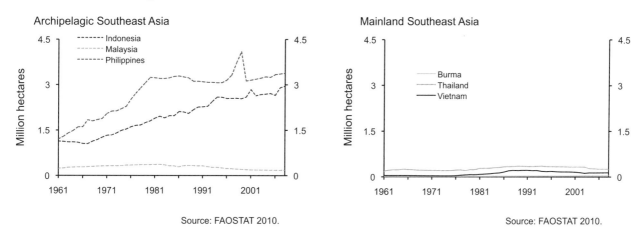

Source: FAOSTAT 2010.

Source: FAOSTAT 2010.

Figure 7.31 Percentage of agricultural area allocated to coconut cultivation in selected countries, 1961–2007

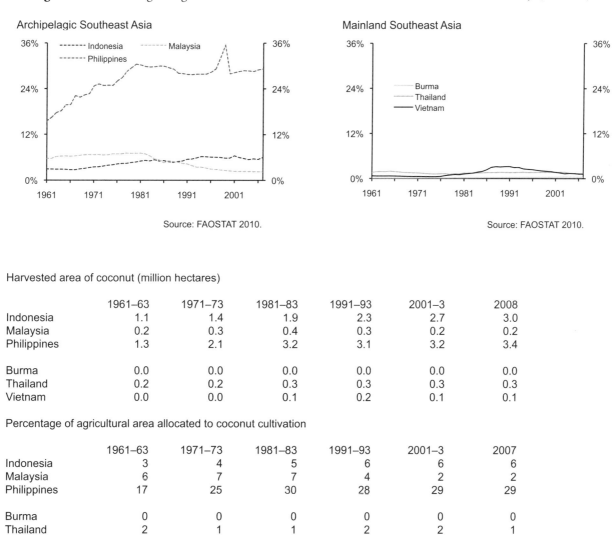

Source: FAOSTAT 2010.

Source: FAOSTAT 2010.

Harvested area of coconut (million hectares)

	1961–63	1971–73	1981–83	1991–93	2001–3	2008
Indonesia	1.1	1.4	1.9	2.3	2.7	3.0
Malaysia	0.2	0.3	0.4	0.3	0.2	0.2
Philippines	1.3	2.1	3.2	3.1	3.2	3.4
Burma	0.0	0.0	0.0	0.0	0.0	0.0
Thailand	0.2	0.2	0.3	0.3	0.3	0.3
Vietnam	0.0	0.0	0.1	0.2	0.1	0.1

Percentage of agricultural area allocated to coconut cultivation

	1961–63	1971–73	1981–83	1991–93	2001–3	2007
Indonesia	3	4	5	6	6	6
Malaysia	6	7	7	4	2	2
Philippines	17	25	30	28	29	29
Burma	0	0	0	0	0	0
Thailand	2	1	1	2	2	1
Vietnam	1	0	1	3	1	1

Plate 52

Coconut trees take about seven years to reach maturity (Clarete and Roumasset 1983: 9), while their replanting is based on 40-year cycles (Arancon 1997: 8). In other words, they are relatively slow to mature but have a longer life cycle than most other major cash crops cultivated in the region. Whatever the case, in comparison with other cash crops, whether rubber, oil palm, coffee or even tea (Figures 7.3, 7.11, 7.17 and 7.25), yield increases in coconut cultivation have not been substantial since the 1960s, particularly in the archipelago countries. In fact, in Malaysia they have even been dropping rapidly, which is not too surprising given the equally rapid marginalization of coconut tree cultivation in this country. In the Philippines, after going through a prolonged slump beginning in the late 1960s, yields have climbed back, although somewhat erratically, to a point where they have remained stable since the early years of the twenty-first century, but at a level not higher than the one attained in the early 1960s. On the other hand, Indonesian coconut yields have increased since the early 1960s, when they were still comparable with Philippine ones. But this growth has been modest, with yields in 2008 being about 33 per cent higher than some 50 years earlier.

On the mainland, where coconut tree cultivation remains much less widespread, land productivity has been increasing much more significantly, particularly in Burma and Vietnam, where average yields are now the highest in the region. Considering that nearly 95 per cent of Southeast Asia's coconut areas are located in the archipelago, this mainland/archipelago yield advantage is hardly reflected in overall production growth. Although yield increases have been proportionately superior on the mainland, the latter's actual share of regional crop production is still inferior, standing at 10 per cent. The bulk of the production, some 90 per cent of it, is thus provided by Indonesia and the Philippines, which together — for at least the past half century — have been responsible for 45 per cent to 60 per cent of the global harvest, depending on the year. Among those two production leaders, the Philippines stood ahead during most years, until the late 1980s. Since then, Indonesia, whose production growth has been strong and steady throughout the period examined here, has become and remained the top producer. The large country's predominance is attributable to yield increases, largely achieved during the years when market prices were following wild fluctuations and an overall downward trend. This trend, which began in 1980 and bottomed out in 2001, has since been reversed, with 2008 prices being the highest in the past half century. Whether this upward trend will continue and will contribute to sustained growth in yields and production remains impossible to predict. But it seems probable that, whatever happens with market prices and given past trends with what remains largely a "poor man's crop", particularly in the Philippines, both productivity and production will keep increasing.

Figure 7.32 Coconut yields in selected countries, 1961–2008

Archipelagic Southeast Asia

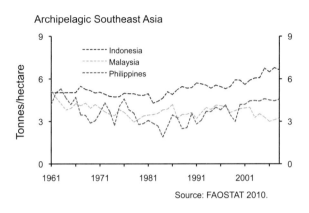

Source: FAOSTAT 2010.

Mainland Southeast Asia

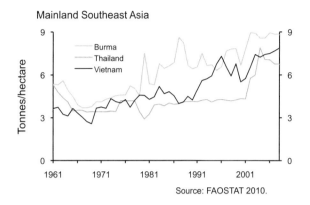

Source: FAOSTAT 2010.

Figure 7.33 Coconut production in selected countries (with copra oil prices), 1961–2008

Archipelagic Southeast Asia

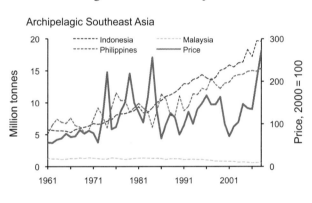

Sources: FAOSTAT 2010; UNCTADstats 2010.

Mainland Southeast Asia

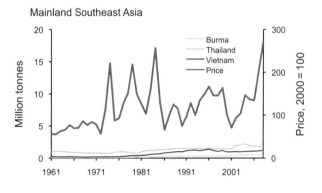

Sources: FAOSTAT 2010; UNCTADstats 2010.

Coconut yields (tonnes/hectare)

	1961–63	1971–73	1981–83	1991–93	2001–3	2008
Indonesia	5.0	4.9	4.5	5.6	5.8	6.6
Malaysia	4.7	3.7	3.5	3.6	3.7	3.2
Philippines	4.8	3.9	2.8	3.2	4.3	4.5
Burma	5.4	4.2	5.8	6.9	8.5	8.8
Thailand	4.8	3.4	3.7	4.2	5.3	6.7
Vietnam	3.5	3.9	4.6	5.4	6.5	7.9

Coconut production (million tonnes)

	1961–63	1971–73	1981–83	1991–93	2001–3	2008
Indonesia	5.6	6.6	8.7	13.1	15.8	19.5
Malaysia	1.1	1.2	1.2	1.0	0.7	0.6
Philippines	6.3	8.1	9.1	9.8	13.8	15.3
Burma	0.0	0.1	0.1	0.2	0.4	0.4
Thailand	1.0	0.7	1.0	1.4	1.7	1.7
Vietnam	0.1	0.1	0.4	1.1	0.9	1.1
Price (Y2000 = 100)	58	83	131	108	89	272

Plate 53

Copra oil is made from copra, the unprocessed inner flesh of the coconut. It is also the most widely traded commodity made from coconut. According to data quoted by Clarete and Roumasset (1983: 6), the Philippines produced 15.93 billion coconuts in 1980, equivalent to 3.9 million metric tonnes of copra oil. The same year, according to the FAO, the country's coconut production totalled 9.1 million tonnes. This implies that some 1,750 nuts were needed to produce one tonne of coconut while 2.3 times more were required to produce one tonne of copra oil.

As their local market for coconut is much smaller than that of Indonesia, the Philippines have systematically produced more copra oil since 1962, although Indonesia's coconut harvest has been more substantial for the last two decades (Figure 7.33). Between the late 1960s and 2007, the Philippines' annual copra oil production never amounted to less than 25 per cent of the global total. Also, while the country's coconut production grew by 260 per cent between 1970 and 2007, its copra oil production grew more than threefold, reaching over 1.5 million tonnes in 2007. This means that an ever-increasing share of the Philippines' harvest is milled into copra oil for the export market. It is therefore not surprising that the country's overseas sales grew at a faster rate than its production. In total, since 1961, 60 per cent of all copra oil traded on global markets has come from the Philippines. Peter Warr's

reference to the Philippines' "apparent monopoly power in the international market for coconut oil" does not seem exaggerated (Warr 2002: 438).

Indonesia's copra oil production rivalled that of the Philippines during the 1960s and has since then systematically remained the second most important in both Southeast Asia and the world. It reached almost 1 million tonnes in 2008, a total some 3.5 times higher than in 1961. However, the size of the Indonesian market meant that for a long time most of the national production was consumed locally and the country's export ratio remained low. The export ratio began to climb very significantly only in the early 1990s. Since then, the share of locally produced copra oil consumed on the domestic market has been decreasing, most likely because of the increasing availability of locally produced palm oil (Figure 7.5). More copra oil has thus been made available for exports, to such an extent that since the late 1990s Indonesia's export ratio has been more or less equivalent to the Philippines', averaging some 75 per cent. Indonesia's copra oil exports have also definitely overtaken those of Malaysia, which nonetheless remains a major regional importer and re-exporter of the commodity.

Finally, the increase in Vietnam's own copra oil production has somewhat made up for the reduction in Malaysia's, but most of that increase has served to feed the domestic market.

Figure 7.34 Copra oil production in selected countries (with prices), 1961–2008

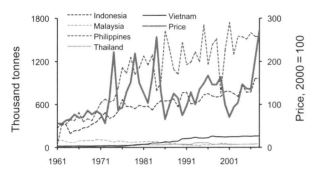

Sources: FAOSTAT 2010; UNCTADstats 2010.

Figure 7.35 Copra oil exports in selected countries (with prices), 1961–2007

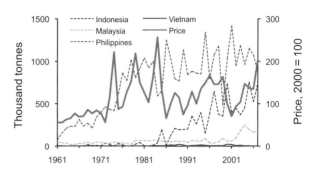

Sources: FAOSTAT 2010; UNCTADstats 2010.

Figure 7.36 Copra oil export ratio in selected countries, 1961–2007

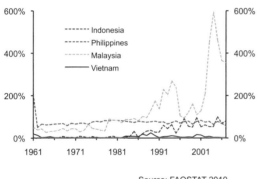

Source: FAOSTAT 2010.

Figure 7.37 Copra oil imports in selected countries, 1961–2007

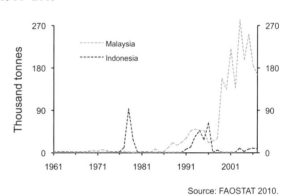

Source: FAOSTAT 2010.

Copra oil production (thousand tonnes)

	1961–63	1971–73	1981–83	1991–93	2001–3	2008
Indonesia	309.0	434.0	553.4	661.6	745.3	958.4
Malaysia	91.5	97.6	80.0	29.4	43.6	49.0
Philippines	225.1	640.6	1,239.0	1,225.0	1,529.0	1,544.6
Thailand	12.8	22.2	35.3	47.4	38.2	46.4
Vietnam	16.3	16.2	47.5	129.6	148.1	157.4

Copra oil exports (thousand tonnes)

	1961–63	1971–73	1981–83	1991–93	2001–3	2007
Indonesia	0.0	17.2	3.9	269.2	402.1	739.9
Malaysia	38.7	34.0	63.4	55.1	110.1	168.1
Philippines	145.0	429.6	986.5	860.4	1,183.1	870.0
Vietnam	1.6	0.0	1.5	4.7	10.5	0.0

Copra oil export ratio (%)

	1961–63	1971–73	1981–83	1991–93	2001–3	2007
Indonesia	0	4	1	42	54	77
Philippines	105	67	80	70	77	56
Malaysia	42	35	79	189	261	355
Vietnam	10	0	3	4	7	0

Copra oil imports (thousand tonnes)

	1961–63	1971–73	1981–83	1991–93	2001–3	2007
Malaysia	2.0	4.4	0.9	41.6	212.8	165.3
Indonesia	0.1	0.1	0.6	17.1	3.0	7.4

| Price (Y2000 = 100) | 58 | 83 | 131 | 108 | 89 | 272 |

Plate 54

During the late seventeenth century, cocoa was introduced in the Philippines by the Spaniards, who had brought the plant from Mexico (Burger and Smit 2001: 41). But its cultivation never really expanded, and even today it remains a marginal crop in the country.

There were several experiments in cocoa cultivation by colonial authorities in Malaya and North Borneo during the late nineteenth century as well as the first half of the twentieth (Kaur 1995). But commercial plantings in the Malayan peninsula began only during the 1950s and were followed by a period of very slow expansion — involving renewed and unfruitful attempts to intercrop cocoa with other tree crops — until the mid-1980s, by which time a real mini boom had begun. Triggered by the ballooning price cycle of the late 1970s and early 1980s, expansion took off first in Malaysia and then in Indonesia. By 1991, Malaysian cocoa plantations totalled 400,000 hectares, with less than a third in the Peninsula, half in Sabah and some 56,000 hectares in Sarawak (Härdter, Chow and Hock 1997: 94), covering over 5 per cent of the country's agricultural area. Then, faced with both price and yield declines, together with agricultural wage increases, the Malaysian cocoa adventure ended as quickly as it had begun. By the mid-1990s it was already petering out, apparently for good. Nowadays, cocoa trees have almost completely disappeared from the Malaysian agricultural scene and given way to less labour-intensive palm tree plantations (Burger and Smit 2001: 41–2). The Malaysian experiment with cocoa cultivation was more of a one-off gamble than a typical "boom and bust" cycle.

In Indonesia, where cocoa was apparently introduced almost as early as in the Philippines, from whence it was transferred in 1690 (Durand 1995: 316), its cultivation was also slow to develop. The Dutch colonial authorities made several attempts at it, but its extent never rivalled that of other cash crops. Real expansion only picked up well after the end of the colonial era, in the late 1980s, primarily on Sulawesi island. In the mid-1990s, the island's smallholders cultivated some 75 per cent of all cocoa lands in Indonesia (Akiyama and Nishio 1997: 100), by then a leading world producer, only behind Côte d'Ivoire and Ghana. Initially favoured by growth in yields and rising market prices, Sulawesi smallholders prospered and migratory flows to cocoa highlands were accelerated. But the tree's cultivation is very sensitive to diseases, in particular the cocoa pod borer, which can have a strong impact on yields. As these fluctuate and decline, and as prices tend to do the same, the fortunes of cocoa production and those responsible for it remain at risk.

Up to this day, cocoa has remained rare outside the archipelago countries, even in Thailand, where only some 400 hectares were recorded under cultivation in 2008. Nevertheless, the region's recent history and geography of cocoa provide yet another illustration of the versatility and adaptability of its agricultures, with several countries and regions trying their hand at the cultivation of boom crops, at times leaving the field, so to speak, to a neighbour.

Figure 7.38 Harvested area of cocoa in countries of archipelagic Southeast Asia, 1961–2008

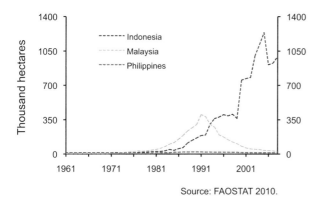

Source: FAOSTAT 2010.

Figure 7.39 Percentage of agricultural area allocated to cocoa cultivation in countries of archipelagic Southeast Asia, 1961–2007

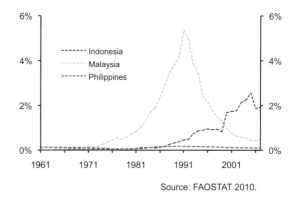

Source: FAOSTAT 2010.

Figure 7.40 Cocoa yields in countries of archipelagic Southeast Asia, 1961–2008

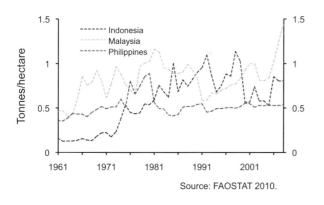

Source: FAOSTAT 2010.

Figure 7.41 Cocoa production in countries of archipelagic Southeast Asia (with prices), 1961–2008

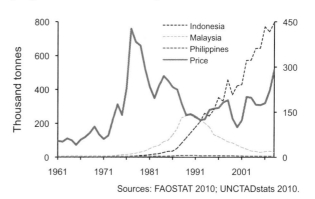

Sources: FAOSTAT 2010; UNCTADstats 2010.

Harvested area of cocoa (thousand hectares)

	1961–63	1971–73	1981–83	1991–93	2001–3	2008
Indonesia	6.9	9.3	24.8	224.4	847.1	990.1
Malaysia	1.2	7.0	56.2	359.2	50.3	20.6
Philippines	9.3	7.1	9.9	17.3	11.5	9.8

Percentage of agricultural area allocated to cocoa cultivation

	1961–63	1971–73	1981–83	1991–93	2001–3	2007
Indonesia	0	0	0	1	2	2
Malaysia	0	0	1	5	1	0
Philippines	0	0	0	0	0	0

Cocoa yields (tonnes/hectare)

	1961–63	1971–73	1981–83	1991–93	2001–3	2008
Indonesia	0.1	0.2	0.7	1.0	0.6	0.8
Malaysia	0.4	0.8	1.1	0.6	0.9	1.5
Philippines	0.4	0.5	0.5	0.5	0.5	0.5

Cocoa production (thousand tonnes)

	1961–63	1971–73	1981–83	1991–93	2001–3	2008
Indonesia	0.9	1.9	16.7	213.4	524.0	792.8
Malaysia	0.5	5.4	59.4	216.7	47.2	30.0
Philippines	3.4	3.6	5.0	8.4	6.0	5.1

| Price (Y2000 = 100) | 56 | 87 | 223 | 128 | 174 | 291 |

Plate 55

The FAO provides export data for three different cocoa products: cocoa beans, cocoa butter and cocoa paste. Cocoa beans have traditionally been the most widely traded in terms of quantity, which is no surprise as they consist of a raw and untransformed product. Cocoa beans also represent the only cocoa product listed on the New York and London commodity exchanges. The current figures are therefore devoted to that sole product. However, it should be noted that commodities that have been through some transformation — such as cocoa butter and cocoa paste — represent an ever-increasing proportion of cocoa products' global market share. For instance, global exports of such products amounted to 14 per cent (in market value) of all exported cocoa products in 1961 but grew to reach 47 per cent in 2007. Such a trend is particularly significant in Southeast Asia, where nearly 60 per cent of 2007 export earnings were provided by overseas sales of transformed products. This is, of course, a consequence of the importance of the region's food industry, more important than that of other significant cocoa producers, mostly located in Western Africa.

Most of the major trends already identified concerning cocoa cultivation and production (Figures 7.38–7.41) are applicable to its trade. Accordingly, only archipelago countries figure among the region's major exporters. Thus, Malaysia's boom and bust cycle in cocoa harvesting and production is also reflected in the evolution of its exports. However, cocoa bean exports peaked in the mid-1980s, a few years before the country's cocoa production did. The reason for this relates to what was said earlier: initially Malaysia exported primarily unprocessed beans, but by the 1990s it had begun to develop exports of cocoa butter, which then rose rapidly. This not only explains the early decline of its cocoa bean exports, but also that of the country's export ratio, as an increasing share of the cocoa beans produced in the country were diverted to downstream industries rather than being exported raw. This means that the conversion of cocoa plantations into palm tree estates by no means signified the end of the cocoa transformation industry, as suggested by Malaysia's growing imports of the commodity. Unsurprisingly, the Malaysian cocoa industry took advantage of the proximity of Indonesia, which provided more than 70 per cent of its overseas purchases in 2007. Malaysia was by then the world's second largest importer (behind the Netherlands and ahead of the United States) and Indonesia the world's third largest exporter, its overseas sales being inferior only to those of Côte d'Ivoire and Ghana. Reaching some 100,000 tonnes in 1990, the large island country's exports climbed to 490,000 tonnes in 2006, then dropped to 380,000 in 2007, a typical illustration of the highly fluctuating nature of production, trade and prices. In addition, quality does not always rhyme with quantity, as Indonesian cocoa beans, along with those grown in Brazil, are usually traded below world market price, the "markdown" sometimes reaching 10 per cent (Hass 2006: 246).

Figure 7.42 Cocoa bean exports in countries of archipelagic Southeast Asia (with prices), 1961–2006

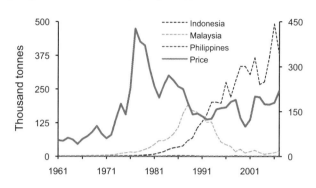

Sources: FAOSTAT 2010; UNCTADstats 2010.

Figure 7.43 Cocoa bean export ratio in countries of archipelagic Southeast Asia, 1961–2006

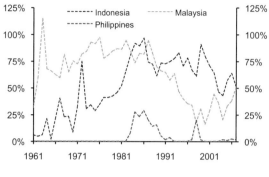

Source: FAOSTAT 2010.

Figure 7.44 Cocoa bean imports in selected countries, 1961–2006

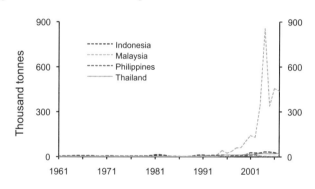

Source: FAOSTAT 2010.

Cocoa bean exports (thousand tonnes)

	1961–63	1971–73	1981–83	1991–93	2001–3	2007
Indonesia	0.0	0.8	11.4	160.6	311.4	379.8
Malaysia	0.3	4.3	52.4	133.7	16.8	17.8
Philippines	0.0	0.0	0.1	0.1	0.0	0.1

Cocoa bean export ratio (%)

	1961–63	1971–73	1981–83	1991–93	2001–3	2007
Indonesia	5	46	66	75	60	51
Malaysia	69	79	88	62	36	51
Philippines	0	0	3	2	0	1

Cocoa bean imports (thousand tonnes)

	1961–63	1971–73	1981–83	1991–93	2001–3	2007
Indonesia	0.0	0.1	7.9	0.2	24.5	19.7
Malaysia	0.0	0.7	0.8	1.9	201.2	438.5
Philippines	3.0	3.9	10.6	8.9	7.0	0.1
Thailand	0.0	0.0	0.0	3.5	16.0	20.1
Price (Y2000 = 100)	56	87	223	128	174	220

Plate 56

Although sugar has long been produced in non-tropical areas, where it is extracted from sugar beet, a typical tropical crop remains the world's most important provider of the sweet product. Sugar cane has been used to produce sugar for a much longer period than sugar beet, which by 2000 provided only 27 per cent of the world's sugar production. The bulk of the rest was made from sugar cane, with corn-derived sugar production remaining marginal due to its significant production cost (Mitchell 2004: 8). Some doubts remain about the origin of sugar cane, located in the Indonesian islands by Li Hui-Lin (1970: 15) and in New Guinea by Gerald Nelson and Martin Panggabean (1991: 704). In fact, the cultivation of sugar cane has a long and complex history in Indonesia, particularly in the archipelago's command island of Java. There the *cultuurstelsel* or "culture system" imposed by the Dutch colonial government between 1830 and 1870 involved the compulsory cultivation of sugar cane and made a deep impact on the country's agrarian structure (Geertz 1963: 52–82). The same can be said of the Philippines' own agrarian history. In fact, the importance of the Philippines' sugar industry on the eve of the nineteenth century was allegedly "one of the main compelling reasons for the American annexation of the Philippines" (Cherniguin 1988: 187). Since then, the relationship between the Philippines and its American "protector" has had much to do with the United States' sugar import quotas and overall "sugar politics".

Sugar cane is cultivated on several of the archipelago's islands, including the command island of Luzon. But Negros island, located at the heart of the Visayas, is the main production platform, with sugar haciendas dominating the landscape and hiring a large number of poorly paid workers. Sugar cane is also cultivated on smallholdings; but even more than coconut cultivation, small-scale cane cultivation has never been enough to ensure a family's livelihood, hence the huge concentration of land in the hands of large-scale operators. Since the early 1960s, the extent of sugar cane cultivation in the Philippines has fluctuated considerably along with the price of the commodity. For example, the mid-1970s massive price surge gave rise to an equivalent expansion of harvested areas. The ensuing two-phased price collapse was itself followed by a significant reduction in harvested areas, which had been halved by the late 1980s.

In the meantime, in Thailand and Indonesia, where agricultural wages are even lower, sugar cane harvested areas had continued to expand, in the first case way beyond the size of the Philippines'. Thailand's impressive sugar cane production boom does not necessarily rest on a geographic comparative advantage, as the Philippines and Indonesia are said to be better suited for cash crop cultivation, including sugar cane, than the kingdom (Hayami 2000: 8). Whatever all the reasons, the expansion of sugar cane plantations in Thailand has gone along with the increasing efficiency of its sugar cane industry (Ibid.: 18). Indeed, along with tea and bananas aimed at export markets, sugar cane is a typical example of a crop that allows great economies of scale when processed rapidly after harvest (Binswanger and Rosenzweig 1987: 528). By 2008, Thailand's sugar cane plantations covered more than a million hectares, representing over 45 per cent of the regional total, and ranking the country fifth in the world.

As of 2008, the size of Indonesia's harvested areas was also more extensive than the Philippines'. Java was historically the most important production island in the Indonesian archipelago and still totalled over 80 per cent of its sugar lands by the mid-1980s (Nelson and Panggabean 1991: 705). Finally, although Burma and Vietnam were latecomers on the scene, between 1990 and 2007 their harvested areas increased faster than those of all other countries in the region.

Figure 7.45 Harvested area of sugar cane in selected countries, 1961–2008

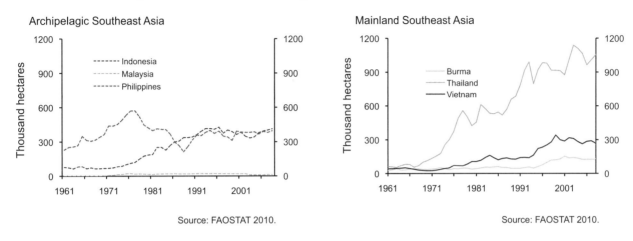

Source: FAOSTAT 2010.　　　　　Source: FAOSTAT 2010.

Figure 7.46 Percentage of agricultural area allocated to sugar cane cultivation in selected countries, 1961–2007

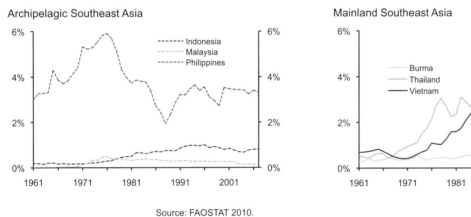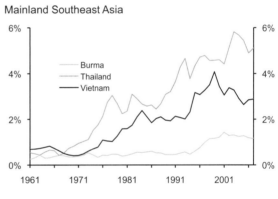

Source: FAOSTAT 2010.　　　　　Source: FAOSTAT 2010.

Harvested area of sugar cane (thousand hectares)

	1961–63	1971–73	1981–83	1991–93	2001–3	2008
Indonesia	73.7	77.1	234.5	392.4	357.5	415.6
Malaysia	1.1	10.8	19.1	22.9	18.4	14.3
Philippines	248.6	445.9	409.3	366.7	384.9	398.0
Burma	36.2	48.6	52.1	54.7	148.9	130.0
Thailand	59.4	159.3	549.0	897.0	1,009.2	1,054.4
Vietnam	45.3	33.2	125.6	144.8	308.0	271.1

Percentage of agricultural area allocated to sugar cane cultivation

	1961–63	1971–73	1981–83	1991–93	2001–3	2007
Indonesia	0	0	1	1	1	1
Malaysia	0	0	0	0	0	0
Philippines	3	5	4	3	3	3
Burma	0	0	0	1	1	1
Thailand	0	1	3	4	5	5
Vietnam	1	1	2	2	3	3

Plate 57

Sugar cane needs to be processed rapidly so as to avoid fermentation and any ensuing waste. Also, unlike most other cash crops, including all those examined in this study, sugar cane is not a tree or a bush, but a perennial grass. Consequently, sugar cane yields often evolve differently from those of cocoa, coffee, tea, oil palm, rubber and the like. For the latter, a typical cycle is characterised by a strong yield increase during the years following intensive expansion. The productivity of Indonesian sugar cane plantations has followed the opposite trend, as yields started declining the very moment harvested areas started increasing and levelled off when the latter did more or less the same. This might suggest that inputs (manpower, fertilizers, etc.) allocated to this crop remained stable while surfaces grew exponentially and/or that this expansion was carried out on poorer lands (Figure 7.45). Indonesia nevertheless managed to remain Southeast Asia's second most important producer during most of the 1961–2007 period, except between the mid-1970s and mid-1980s. During that interval, while its production was overtaken by that of a booming producer, Thailand, it had not yet overtaken that of the former leading producer in the region, the Philippines. Sugar cane expansion in the latter led to similar outcomes. A massive expansion of harvested areas was accompanied by a significant drop in average yields, from 77 to 60 tonnes per hectare, in 1961–63 and 1971–73. In 1976, when the Philippines' sugar cane production peaked at nearly 40 million tonnes, harvested areas had also reached their maximum extent, and yields were themselves still below 70 tonnes per hectare. By 2008, the extent of the harvested area as well as national production had dropped to more or less two-thirds of the 1976 level and average yields wavered around ~60 tonnes per hectare.

Such a setback had to do with, among other things, the end of the American preferential buying programme and the 1984–85 "Caribbean Sugar Crisis". The latter was the consequence of a global oversupply, partly driven by Southeast Asia's rapidly growing production, which led to major price drops (MacDonald and Demetrius 1986: 35, 54). Unlike the Philippines' sugar industry, which was badly hurt — Serge Cherniguin (1988: 189) refers to 1984 as the "collapse of sugar industry" — Thailand's production was less affected: instead of falling, it levelled off for a few years. Among the reasons is that before and during the crisis, the Thai government took the initiative of monitoring more closely the country's sugar producers as well as buyers. In the early 1980s, it initiated a risk-sharing mechanism between these stakeholders, the so-called 70-30 Revenue Sharing System (Ramsay 1987: 259). Although this process was marred by conflict, and sometimes even violence, Thailand's sugar production rebounded rapidly after the crisis, increasing from 24 million to over 73.5 million tonnes between 1986 and 2008. By then, the country was the world's fourth largest producer, but still far behind the first, Brazil. That year, the South American giant's output reached 645 million tonnes, a large proportion of which was processed into ethanol (José Goldemberg [2007] estimates that sugar-derived ethanol production monopolizes over 50 per cent of Brazilian sugar lands).

Contrary to what occurred in the archipelago, mainland Southeast Asian countries' sugar cane yields nearly doubled between 1961 and 2008 as production shot up in Burma, Vietnam and, of course, Thailand. This tends to confirm that territorial expansion can go hand in hand with yield increases, given that proper support and regulation are made available and enforced by the state.

Figure 7.47 Sugar cane yields in selected countries, 1961–2008

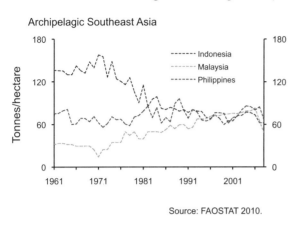

Archipelagic Southeast Asia

Source: FAOSTAT 2010.

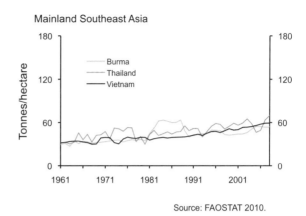

Mainland Southeast Asia

Source: FAOSTAT 2010.

Figure 7.48 Sugar cane production in selected countries (with sugar prices), 1961–2008

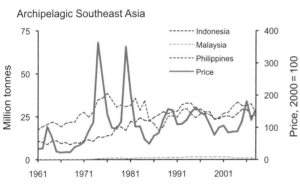

Archipelagic Southeast Asia

Sources: FAOSTAT 2010; UNCTADstats 2010.

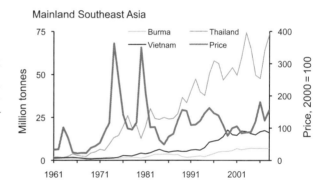

Mainland Southeast Asia

Sources: FAOSTAT 2010; UNCTADstats 2010.

Sugar cane yields (tonnes/hectare)

	1961–63	1971–73	1981–83	1991–93	2001–3	2008
Indonesia	136.2	146.9	98.9	79.1	70.3	62.6
Malaysia	33.2	21.5	46.7	59.4	76.1	48.4
Philippines	77.0	60.1	78.2	75.8	74.1	66.8
Burma	29.6	34.9	53.5	44.1	45.1	53.8
Thailand	31.8	45.9	45.0	48.0	60.3	69.7
Vietnam	33.0	37.2	37.6	43.0	52.6	59.5

Sugar cane production (million tonnes)

	1961–63	1971–73	1981–83	1991–93	2001–3	2008
Indonesia	10.0	11.2	22.8	31.0	25.1	26.0
Malaysia	0.0	0.2	0.9	1.4	1.4	0.7
Philippines	19.1	26.8	32.0	27.8	28.5	26.6
Burma	1.1	1.7	2.8	2.4	6.7	7.0
Thailand	1.9	7.3	24.8	42.7	61.3	73.5
Vietnam	1.5	1.2	4.7	6.2	16.2	16.1
Price (Y2000 = 100)	57	87	138	114	92	156

Plate 58

Data about *sugar* production are rare, and none are made available by the FAO, even if it does post figures about *sugar cane* production. However, it is known that in 2007, Thai sugar mills produced an average 103.6kg of sugar per harvested tonne of sugar cane (Nguyen *et al.* 2008: 725). Unfortunately, we cannot extrapolate about the production level of other countries from such a benchmark, as Thailand's sugar industry is considered to be exceptionally efficient (Figures 7.45 and 7.46).

Export and import figures posted here refer to both raw and refined (white) sugar. Refined sugar accounted for 84 per cent of all Southeast Asia's sugar imports in 1961, compared to 55 per cent in 2007. But refined sugar made up only 6 per cent of Southeast Asia's total sugar exports in 1961, and over 50 per cent 46 years later.

The efficiency and productivity of Thailand's sugar industry is one of the main reasons behind the impressive growth of the country's exports between 1961, when they were close to nil, and the first decade of the twenty-first century. Although fluctuating a lot from year to year, the kingdom's annual sugar exports nevertheless averaged 4 million tonnes between 2000 and 2006, the second best performance after Brazil's. In the early 1960s, Cuba was the world's number one exporter and the Philippines number two. This was an era when exports from new European powerhouses such as France, Belgium and Germany remained very low,

but also a time when American and Soviet sugar purchases were driven more by politics than market forces. The Philippines were then benefiting from advantageous American buying policies enshrined in a treaty that ended in 1977 (Cherniguin 1988: 187). That year Philippine overseas sales of sugar peaked, reaching 2.4 million tonnes, or some 8 per cent of world exports. The country's sales were halved the following year, as prices were collapsing. This came as an additional blow to its sugar exports, which continued their decline to such an extent that by 1995 the country had become a net sugar importer. This embarrassing situation was finally reversed in 2004, a fortunate outcome given the importance of the overall Philippine sugar industry, which, including all sugar-related activities, employs nearly 5 million persons (Padilla-Fernandez and Nuthall 2009: 77).

Although the Cold War is well over, sugar is still considered as "one of the most policy distorted of all commodities" (Mitchell 2004: 3). Along with Japan, the United States and several sugar-producing countries in Europe, Indonesia is also considered a country where sugar producers are highly protected (Ibid.: 5). In spite of this, its imports have soared since the mid-1990s, making it the region's leading importer, ahead of Malaysia, whose own purchases have been climbing steadily and substantially since the 1980s. As a result, in 2006 Southeast Asia had become a net importer of sugar.

Figure 7.49 Sugar exports in selected countries (with prices), 1961–2007

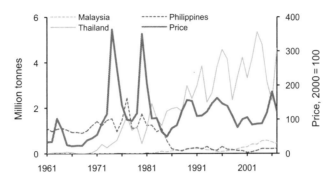

Sources: FAOSTAT 2010; UNCTADstats 2010.

Figure 7.50 Sugar imports in selected countries, 1961–2007

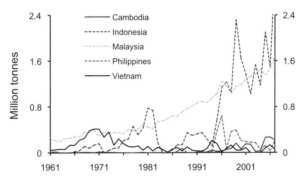

Source: FAOSTAT 2010.

Sugar exports (million tonnes)

	1961–63	1971–73	1981–83	1991–93	2001–3	2007
Malaysia	0.0	0.0	0.1	0.2	0.4	0.4
Philippines	1.1	1.4	1.2	0.3	0.1	0.2
Thailand	0.0	0.3	1.6	3.0	4.3	4.6

Sugar imports (million tonnes)

	1961–63	1971–73	1981–83	1991–93	2001–3	2007
Cambodia	0.0	0.0	0.0	0.0	0.1	0.2
Indonesia	0.0	0.1	0.6	0.3	1.3	3.2
Malaysia	0.2	0.3	0.5	0.9	1.3	1.7
Philippines	0.0	0.0	0.0	0.0	0.2	0.2
Vietnam	0.1	0.4	0.1	0.0	0.0	0.1
Price (Y2000 = 100)	57	87	138	114	92	123

Plate 59

Between 1961 and 2008, just about every major crop cultivated throughout the region was the object of intensification and expansion. By 2008, food crops* were still substantially more widespread than cash crops,† covering some 63 million versus 28 million hectares. But over the 47-year period, the expansion of cash crops was much more rapid, in fact twice as rapid, chalking up an average annual rate of territorial growth of 3 per cent against 1.2 per cent for food crops. In fact, strictly speaking, the difference is even more significant because the "expansion" of rice, by far the number one crop — in 2008 it covered about 47 million hectares versus 9.5 million and 9.4 million hectares for maize and palm fruit, respectively numbers two and three — is largely attributable to the increase in double cropping. The faster expansion of cash crops is also illustrated by their increasing share of total agricultural area.‡ That cash crops, most of which are predominantly intended for exports, have been occupying a growing proportion not only of the overall but also of the cultivated territory — and seem geared to continue to do so — has a number of meanings and implications. Three major ones must be singled out.

First, expansion of the cash crop domain as well as its intensification, along with that of food crops, some of which — notably rice — are also at least partly headed for the export market, contributes to the acceleration in the commercialization of the region's agriculture. Second, this is to be associated with its increasingly evident externalization and hence globalization, with several financial and economic consequences, including in terms of national and regional food security. Third, overall agricultural expansion contributes to the "agriculturalization" of the region's landscapes, achieved basically at the expense of its forests. It can be estimated that in the early 1960s, the ratio between the extent of forest cover versus that of food and cash crops was of the order of eight to one. By 2008, this ratio had declined to 2.6 to one, forest cover having been reduced from about 310 million hectares (Figure 2.6) to some 197 million (Figure 8.9), and areas sown with food and cash crops ranging from about 45 million to over 90 million hectares. This agriculturalization of Southeast Asia's overall territory compares to that currently taking place in Brazil, through the same process — the take-over of forestlands — and in comparable proportions. It is also reminiscent of the one that occurred in Europe over several centuries, beginning in the Middle Ages (Duby 1977), accelerating and culminating from the late eighteenth century onwards, throughout the nineteenth and well into the twentieth, at a time when European countries were driving the globalization processes, eventually obtaining the help of the United States, where the agriculturalization of the land has been achieved much more recently and rapidly (Figure 2.2).

Since then, the global scene has fundamentally changed but Southeast Asia seems to have nonetheless launched itself into a process of increasingly betting on the resources of its lands, to the point of at times gambling with them and having to turn increasingly to those of its seas.

---

* Includes rice, maize, fruit and vegetables dealt with previously. Admittedly, numerous other food crops are cultivated in the region, but it can be estimated that put together these account for at least 95 per cent of all lands devoted to the cultivation of food crops.

† Includes oil palm, rubber, coffee, tea, coconut, cocoa and sugar cane, also dealt with previously. Other commercial crops are grown throughout Southeast Asia, but put together these account for at least 95 per cent of all lands devoted to the cultivation of cash crops.

‡ "... the sum of areas under a) arable land ...; (b) permanent crops ...; and (c) permanent meadows and pastures ..." (FAOSTAT).

Figure 7.51 Cash crops versus food crops in Southeast Asia, 1961–2008

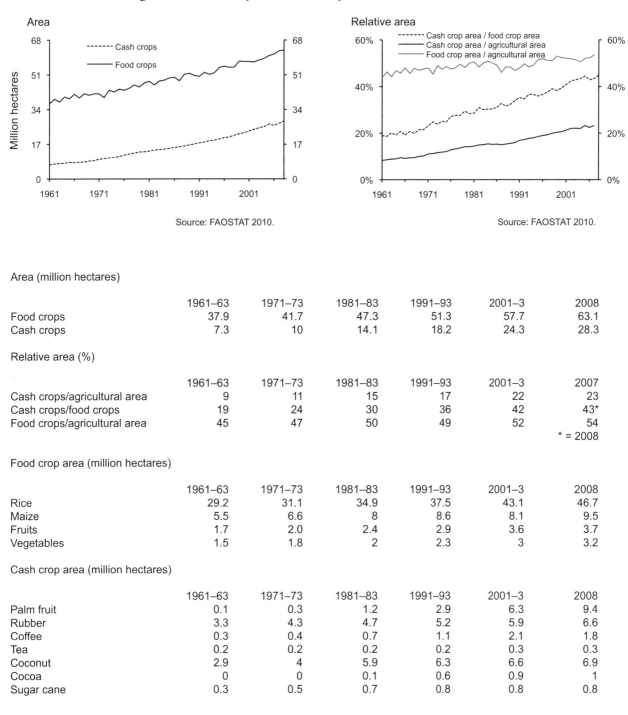

Source: FAOSTAT 2010.

Source: FAOSTAT 2010.

Area (million hectares)

	1961–63	1971–73	1981–83	1991–93	2001–3	2008
Food crops	37.9	41.7	47.3	51.3	57.7	63.1
Cash crops	7.3	10	14.1	18.2	24.3	28.3

Relative area (%)

	1961–63	1971–73	1981–83	1991–93	2001–3	2007
Cash crops/agricultural area	9	11	15	17	22	23
Cash crops/food crops	19	24	30	36	42	43*
Food crops/agricultural area	45	47	50	49	52	54

* = 2008

Food crop area (million hectares)

	1961–63	1971–73	1981–83	1991–93	2001–3	2008
Rice	29.2	31.1	34.9	37.5	43.1	46.7
Maize	5.5	6.6	8	8.6	8.1	9.5
Fruits	1.7	2.0	2.4	2.9	3.6	3.7
Vegetables	1.5	1.8	2	2.3	3	3.2

Cash crop area (million hectares)

	1961–63	1971–73	1981–83	1991–93	2001–3	2008
Palm fruit	0.1	0.3	1.2	2.9	6.3	9.4
Rubber	3.3	4.3	4.7	5.2	5.9	6.6
Coffee	0.3	0.4	0.7	1.1	2.1	1.8
Tea	0.2	0.2	0.2	0.2	0.3	0.3
Coconut	2.9	4	5.9	6.3	6.6	6.9
Cocoa	0	0	0.1	0.6	0.9	1
Sugar cane	0.3	0.5	0.7	0.8	0.8	0.8

CHAPTER 8

Pressuring the Land and the Sea

"There are other curious little exchanges of material between sea and land."

(Carson 1951: 143)

"Fish and other marine organisms constitute one of the most important of the marine resources in Southeast Asian seas. ... All states in the region have reason to protect the marine environment from pollution. ... At the same time the Southeast Asian nations are eager to stimulate economic development, which calls for the exploitation of terrestrial as well as marine resources that could create pollution of nearby seas."

(Morgan and Valencia 1983: 1, 4, 6)

Plate 60

For centuries, fish* and seafood† have represented key elements in the diet of a large number of Southeast Asian communities. In 2001, as sources of protein, they were at least as important as meat in all countries except Vietnam, and contributed more to fulfilling daily energy needs than meat in Indonesia, Burma and Cambodia (Table A3). Furthermore, since the 1960s, in Indonesia, Thailand and Cambodia protein intake derived from fish and seafood consumption has increased more rapidly than that provided by all other types of food. Given the growing international demand for the region's fish and seafood products, it is therefore not surprising that the regional output has itself grown more rapidly than that of most other agro-food items.

In Figures 8.1 and 8.2, "Fish and seafood production" refers to the total combined production of the fisheries and aquaculture sectors. "Fish and seafood captures" refers to the production resulting solely from fishing activities, the latter being mostly carried out at sea, and partly in inland waters, such as rivers and lakes. In the case of Cambodia, that is very significant, given the volume of captures coming from the Tonle Sap, Southeast Asia's largest and more importantly most productive body of inland water and possibly in the world (Van Zalinge *et al.* 2001).

Just like many types of agricultural production, that of fish and seafood did not increase equally in all countries, although most have been involved in the growth trend. As could be expected, the two large archipelagic countries, Indonesia and the Philippines, are those whose production has increased the most since the early 1960s. Adding to this, both countries' total production was multiplied by more than ten over the same period, approaching the level of growth achieved in the most dynamic

mainland countries, where the fish and seafood industry remains smaller. In the case of Indonesia, between 1980 and 2008, the average annual rate of growth stood at 5.7 per cent, nothing equivalent having been achieved with any of the major food crops. Among mainland countries, Thailand got off to an early start, its production rivalling and even overtaking that of the Philippines in the 1970s. But it peaked by the mid-1990s, and then levelled off during a decade, until it started to decrease rather sharply in 2005–6. As for Vietnam's own production, it has followed a familiar pattern, i.e., beginning to catch up in the 1980s then starting to boom in the 1990s, the boom having since continued, to such a point that, between 1998 and 2008, total output has nearly tripled. Over the same period, Burma did nearly as well, having thus joined the ranks of the mainland region's major producers. Cambodia, also a late starter and still a modest producer, has nevertheless seen its own output increase rapidly since the turn of the century. Only landlocked Laos remains uninvolved in this general growth trend.

From the early 1960s to the late 1970s, over 90 per cent of the region's fish and seafood production came from captures, most of which occurred in marine ecosystems. The regions' captures almost doubled during the 1960s, a period when this activity grew particularly rapidly in Thailand. Regional captures have kept on increasing since, but at a more moderate pace dictated by the limits of the seas, and because of the enforcement of some regulation. As a result, by 2008 captures totalled less than 60 per cent of Southeast Asia's entire fish and seafood production. In the meantime, people had once again turned to their land with aquaculture going through a major boom.

---

* Fish: "Used as a collective term it includes fish, mollusks, crustaceans and any aquatic animal which is harvested" (FAO Glossary of Aquaculture).
† Seafood: "Human food derived from the sea or from marine aquaculture" (FAO Glossary of Aquaculture).

Figure 8.1 Fish and seafood production by country, 1960–2008

Archipelagic Southeast Asia

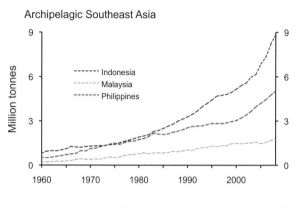

Source: FAO Fisheries and Aquaculture Department 2010.

Mainland Southeast Asia

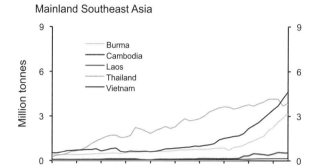

Source: FAO Fisheries and Aquaculture Department 2010.

Figure 8.2 Fish and seafood captures by country, 1960–2008

Archipelagic Southeast Asia

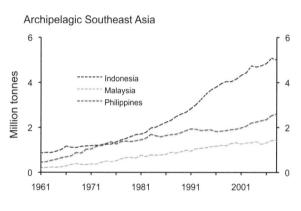

Source: FAO Fisheries and Aquaculture Department 2010.

Mainland Southeast Asia

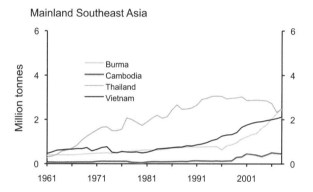

Source: FAO Fisheries and Aquaculture Department 2010.

Fish and seafood production (million tonnes)

	1960–62	1970–72	1980–82	1990–92	2000–2	2008
Indonesia	0.9	1.3	2.0	3.4	5.3	8.8
Malaysia	0.2	0.4	0.8	1.0	1.4	1.8
Philippines	0.5	1.2	1.8	2.6	3.2	5.0
Burma	0.4	0.4	0.6	0.7	1.3	3.2
Cambodia	0.0	0.1	0.0	0.1	0.4	0.5
Laos	0.0	0.0	0.0	0.0	0.1	0.1
Thailand	0.3	1.6	2.0	3.0	3.7	3.8
Vietnam	0.5	0.7	0.6	1.0	2.3	4.6

Fish and seafood captures (million tonnes)

	1960–62	1970–72	1980–82	1990–92	2000–2	2008
Indonesia	0.8	1.2	1.7	2.8	4.3	5.0
Malaysia	0.2	0.3	0.7	1.0	1.3	1.4
Philippines	0.4	1.0	1.4	1.9	2.0	2.6
Burma	0.4	0.4	0.6	0.7	1.2	2.5
Cambodia	0.0	0.1	0.0	0.1	0.4	0.4
Thailand	0.3	1.5	1.9	2.7	2.9	2.5
Vietnam	0.5	0.6	0.5	0.8	1.7	2.1

Plate 61

Although not as ancient as in China, aqua-culture production in Southeast Asia is several centuries old (Hishamunda *et al.* 2009). Until recent decades, however, its share in total fish and seafood production had remained modest. In 1960, just over 200,000 tonnes of produce came from the region's aquaculture sector. But in 2008, production had reached 11.3 million tonnes, the boom having begun during the late 1970s in the archipelago countries, with Thailand joining in a few years later, Vietnam in the mid-1990s and Burma by the early years of the twenty-first century. From the late 1970s until the turn of the century, production has expanded at a more or less equal rate in Indonesia and the Philippines, the total volume of production remaining almost equivalent in the two countries. However, since the middle of the first decade of the twenty-first century, Indonesian growth has rapidly outpaced the growth of its archipelagic neighbour, to such an extent that in 2007 and 2008 its annual production was superior by some 60 per cent. In both countries, but particularly in Indonesia, this expansion has been accompanied by a major shift in the structure of production, traditionally dominated by fish cultivation, but now shifting increasingly towards that of aquatic plants, primarily seaweeds, whose extracts are used in processed foods, cosmetics and pharmaceuticals. In Indonesia alone, between 2003 and 2008, aquatic plant production was multiplied by more than nine, from some 232,000 to over 2.1 million tonnes, accounting by then for well over half of total aquaculture production (FAO Fisheries and Aquaculture Department 2010). Of the two other major production categories, fish and crustaceans, the first has also expanded very rapidly, accounting for about a third of the 2008 total. The remaining 10 per cent is made up of crustaceans, whose production increase has been much more modest. In many regions, such as in the Karimunjawa Archipelago National Park, just off Central Java, seaweed farming has been virtually replacing all shrimp aquaculture and, to a lesser extent, fish aquaculture (Maillet 2012).

In most countries of the region, the rate of growth of aquaculture production has been much more rapid than that of fish captures, particularly since the early 1980s. Consequently, the proportion of fish and seafood production coming from aquaculture has jumped. This growth in the relative importance of fish and seafood cultivation has been substantial in both the archipelago countries and the mainland ones, Vietnam and Laos showing the fastest growth rates. In these two countries the aquaculture sector's share has even become dominant. While that is not surprising on the part of landlocked Laos, it is more so in the case of Vietnam, given the demographic importance of its coastal fishing communities and the extent of the country's coastline and territorial waters. The same can be said of the Philippines, whose aquaculture sector accounted for nearly half of its very substantial production of fish and seafood in 2008. All things considered, the most spectacular example in this shift from capture to cultivation of fish and seafood is provided by Indonesia, which possesses the largest expanse of territorial waters and where the share of aquaculture, which still stood at a relatively modest 20 per cent of the total at the beginning of the first decade of the twenty-first century, had reached nearly 44 per cent by 2008. By the late 1970s, region wide, aquaculture accounted for slightly more than 10 per cent of total fish and seafood production. By 2008, while that total had quadrupled, the aquaculture sector's share had reached over 40 per cent.

Throughout Southeast Asia, the pressure exerted on agriculture for the production of food and non-food cash crops is increasingly shared with aquaculture, which is itself expanding very rapidly into the coastal and maritime domain, thus joining the fishing sector per se in putting pressure on the seas, which are being increasingly cultivated, literally, and increasingly polluted (Sodhi *et al.* 2010).

Figure 8.3 Aquaculture production by country, 1960–2008

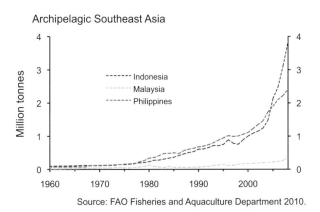

Archipelagic Southeast Asia

Source: FAO Fisheries and Aquaculture Department 2010.

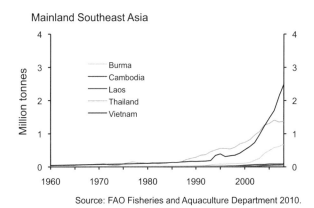

Mainland Southeast Asia

Source: FAO Fisheries and Aquaculture Department 2010.

Figure 8.4 Ratio of fish and seafood production from aquaculture by country, 1960–2008

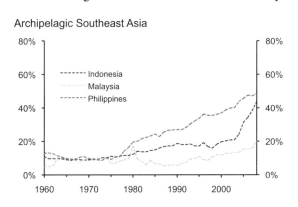

Archipelagic Southeast Asia

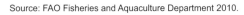

Source: FAO Fisheries and Aquaculture Department 2010.

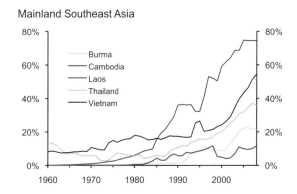

Mainland Southeast Asia

Source: FAO Fisheries and Aquaculture Department 2010.

Aquaculture production by country (million tonnes)

	1960–62	1970–72	1980–82	1990–92	2000–2	2008
Indonesia	0.1	0.1	0.3	0.6	1.1	3.9
Malaysia	0.0	0.0	0.1	0.1	0.2	0.4
Philippines	0.1	0.1	0.4	0.7	1.2	2.4
Burma	0.0	0.0	0.0	0.0	0.1	0.7
Cambodia	0.0	0.0	0.0	0.0	0.0	0.1
Laos	0.0	0.0	0.0	0.0	0.1	0.1
Thailand	0.0	0.1	0.1	0.3	0.8	1.4
Vietnam	0.0	0.1	0.1	0.2	0.6	2.5

Ratio of fish and seafood production from aquaculture (%)

	1960–62	1970–72	1980–82	1990–92	2000–2	2008
Indonesia	10	9	13	18	20	44
Malaysia	5	9	11	6	12	20
Philippines	13	9	20	27	38	48
Burma	0	0	1	2	10	21
Cambodia	0	0	1	6	4	11
Laos	0	1	7	36	62	74
Thailand	13	5	5	11	22	36
Vietnam	8	10	17	17	26	54

Plate 62

As classified by the FAO, Southeast Asia's aquaculture production comes from three types of environment, or waters: brackish,* fresh and marine. In each type of environment, production began to increase significantly during the 1970s. By the early 1990s, this increase had become a boom, which is still going on today. In the 1960s, production from marine water was still much less significant than that reaped from the two other types of environment. By the 1980s, all three domains were producing equivalent volumes of fish and seafood. But since then, production totals from freshwater and marine environments have grown at an even faster pace, to a point where, by now, they each account for about 40 per cent of the total volume, against some 20 per cent from brackishwater.

However, in terms of monetary value, the share of brackishwater production is likely to be closer to that of the two other domains, given that it is the dominant source of crustaceans, particularly shrimps and prawns. In fact, within the entire Southeast Asian realm, the value share of crustacean production to total aquaculture production is nearly equal to half (Yap *et al.* 2007: 3). In volume, total Southeast Asian shrimp production more than tripled from 1980 to 2005 (Hishamunda *et al.* 2009: 10), most of the "catch" coming from shrimp aquaculture ponds established along the seashore, on former mangrove forests. Throughout the region, the domestication of these mangrove forests represents a major environmental setback — notwithstanding a few exceptions such as found in East Java — given the key functions they play in several domains, such as serving as feeding and reproduction grounds for a number of marine species, natural filters between land and sea waters and protection barriers against tidal waves. But, because of the high albeit risky rewards that intensive shrimp cultivation provides to small operators, expansion continues, with the combined output of Indonesia, Thailand and Vietnam — the region's three major producers — accounting "for more than 30 per cent of world farmed shrimp in 2005" (Ibid.: 11).

In the marine domain, since the mid-1990s, the most spectacular growth production has concerned seaweed, which has fast become the emblematic product of marine aquaculture, or mariculture, particularly in the Philippines and Indonesia, by far the two largest producers of aquatic plants. In Indonesian waters for example, seaweed cultivation — essentially red seaweeds (*eucheuma cottonii*), whose extracts are used in processed foods, cosmetics and pharmaceuticals — has been expanding extremely rapidly since the early years of the twenty-first century. Red seaweed cultivation is primarily the work of small-scale operators, habitually fishermen who try and diversify their sources of livelihood by going into mariculture. To become part-time "farmers of the sea", they generally borrow from traders the limited capital needed to buy start-up equipment, such as seaweed germs, ropes and bottles, the latter to be used as buoys (Maillet 2012). Among products reaped from the sea, molluscs, particularly mussels and blood cockles, are the most important. In 2005 they accounted for — not taking into account seaweeds — over 80 per cent of the total volume (Hishamunda *et al.* 2009: 12).

Of the three environmental domains under which aquaculture is practised, fresh water is the dominant source of fish, *stricto sensu*, providing about half of the total tonnage, with catfish, carp and tilapia being the most common species, and Vietnam the most important producer. In addition, region wide, fish production from fresh water aquaculture has, since the late 1990s, been growing much faster than from brackish or marine water environments.

Just like in the agricultural sector, the region's countries have been overtaking and relaying each other in the production or harvesting of different fish and seafood species. This has been the case with shrimp production, which is particularly vulnerable to diseases, leading to volatility in prices and, hence, export markets.

---

* Brackishwater: "Water with a salinity intermediate between seawater and freshwater, usually showing wide salinity fluctuations" (FAO Glossary of Aquaculture).

Figure 8.5 Southeast Asian aquaculture production from three types of environment, 1960–2008

Production

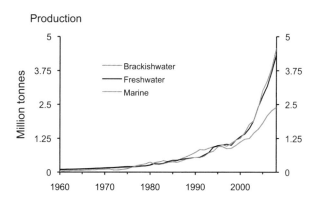

Source: FAO Fisheries and Aquaculture Department 2010.

Percentage of production

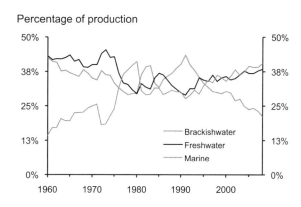

Source: FAO Fisheries and Aquaculture Department 2010.

Figure 8.6 Selected aquaculture productions, 1960–2008

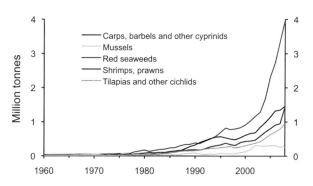

Source: FAO Fisheries and Aquaculture Department 2010.

Amount of aquaculture production from three types of environment (million tonnes)

	1960–62	1970–72	1980–82	1990–92	2000–2	2008
Brackishwater	0.1	0.1	0.3	0.8	1.2	2.4
Freshwater	0.1	0.2	0.3	0.6	1.4	4.3
Marine	0.0	0.1	0.3	0.6	1.5	4.6

Percentage of aquaculture production from three types of environment

	1960–62	1970–72	1980–82	1990–92	2000–2	2008
Brackishwater	42	36	35	41	29	21
Freshwater	42	41	31	30	35	38
Marine	16	23	34	29	36	40

Selected aquaculture productions (million tonnes)

	1960–62	1970–72	1980–82	1990–92	2000–2	2008
Carps, barbels and other cyprinids	0.0	0.0	0.1	0.2	0.4	1.4
Mussels	0.0	0.0	0.0	0.1	0.2	0.3
Red seaweeds	0.0	0.0	0.2	0.4	1.0	4.0
Shrimps, prawns	0.0	0.0	0.0	0.4	0.6	1.4
Tilapias and other cichlids	0.0	0.0	0.0	0.2	0.3	0.9

Plate 63

As with most of the region's agro food productions, fish and seafood products have traditionally targeted the domestic market. Today, that is still the case with the majority of freshwater species captured or harvested in the region. However, over recent decades, fish and seafood exports have increased significantly, in volume as well as in relative importance, with shrimps representing, in terms of value, the leading component and milkfish — also produced primarily in brackishwater environments — a distant second. These exports are predominantly shipped to Japan, Taiwan, South Korea and the United States.

Since the mid-1970s, by which time data on fish and seafood exports had become more reliable, and even more since the mid-1980s, these exports have been provided predominantly by Thailand, Indonesia and Vietnam. In the case of Thailand, by far the leading exporter, the fish and seafood export ratio is exceptionally high, surpassing 40 per cent in 2006. Thailand was already contributing close to two-thirds of the region's fish and seafood exports in the late 1980s. Since then, Indonesia and Vietnam have increased their presence on this rapidly growing market. Indeed, Indonesia, the region's largest producer, became a significant exporter starting in the late 1980s, essentially as the result of policy decisions to boost exports, including through the implementation of a national Aquaculture Intensification Programme and another programme to promote fisheries exports (Hishamunda *et al.* 2009: 25). As for Vietnam, again a late starter, it truly joined in only during the mid-1990s but has since seen its total exports quadruple while its export ratio has doubled to over 20 per cent. In all three cases, shrimps have represented the main export. In fact, throughout the region, shrimp production is predominantly destined for exports. Although "the proportion of the region's shrimp output that is exported varies … it is probably more than 80 per cent" (Ibid.: 26).

Since the mid-1990s, Burma has also become a relatively significant exporter, largely thanks to the development of an apparently thriving export-oriented aquaculture sector. As for Cambodia's sudden appearance in 1992 among the ranks of those with a substantial export ratio, it is attributable to the fact that by then exports had become better accounted for, thanks to the work of a state export agency. But their tabulation has remained problematic, given that these exports seem to be shipped largely through its neighbours, Thailand and Vietnam (Ibid.: 26).

For Malaysia and the Philippines, exports as well as export ratios have remained relatively stable between the mid-1970s and the middle of the first decade of the twenty-first century. But these exports have not been sufficient to counterbalance their imports, both countries having a seafood trade deficit. In fact, although the region does have an overall seafood trade surplus, it has not been increasing significantly, because of price fluctuations and, in some cases, relative price decrease, but mostly because domestic consumption has been increasing faster than exports. As noted earlier, fish and seafood remains a major source of protein intake, even growing in proportionate terms as the overall nutritional levels are improving in all countries of the region. Among the world's major regions, the proportion of protein intake provided by fish and seafood is the highest in Southeast Asia, slightly higher than in East Asia (within the various world regions defined by the FAO, Micronesia and Polynesia are the only ones where fish and seafood derived protein intake is higher, in relative terms, than in Southeast Asia). Within the region, the leading "consumers" of fish and seafood proteins are by far the Malaysians, followed by the Thais and the Filipinos. In Burma and — somewhat surprisingly — Vietnam, per capita fish protein consumption is well below the region's average, barely surpassing the global average. This might contribute to explaining how these two countries maintain a very positive seafood trade surplus.

Figure 8.7 Fish and seafood exports by country, 1976–2006

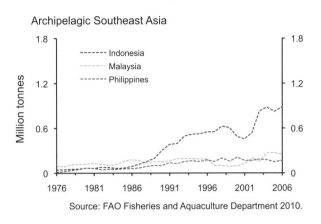

Archipelagic Southeast Asia

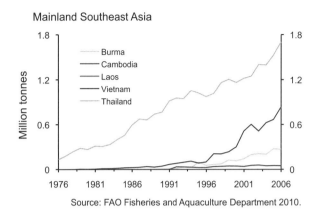

Mainland Southeast Asia

Source: FAO Fisheries and Aquaculture Department 2010.

Source: FAO Fisheries and Aquaculture Department 2010.

Figure 8.8 Fish and seafood export ratio by country, 1976–2006

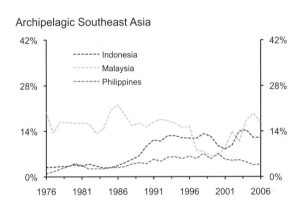

Archipelagic Southeast Asia

Mainland Southeast Asia

Source: FAO Fisheries and Aquaculture Department 2010.

Source: FAO Fisheries and Aquaculture Department 2010.

Fish and seafood exports (million tonnes)

	1976–78	1986–88	1996–98	2006
Indonesia	0.0	0.1	0.6	0.9
Malaysia	0.1	0.2	0.1	0.3
Philippines	0.0	0.1	0.2	0.2
Burma	0.0	0.0	0.1	0.3
Cambodia	0.0	0.0	0.0	0.0
Laos	0.0	0.0	0.0	0.0
Vietnam	0.0	0.0	0.2	0.8
Thailand	0.2	0.6	1.0	1.7

Fish and seafood export ratio (%)

	1976–78	1986–88	1996–98	2006
Indonesia	3	4	12	12
Malaysia	17	19	10	17
Philippines	2	3	6	4
Burma	0	1	8	10
Cambodia	0	0	30	9
Laos	0	0	0	0
Thailand	9	24	30	41
Vietnam	0	4	11	23

Plate 64

As was seen earlier (Figures 2.5 and 2.6), deforestation has for centuries resulted from agricultural expansion throughout the region, the two processes evolving more or less at the same pace, accelerating and slowing down concurrently. This has been particularly so since the nineteenth century. The last two decades have been witness to such a closely interrelated evolution. As far as deforestation (or decrease in forest area) is concerned, it has been particularly significant in the archipelago countries and in two of the mainland ones, Burma and Cambodia, with Thailand and Vietnam the only ones to have stopped and even, in Vietnam's case, clearly reversed the trend. Between 1990 and 2007, Indonesia, Malaysia and the Philippines together lost a quarter of their forest cover, the latter more than a third, Indonesia over 20 per cent and Malaysia some 8 per cent.

Altogether, over the same 17-year period, mainland countries lost only some 10 per cent of their own forest area. But here the differences are quite substantial, particularly between the two extremes, Burma and Vietnam, located on either side of the mainland portion of Southeast Asia. Burma lost over 20 per cent of its forest cover, while Vietnam actually regained more than 40 per cent. This astonishing turn of events may be partly attributed to a change in the country's methods of land classification reporting. But it is quite clear that the massive deforestation that had taken place from the mid-1970s to the early 1990s, largely because of agricultural expansion (De Koninck 1999), has been stopped and in fact reversed. This appears largely attributable both to vigorous state policies favouring forest conservation and reforestation (Meyfroidt and Lambin 2008), as well as to livelihood choices on the part of those most directly concerned, small-holders and peasants (Sikor 2001, Clement and Amezaga 2008). One consequence of this reversal in the nation's forest policy has been an increase in wood imports, including illegal ones from neighbouring countries, such as Laos and Cambodia (Meyfroidt and Lambin 2009). This is yet another example of the intra-regional transfer of production responsibilities and environmental pressure that has been ongoing for decades in Southeast Asia.

But in Vietnam, as elsewhere in the region, one type of forest formation has not stopped receding, perhaps the most ecologically precious and nearly irreplaceable one: mangrove forests. These are being cut down in all countries — except in landlocked Laos — primarily to make way for shrimp farming, the products of which are themselves predominantly intended for exports (Figures 8.7 and 8.8). The ensuing ecological transformations of coastal environments, where mangroves are located, turn out to be particularly damaging. The key role that these environments play in the reproduction of a number of marine species and in the filtering of waters at the intersection between land and sea can hardly be fulfilled by the intensive cultivation of shrimps. These are raised in artificial and densely packed ponds, the polluted waters of which are systematically drained into the sea.

Here again, the archipelago countries have been the most involved, with Indonesia in the lead. Because of the huge extent of its very often swampy coastline (allegedly the second longest in the world behind Canada's), the country is by far the best endowed with mangrove forests. However, it is also the one where their retreat has been the most critical, in both absolute and relative terms. But other countries, particularly Vietnam, have in recent years been intensifying their shrimp production, following a pattern reminiscent of what has been happening in the region with other boom crops, including timber (De Koninck 2006; Hall 2011): when production recedes in one country, another one takes over.

Figure 8.9 Forest area by country, 1990–2007

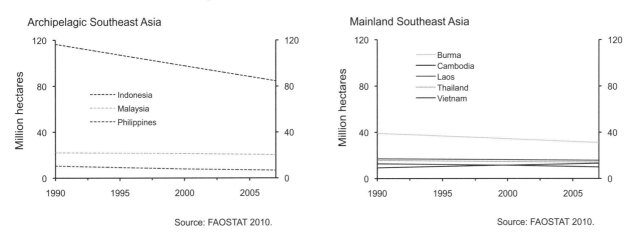

Source: FAOSTAT 2010.

Source: FAOSTAT 2010.

Figure 8.10 Mangrove forest area by country, 1980–2005*

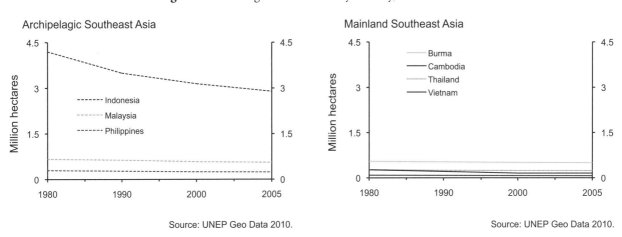

Source: UNEP Geo Data 2010.

Source: UNEP Geo Data 2010.

Forest area (million hectares)

	1990	1995	2000	2005	2007
Indonesia	116.6	107.2	97.9	88.5	84.8
Malaysia	22.4	22.0	21.6	20.9	20.6
Philippines	10.6	9.3	7.9	7.2	6.8
Burma	39.2	36.9	34.6	32.2	31.3
Cambodia	12.9	12.2	11.5	10.4	10.0
Laos	17.3	16.9	16.5	16.1	16.0
Thailand	16.0	15.4	14.8	14.5	14.4
Vietnam	9.4	10.5	11.7	12.9	13.4

Mangrove forest area (million hectares)

	1980	1990	2000	2005
Indonesia	4.2	3.5	3.2	2.9
Malaysia	0.7	0.6	0.6	0.6
Philippines	0.3	0.3	0.3	0.2
Burma	0.6	0.5	0.5	0.5
Cambodia	0.1	0.1	0.1	0.1
Thailand	0.3	0.3	0.2	0.2
Vietnam	0.3	0.2	0.2	0.2

* Data are available for 1980, 1990, 2000 and 2005, which explains the curves' constant gradient.

Plate 65

In 1990, forests covered 54.6 per cent of the total combined land area of the eight Southeast Asian countries examined here. Seventeen years later, the percentage had been reduced to 44.1 per cent, resulting in an average annual deforestation rate of 1.3 per cent. At the outset, the distribution of percentages among the eight countries was very uneven. The three least densely populated, Malaysia, Cambodia and Laos, were unsurprisingly the most heavily forested, each with more than two-thirds of its national territory still covered with forest. This was equivalent to approximately twice the forest cover ratio of the Philippines, Thailand and Vietnam, which also happened to be the most densely populated countries. Thailand's population density then stood just above the regional average of nearly 100 inhabitants per square kilometre; for both the Philippines and Vietnam, the equivalent figure was more than double. As for Indonesia and Burma, which are the largest countries in the region but have population densities below the regional average, their respective territories were still about 60 per cent forested.

Only the Philippines, which was already one of the three most forest-depleted countries in the region in 1990, was unable to slow down the onslaught. In fact, since then the country has lost more than a third of its forest cover, having maintained by far the region's highest annual deforestation rate, nearly 2.5 per cent. This "performance" is attributable to the continuous expansion of agriculture (Figures 5.17 and 5.18), combined with vigorous legal and illegal logging, still a major problem in this corruption-plagued country (Bello *et al.* 2004), where much of the cleared land is not even turned over to agricultural use (Kummer 1992, Van den Top 2003). Thailand, where agricultural expansion has totally ceased, appears well under way to reversing deforestation and to have reached the status of a country undergoing the so-called forest transition (Leblond 2011). The same can be said of Vietnam — assuming the country's land use reporting

methods are reliable — since, as already stated (Figure 8.9) — the reversal has been spectacular, forest cover having increased by an average annual rate of 2.1 per cent between 1990 and 2007.

Among the three countries holding proportionately the most extensive forest heritage in 1990, Malaysia and Laos have lost the smallest proportion and Cambodia the largest, in this case at the rate of 2.6 per cent per year. Countries like Burma, and more so Indonesia, have also maintained a very high annual deforestation rate, both above 1 per cent. In the case of Indonesia, this means nearly 2 million hectares per year, thus accounting for over half of the region's total annual forest loss. At less than 0.5 per cent, the Laotian and Malaysian annual deforestation rate appears relatively low. This is not surprising on the part of the less accessible land-locked state of Laos, by far the least densely populated in the region and with the least developed transport network. It is somewhat surprising on the part of Malaysia, considering rapid expansion of oil palm cultivation in the states of Sabah and Sarawak (Figures 7.1 and 7.2). However, the ensuing deforestation is at least partially offset by the fact that, in Peninsular Malaysia, net expansion of agriculture has considerably slowed down. Although oil palm has here also continued to gain ground, it has largely been at the expense of the receding cultivation of rubber (De Koninck 2007).

Forest area per capita has closely followed the generally downward trend of forest cover. Increasing pressure on the respective nations' forest heritage is increasingly evident. By 2007, Indonesia still held 43 per cent of the region's forested lands and the extent of forest area "available" for each Indonesian was just above the region's average, while in Laos it was way above. In the Philippines, and even in Thailand and Vietnam where reforestation is ongoing, it was exceptionally low, below the world's average of 0.6 hectare per capita (about 400 billion hectares of forested area "available" for 6.7 billion people).

Figure 8.11 Percentage of forest area by country, 1990–2007

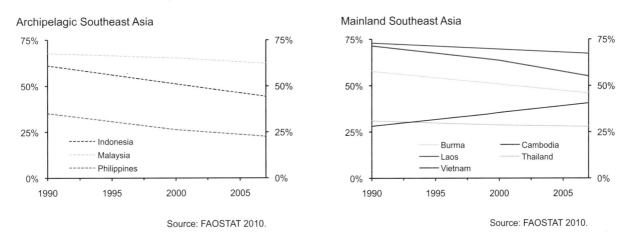

Source: FAOSTAT 2010.

Source: FAOSTAT 2010.

Figure 8.12 Forest area per capita by country, 1990–2007

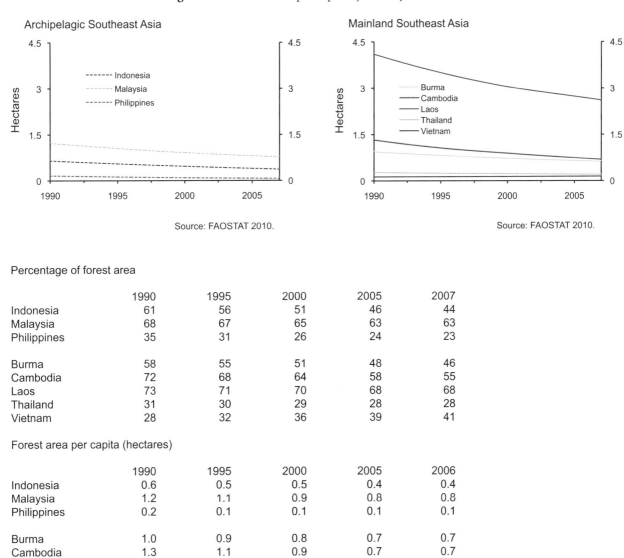

Source: FAOSTAT 2010.

Source: FAOSTAT 2010.

Percentage of forest area

	1990	1995	2000	2005	2007
Indonesia	61	56	51	46	44
Malaysia	68	67	65	63	63
Philippines	35	31	26	24	23
Burma	58	55	51	48	46
Cambodia	72	68	64	58	55
Laos	73	71	70	68	68
Thailand	31	30	29	28	28
Vietnam	28	32	36	39	41

Forest area per capita (hectares)

	1990	1995	2000	2005	2006
Indonesia	0.6	0.5	0.5	0.4	0.4
Malaysia	1.2	1.1	0.9	0.8	0.8
Philippines	0.2	0.1	0.1	0.1	0.1
Burma	1.0	0.9	0.8	0.7	0.7
Cambodia	1.3	1.1	0.9	0.7	0.7
Laos	4.2	3.6	3.2	2.8	2.8
Thailand	0.3	0.3	0.2	0.2	0.2
Vietnam	0.1	0.1	0.1	0.2	0.2

Plate 66

Forest plantations have a long history in the region, having played a significant economic role both prior to and during the colonial period.* This has particularly been the case with teak wood plantations. Teak is indigenous to South Asia and mainland Southeast Asia, where it is found in Burma, Thailand and Laos. Its very hard and precious wood — formerly widely used in the shipbuilding industry — represents a valuable export commodity, especially when transformed into high value furniture. It has also long been cultivated in Southeast Asia, not only in mainland countries but even more so in Indonesia, reportedly from seedlings imported centuries ago from Thailand. Since at least the nineteenth century, the largest teak wood plantations in the region have been found in Java, where they still cover more than a million hectares, predominantly under state management (Peluso 1992). Other trees grown commercially in the region include eucalyptus — with plantations dating back to the colonial period, for example in Vietnam (Tran n.d.) — acacia and various species of pine trees, most of them catering to the wood pulp industry, which is rapidly expanding, notably in Indonesia (Pirard and Cossalter 2006).

Though still relatively modest, accounting for only some 6 per cent of total forest cover, forest plantations in the region have been expanding at the relatively rapid rate of some 1.5 per cent per year between 1990 and 2005. But the gain of some 2.5 million hectares in forest plantations during

that 15-year period pales in comparison with the loss of some 47 million hectares in the extent of the total regional forest cover during the same period. Thailand, Indonesia and Vietnam together account for some three quarters of the regional total of forest plantation gain, with the share of the latter two, particularly Vietnam, having increased markedly since 1990. Within Thailand and Vietnam, planted forests actually represented over 20 per cent of total forests in 2005, an exceptional proportion. In the case of Vietnam, where that percentage had doubled over the course of the 15 preceding years, it largely explains the reversal in the evolution of the country's forest cover, which had been dramatically decreasing between 1975 and the early 1990s and has since been expanding (Figures 2.6 and 8.9). Part of the explanation for this impressive recovery might be attributable to Vietnam's policy decision to classify an increasing number of tree crops as production forest. As donor agencies from industrial countries have a tendency to reward countries that give signs of caring for their "forests", this may also explain why Indonesia has also recently reclassified its fast expanding oil palm covered lands as production forests.

The plight of the Philippines' forests shows up here again. It is the only country in the region where forest plantations have been decreasing markedly, both in absolute and relative terms. Malaysia's forest plantations have also been receding in extent and relatively, but at a much slower pace.

---

* A forest plantation is a forest established by planting and/or seeding in the process of afforestation or reforestation. It consists of introduced species or, in some cases, indigenous species. Forest plantations and natural forests are included in the term "forest", a term that refers to land with a tree cover of more than 10 per cent and area of more than 0.5 hectares (UNEP 2010).

Figure 8.13 Forest plantation area by country, 1990–2005*

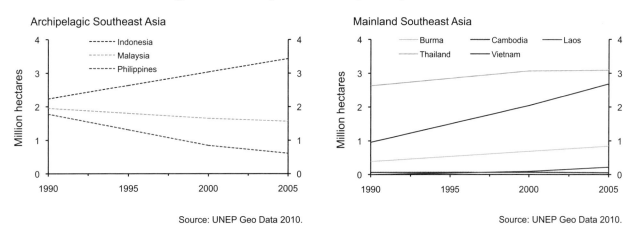

Source: UNEP Geo Data 2010.

Source: UNEP Geo Data 2010.

Figure 8.14 Forest plantations as percentage of forest area by country, 1990–2005*

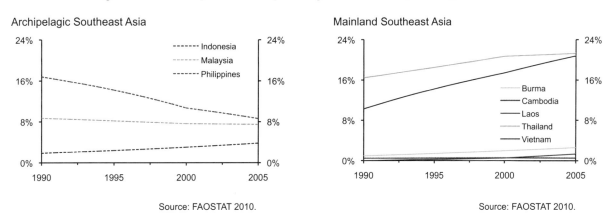

Source: FAOSTAT 2010.

Source: FAOSTAT 2010.

Forest plantation area (million hectares)

	1990	1995	2000	2005
Indonesia	2.2	2.6	3.0	3.4
Malaysia	2.0	1.8	1.7	1.6
Philippines	1.8	1.3	0.9	0.6
Burma	0.4	0.5	0.7	0.8
Cambodia	0.1	0.1	0.1	0.1
Laos	0.0	0.1	0.1	0.2
Thailand	2.6	2.9	3.1	3.1
Vietnam	1.0	1.5	2.1	2.7

Forest plantations as percentage of forest area

	1990	1995	2000	2005
Indonesia	2	2	3	4
Malaysia	9	8	8	8
Philippines	17	14	11	9
Burma	1	1	2	3
Cambodia	1	1	1	1
Laos	0	0	1	1
Thailand	17	19	21	21
Vietnam	10	14	17	21

* Data are available for 1980, 1990, 2000 and 2005, which explains the curves' constant gradient.

Plate 67

In Southeast Asia, as in most other regions of the world, CO_2 emissions have been growing very fast, although not as rapidly as the GDP (Figure 3.5). But, in general, the increase in the emissions has been more or less parallel to that of the individual national economies and proportionate to them. The three major economies are those that pollute the atmosphere the most. Thus, Indonesia, which accounts for nearly a third of the regional GDP, is also responsible for about the same proportion of total regional CO_2 emissions. However, Malaysia's, and even more Thailand's, participation in these emissions is disproportionately high, the mainland country's own contributions having reached about 18 per cent of regional GDP and 26 per cent of regional CO_2 emissions in 2007, while in Malaysia these values amounted to 14 per cent and 18 per cent. On the other hand, the Philippines' own share in total regional emissions stands well below its corresponding share in the regional GDP. In that regard, Vietnam's profile resembles those of Thailand and Malaysia: its share in total CO_2 emissions has become much more significant than its relative economic weight. As for Burma, Laos and Cambodia, their emissions remain more or less at the same level as their contribution to the regional GDP, that is, very low.

CO_2 emissions from the four main polluters have also been increasing at a much faster rate. In Indonesia and Malaysia, emission growth picked up in the 1970s and 1980s. In the case of Malaysia, the increase can be attributed to rapid urbanization and industrialization, coupled with the growth of a particularly fuel inefficient transport system (Timilsina and Shrestha 2009) along with deforestation cum agricultural expansion. The same can be said of Indonesia, but forest destruction — especially of peat swamp forest — and forest fires also played a dramatic role in massive emissions, which peaked following the 1997 fires in Kalimantan (Page *et al.* 2002, Lazaroff 2002). Total national emissions, however, declined markedly in 1998 and only regained their pre-1998 level by 2001, having since continued their very rapid increase. The 1998–2000 decrease can be attributed to the economic slowdown that followed the 1997–98 financial and economic crisis. In Thailand and Malaysia, the two other Southeast Asian countries to have been impacted significantly by the crisis, total emissions also declined temporarily.

In Thailand a combination of the same factors has been at play until recently, but with one significant difference: deforestation has actually been reversed. However, the positive impacts of this transition on atmospheric pollution have yet to be demonstrated, as the kingdom's annual carbon dioxide emissions have grown as fast as the regional average between 1990 and 2007. Vietnam's own increasing contribution to CO_2 emissions is related to its rapid economic expansion, which tolerates hardly any environmental regulation, particularly for its exploding transportation system, whose fuel inefficiency is nearly as high as Malaysia's (Timilsina and Shrestha 2009).

In per capita CO_2 emissions, Malaysia stands way ahead of all other countries in the region except Thailand, which is not very far behind. Their "performances" nevertheless remain well behind those of major industrial countries. For instance, the emissions from OECD countries totalled over 12 million kilotonnes and reached an average 12 tonnes per capita in 2007, against 7 tonnes per capita in Malaysia. The United States alone then contributed to almost half of the OECD total, and each American for an annual average of 19 tonnes of CO_2.

Figure 8.15 CO_2 emissions in total and per capita by country, 1960–2007

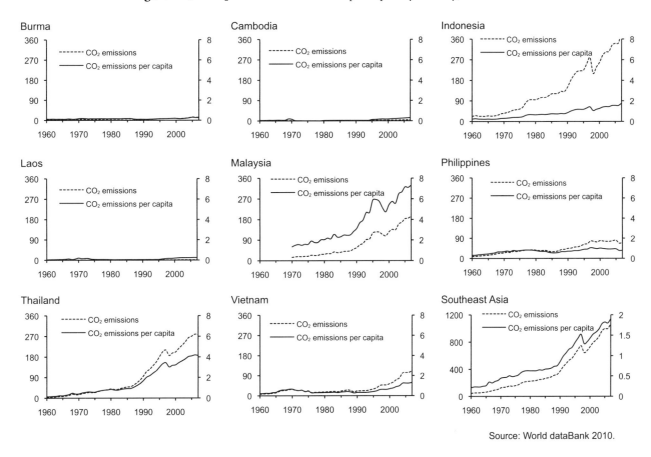

Source: World dataBank 2010.

Left Y axis = CO_2 emissions (thousand Kt); Right Y axis = Metric tonnes per capita

Total CO_2 emissions (thousand Kt)

	1960–62	1970–72	1980–82	1990–92	2000–2	2007
Burma	2.7	4.9	5.6	4.4	8.1	13.2
Cambodia	0.3	0.5	0.3	0.5	2.6	4.4
Indonesia	23.5	39.4	100.0	177.1	283.3	396.8
Laos	0.1	0.5	0.2	0.3	1.2	1.5
Malaysia		16.4	29.8	66.8	132.7	194.3
Philippines	9.2	26.3	35.7	46.9	77.1	70.9
Thailand	4.3	18.8	38.7	112.8	216.2	277.3
Vietnam	8.3	25.2	17.6	21.7	61.6	111.3
Southeast Asia	48.4	131.9	227.9	430.5	782.9	1,069.7

CO_2 emissions per capita (metric tonnes)

	1960–62	1970–72	1980–82	1990–92	2000–2	2007
Burma	0.1	0.2	0.2	0.1	0.2	0.3
Cambodia	0.0	0.1	0.0	0.0	0.2	0.3
Indonesia	0.2	0.3	0.7	1.0	1.4	1.8
Laos	0.0	0.2	0.0	0.1	0.2	0.3
Malaysia		1.5	2.1	3.6	5.6	7.3
Philippines	0.3	0.7	0.7	0.7	1.0	0.8
Thailand	0.2	0.5	0.8	2.0	3.4	4.1
Vietnam	0.2	0.6	0.3	0.3	0.8	1.3
Southeast Asia	0.2	0.5	0.6	1.0	1.5	1.9

CHAPTER 9

Conclusion: Gambling with the Land

"There are multiple agrarian paths and, moreover, there is 'continuous revolution'. ... The experiences of other parts of the world may offer insights into the possible, they in no sense offer a model of the agrarian transition as it will emerge in Southeast Asia."

(Rigg 2001: 147)

Salient Characteristics and Processes

This documented survey of the major trends in Southeast Asian agricultures since the 1960s allows us to identify a number of salient characteristics and processes which can be summarized as follows:

1) Throughout the colonial period, cropland expansion has been a dominant process in the region and has gone through various phases of acceleration (Chapter 2). More importantly, since the 1960s, the pace of expansion has increased. As a result, in comparison with the rest of the world, Southeast Asia's ratio of cropland expansion over population growth does appear unusual, with perhaps only Brazil's performance being comparable. This territorial expansion of agriculture has largely been occurring and continues to do so at the expense of the forest cover. The latter has been receding rapidly in all countries, which seem to be taking turns in an apparent deforestation cycle and in a context where tree crops, such as oil palm, rubber and coffee, represent the dominant spearhead in the conquest of the forest.

2) As should be expected of countries undergoing rapid urbanization and industrialization (Chapter 3), the share of agriculture in the gross domestic product and as a source of employment has been fast decreasing, although at very different rhythms among the countries concerned. But the overall picture is clear: the agrarian transition, whereby the city and industry are gradually overtaking the countryside and agriculture as the major locus of life, employment, and production, is well under way. This process is neither spatially nor structurally uniform among and within each of the respective countries. Even if the industrial and service sectors are employing a growing proportion of the labour force, it is not increasing nearly as rapidly as their share of the GDP. While that is to be expected or normal, so to speak, given the greater productivity of industrial labour, the employment retaining capacity of the agricultural sector in the region remains very significant.

3) This can be attributed to a number of negative factors, including the insufficient size and quality of the non-agricultural job market as well as the inadequate qualifications of the agricultural labour force for the market. But additional factors are involved. From an analysis of employment patterns (Chapter 4) — although, given the nature of our data, we can only make inferences — it is also obvious that farming activities alone are increasingly insufficient to keep people on the land and pluriactivity is spreading. Yet agriculture has been showing a remarkable resilience throughout much of the region. Agricultural dependency ratios remain high and in some countries are hardly decreasing, notwithstanding the overall diversification of sources of employment, the more rapid increase of non-agricultural sources of employment and the growth of pluriactivity. In fact, in four of the eight countries examined, namely Indonesia, Laos, the Philippines and Burma, the tendency has been for the share of agricultural employment in the rural areas to actually increase, which would mean that de-agrarianization of the countryside is not proceeding as rapidly as expected. Put differently, in rural areas, particularly those of Indonesia and Laos, agriculture more than holds its ground as a source of employment. This suggests that throughout much of the region, farming, whether full time or part time, remains an activity many people turn to when fearing for their subsistence security. Southeast Asians still bet largely on the land (Figures 4.5 and 4.6). By Southeast Asians, we refer not only to farm operating households but also to state authorities who throughout the years have adopted policies of agricultural intensification and territorial expansion, and have increasingly adopted a laissez-faire attitude towards the expansionist policies of multinationals involved in agricultural land development.

4) There are several additional illustrations of the region's overall agricultural resilience through growth and diversification (Chapter 5). Between 1961 and 2007, Southeast Asian net agricultural and food production per capita indices clearly outpaced global trends. In addition, the total value of the region's agricultural production increased almost twice as fast as the world's, while also growing faster than did its share of global population. This growth

has been attributable both to the expansion of boom crops, whether grown on plantations or on family smallholdings, and to the resilience of traditional food agriculture, primarily rice cultivation. Not only has the rice-growing sector been providing a rising proportion of the local demand for what remains by far the region's number one staple food, its share of world rice production has also been increasing. In 1961, some 21 per cent of all rice produced in the world was grown in Southeast Asian fields. In 2007, the proportion had reached over 28 per cent. In the meantime Vietnam had joined Thailand to become one of the world's two leading rice exporters, and the region as a whole remained the leading contributor to the global rice market.

5) A fundamental factor behind the growth of the region's agricultural sector — in fact, the capacity of agriculture to expand in just about all Southeast Asian countries — has clearly been the dynamic association between crop intensification and territorial expansion (Chapters 6 and 7). Of course, among the various countries, timings have been different, but in every place where the green revolution has taken hold of the land, there has been a more or less concurrent rapid increase in the extent of that very land being brought under cultivation largely at the expense of various forms of forestland, whether rainforest, secondary, degraded or logged over, even fallow forestland. And the rate of expansion has been exceptional. Between 1961 and 2007, for the region as a whole, the percentage of agricultural area over total area increased from 19 per cent to nearly 27 per cent. As stated earlier, Southeast Asia is obviously evolving well beyond the image suggested in the classical geographical literature, of a region underpopulated and under-cultivated, particularly when compared to China (Figure 5.19). Its population has more than doubled over the period, reaching an estimated 600 million people in 2010, and an average population density of nearly 135, not far behind China's own average of 143 inhabitants per square kilometre. The still substantial difference between the population

growth rate and the agricultural land expansion rate during the last half century has been fully compensated by increases in land productivity.

In fact, overall yield increases have been even more significant, notably in rice agriculture, than territorial expansion. These yield increases have been largely attributable to systematic improvements in irrigation and water management as well as to the increased reliance on higher yielding seed varieties, industrial inputs and the overall betterment of farming practices, in short, the green revolution. All of this has actually been raising the pressure on land resources. This seems to contradict the frequent claim that intensification reduces the need for expansion and relieves the pressure on forestlands (Balisacan and Fuwa 2007: 25). For the moment, throughout the region, except in Thailand, it is quite clear that intensification and expansion are continuing hand in hand, as overall population is also expanding and the demand for upland crops grows.

The generally rapid rate of adoption of yield-raising food crop technologies has largely contributed to the equally rapid rise in agricultural labour productivity. This has also been occurring in the commercial crop sector, particularly in the cultivation of oil palm. One consequence of this generalized increase in productivity in just about all forms of crop cultivation, including that of fruit and vegetables, has been the maintenance of the strong predominance of crop over livestock production. But since the early 1960s, the latter has grown slightly faster in several of the region's countries, with an increasing amount of land being devoted to the cultivation of maize, much of it intended as animal feed. In addition, large cattle herds can frequently be seen in lowland plains such as those in East Java, while the practice of raising livestock in house yards and feeding it with crop residues appears to be spreading, particularly in those same densely cultivated and populated areas. Whether this apparent, and for the moment modest, livestock revolution is likely to accelerate or not is yet to be seen. So far, the region's agriculture has remained exceptionally "vegetarian". By 2007, crops still accounted for 87 per cent of Southeast Asia's agricultural production index versus a world average of around 62 per cent (Figure 5.10).

6) These competing claims and dynamisms of the food and non-food crop sectors have dual consequences. On the one hand, Southeast Asia has been quite successful in improving its level of self-sufficiency in rice, its number one staple food crop, while total food crop production remains largely dominant, but with the following caveat: a significant proportion of this food production is for exports, while several of the so-called food crops are not really such, as is the case with much of palm oil derived products. On the other hand, the relative share of rice production — as measured by its contribution to overall agricultural production value — has been declining while the relative value of cash crops has increased, a trend corroborated by the latter's faster territorial expansion (Figure 7.51). This has allowed the region to consolidate and in fact accentuate its long established role as a supplier of agricultural commodities to the global market. Finally, the combination of yield increases and territorial expansion has also led to sustained and substantial increases in fruit and vegetable production, also for both the domestic and export markets.

7) Throughout the region, the pressure exerted on agriculture by the cultivation of food and non-food cash crops is now extending to aquaculture, which itself is expanding very rapidly into the coastal and maritime domain (Chapter 8), thus joining the fishing sector per se in putting pressure on the seas. The seas are being increasingly cultivated (Figures 8.3 and 8.4) to such an extent that fish and seafood production has been increasing at a faster rate than food crop production. And in this case external demand plays an exceptional role, as illustrated by the fact that the proportion of the region's shrimp output — the dominant one in terms of value — that is exported is probably more than 80 per cent.

The pressure exerted on the coastal and marine environments by the expansion of such forms of

production is constantly intensifying with the consequence that just like in the agricultural sector, the region's countries have been overtaking and relaying each other in the production or harvesting of different fish and seafood species. This has been precisely the case with shrimp production, which is particularly vulnerable to diseases, leading to volatility in prices and, hence, export markets. For example, while in recent years the pace of shrimp production expansion has slackened in several countries, Vietnam has been intensifying its own production. This is a pattern reminiscent of what has been happening in the region with other boom crops, including timber: when production recedes in one country, another one takes over.

In short, the agricultures and agriculturalists of Southeast Asia, whether individual operators or multinationals, are not only gambling with and betting on its land and soil, but also, increasingly, with and on its seas and inland waters, the continental, coastal and maritime domains thus sharing the increasing pressure.

The Four Fundamental Processes

This intensification of the demand on Southeast Asia's environmental resources is the result of at least four major and interrelated processes. The first is the fast-increasing *commoditization* of the region's agriculture, aquaculture and fishing sectors. The second is their equally accelerating *externalization* and hence *globalization*. Third, these and particularly the continuing agricultural expansion of agriculture contribute in turn to the "*agriculturalization*" of the region's landscapes, achieved basically at the expense of its forests, Indonesia representing perhaps the ultimate example. This agriculturalization does constitute the most original as well as paradoxical major process as it is achieved concurrently with what has aptly been described as the deagrarianization of Southeast Asia (Rigg and Nattapoolwat 2001, Rigg 2003). Fourth, relays and complementarities appear exceptionally dynamic, being constantly redeployed among nearly all Southeast Asian countries' agricultural sectors.

All four of these processes are necessarily unfolding unevenly throughout the region, both between and within the various countries, as they are all individually influenced by a number of specific, regional and international agents. Also, beyond the very nature of the individual political regimes, which obviously impact a great deal on national policies, there are a number of political events as well as policy decisions that facilitate or hinder them. These include wars, such as those that took place in former Indochina, along with their aftermath. Thus the disaster that the Khmer Rouge regime brought upon Cambodian society was accompanied by a number of profound setbacks for the agricultural sector itself, including in the long term. On the other hand, the war's aftermath in Vietnam led to such rejuvenation that, since the adoption of *Doi Moi* in 1986, the country's agriculture has become the region's most dynamic. In Malaysia, it was the adoption of the New Economic Policy that, starting in the 1970s and through the adoption of costly but efficient policies privileging the rural and agricultural sectors during nearly three decades (De Koninck 2000, De Koninck and Bernard 2000), provided added impetus to an already expanding agricultural sector, to such an extent that the country's exceptional economic growth and rapid industrialization go hand in hand with the equally exceptional territorial expansion of its agriculture. The list of such internal "turning points" is long. It ranges from the accelerating deterioration of the Filipino political body, which began, arguably, in the 1980s and led to a long list of ill-inspired policies which in turn resulted in the deterioration of the country's agriculture, including its level of self-sufficiency in food production; to the fall of the Suharto regime in 1998, in the aftermath of the 1997–98 Asian financial crisis, which has been followed by a number of new policy decisions whose impacts on the agricultural scene have yet to be fully assessed. Such international agencies include the research centres that helped give rise to the green revolution itself, which has been unfolding throughout the region since the 1960s, with major consequences everywhere, beginning with Indonesia itself.

In fact, the region has been sharing a number of these transnational agencies, processes and events, including dramatic ones such as the sanitary crises of the first decade of the twenty-first century, which affected in particular several of the mainland countries. These in turn revealed the increasing intensity in the dynamic links, notably commercial, technological and financial, that exist among the region's countries. Within the agricultural sector, these links have complementary as well as competitive features. When a given boom crop brings prosperity or apparent prosperity in one country, its production tends to spread to neighbouring ones. This has for a long time been the case with rubber, and more recently with oil palm and shrimp production. Boom crops in fact tend to go through various forms of geographical cycles. Thus, when a country reduces the cultivation of a given crop, another takes over and fills the gap in the international market. This has been the case with rubber and cocoa, where the reduction of Malaysia's involvement — largely attributable in the case of rubber to the long-term upward trend in rural wages in what has become a middle income country (Barlow 1997) — has been followed by an increase in that of, respectively, Thailand and Indonesia. But when a country shares, relays or cedes the cultivation of a crop to its neighbours, as Malaysia has done with cocoa and rubber, the downstream industries related to it remain, as illustrated by that same country's rubber and cocoa imports and re-exports.

Complementarities and relays are also what characterize the timber industry. Thus, one consequence of the reversal in Vietnam's forest policy, which until the 1990s had been fast depleting its forest resources, has been an increase in wood imports, including illegal ones from neighbouring countries, such as Laos and Cambodia. This represents yet another example of the intra-regional transfer of production responsibilities and environmental pressure that has been ongoing for decades in Southeast Asia. Finally, another good illustration of competition cum complementarities in the region is provided by the case of oil palm cultivation in Malaysia and Indonesia. Much of the capital fuelling its rapid expansion in Indonesia — as well as in Cambodia — is provided by Malaysian multinationals, while Indonesia is the major provider of foreign workers toiling on Malaysian plantations.

Unfortunately, as pointed out in the Introduction, the nature and the scale of our approach have not allowed us to address closely a number of key issues, such as capital investment, migrant labour, livelihood and communities, including those of minority people. This caveat also applies to the limited number of indicators we have been able to harness to document our contention that gambling is also occurring with the region's seas and their resources. The list of challenging themes which we haven't been able to pursue is indeed very long and even includes land issues themselves, such as international land-grabbing, likely to accelerate in the region along with the predicted intensification of agrofuel production. But we remain confident that we have provided a useful background against which all of these questions can be investigated.

Appendices

Table A1 Southeast Asia: Countries and islands, dimensions and population in 2010

Regions (including Brunei, Singapore and East Timor)	Population (million)	Area (sq. km)
Archipelagic Southeast Asia	231.5	1,938,743
Peninsular Southeast Asia	367.0	2,552,879
Total	598.5	4,491,622

Countries	Population (million)	Area (sq. km)
Burma	50.5	676,578
Cambodia	15.2	181,035
Indonesia	239.6	1,904,443
Laos	6.2	236,800
Malaysia	27.9	329,847
Philippines	93.0	297,190
Thailand	68.8	513,120
Vietnam	90.8	331,210
Total	592.0	4,470,223
Brunei	0.4	5,765
Singapore	5.1	724
East Timor	1.1	14,910
Total	6.6	21,399

Main archipelagic territories	Population (million)	Area (sq. km)
Bali	3.9	5,678
Java	125.9	132,519
Kalimantan	13.8	538,161
Moluccas	2.6	78,111
Nusa Tengarra	9.2	66,315
Papua	3.6	411,941
Sulawesi	28.0	187,020
Sumatra	50.6	477,310
Peninsular Malaysia	22.2	132,351
Sabah	3.2	74,439
Sarawak	2.5	124,126
Luçon	48.5	107,898
Mindanao	19.4	96,792
Palawan	1.0	14,552
Mindoro	1.4	10,262
Western Visayas	6.7	18,895
Eastern Visayas	4.5	21,068
Central Visayas	7.8	15,345
Masbate	0.9	4,038
Other Philippine islands	2.8	8,341

Sources: Central Bureau of Statistics 2010 (Indonesia); Department of Statistics 2010 (Malaysia); National Statistics Office 2000 (Philippines); UNPOP 2010.

Table A2 Southeast Asia: Some basic statistics by country, 1961–2010

	Population (million) (a)*	Population density (hab/km²) (a)*	Urban population (%)	Agricultural population (%) (b)*	Life expectancy* (a)*	GDP (current million US$) (c)	GDP per capita (current US$) (c)
Burma							
1960	21.1	31	19	81	42.3	N/A	N/A
1970	26.4	39	23	78	47	2,692.4	102.0
1980	33.3	50	24	76	50.5	5,905.2	176.0
1990	40.1	60	25	73	54.9	5,179.1	126.8
2000	45.9	69	28	70	58.6	7,275.3	156.1
2010	50.1	75	34	67	61.8	28,663.5†	578.3†
Cambodia							
1960	5.4	30	10	83	41.4	N/A	N/A
1970	6.9	38	16	79	45.4	630.3	90.9
1980	6.7	37	9	76	31.2	593.9	88.0
1990	9.7	54	13	74	53.6	1,404.4	144.9
2000	12.8	70	17	70	55.5	3,666.6	287.4
2010	15.2	83	23	66	58.0	11,192.7†	768.6†
Indonesia							
1960	95.9	49	15	71	39.9	N/A	N/A
1970	120.5	61	17	62	46.0	9,805.0	83.4
1980	151.1	77	22	54	52.7	79,636.5	541.1
1990	182.8	93	31	51	60.1	125,720.2	705.8
2000	211.7	108	42	44	64.9	165,021.0	803.9
2010	239.6	122	54	38	68.7	510,779.3†	2,246.7†
Laos							
1960	2.0	9	8	83	40.4	N/A	N/A
1970	2.6	11	10	81	40.4	114.4	42.5
1980	3.1	14	12	80	43.5	321.8	99.4
1990	4.1	18	15	78	48.3	865.7	205.8
2000	5.2	23	22	76	52.5	1,653.5	306.0
2010	6.2	27	33	75	56.5	5,326.5†	858.4†

continued

Table A2 *continued*

	Population (million) (a)*	Population density (hab/km²) (a)*	Urban population (%)	Agricultural population (%) (b)*	Life expectancy* (a)*	GDP (current million US$) (c)	GDP per capita (current US$) (c)
Malaysia							
1960	8.1	25	27	62	52.1	N/A	N/A
1970	10.9	33	33	52	59.4	3,591.6	330.9
1980	13.8	42	42	39	65.3	25,429.0	1,847.6
1990	18.1	55	50	26	69.5	45,716.0	2,525.3
2000	23.3	71	62	18	71.9	93,789.7	4,029.9
2010	27.9	85	72	12	74.1	221,437.0†	8,197.0†
Philippines							
1960	27.1	90	30	63	51.3	N/A	N/A
1970	36.6	122	33	58	56.4	6,690.8	183.0
1980	48.1	160	37	52	60.1	32,450.4	674.5
1990	61.2	208	49	46	64.2	44,311.6	709.8
2000	76.2	259	59	39	68.6	75,912.1	977.1
2010	93.0	312	66	33	71.6	168,580.3†	1,865.9†
Thailand							
1960	27.7	54	20	79	54.5	N/A	N/A
1970	37.2	72	21	74	59.1	7,128.6	191.7
1980	46.8	92	27	64	63.1	32,353.5	684.5
1990	54.3	110	29	57	67.2	85,361.0	1,506.2
2000	60.7	122	31	49	69.0	122,725.2	1,968.4
2010	68.8	133	34	41	71.7	282,157.6†	4,187.2†
Vietnam							
1960	33.6	101	15	81	42.9	N/A	N/A
1970	42.9	129	18	77	47.8	2,775.1	64.7
1980	53.0	161	19	73	55.8	2,395.6	44.9
1990	66.2	200	20	71	63.1	6,471.7	97.7
2000	79.1	237	24	67	68.8	31,172.6	396.3
2010	90.8	268	29	63	71.9	90,645.2†	1,040.8†

(a) UNPOP 2010; (b) FAOSTAT 2010; (c) UNSTATS 2010   * Data for 2010 are estimates.   † Data for 2008

Appendices

Table A3 Southeast Asia: Food and protein intake per capita by country, 1961–2007

	All cereals		Rice		Fruits		Vegetables		Meat		Fish & seafood		Poultry meat		Eggs		Total	
	Calories	Protein	Calories	Protein	Calories	Protein	Calories	Protein	Calories	Protein	Calories	Protein	Calories	Protein	Calories	Protein	Calories	Protein
Burma																		
1961	1248	29	1212	28	47	1	14	1	31	2	31	5	5	0	2	0	1674	43
1971	1515	36	1470	34	34	0	21	1	47	2	24	4	8	1	3	0	1986	51
1981	1727	41	1653	39	30	0	27	2	49	3	26	4	10	1	4	0	2231	57
1991	1329	31	1267	30	30	0	31	2	31	2	25	4	8	1	3	0	1810	45
2001	1408	33	1336	31	42	0	49	3	63	4	32	5	24	2	8	1	2150	56
2007	1430	34	1342	31	50	1	59	3	164	9	44	7	62	5	16	1	2465	71
Cambodia																		
1961	1656	34	1573	32	57	1	35	2	31	2	10	2	3	0	3	0	2019	44
1971	1707	35	1551	32	31	0	37	2	76	4	21	3	6	0	4	0	2110	50
1981	1447	30	1328	27	25	0	28	2	27	2	14	2	5	0	4	0	1743	40
1991	1564	32	1541	31	31	0	25	2	85	4	22	4	8	1	4	0	1878	45
2001	1564	32	1468	30	31	0	20	1	112	5	72	10	10	1	4	0	2056	53
2007	1620	34	1453	30	30	0	19	1	122	5	54	8	9	1	4	0	2268	58
Indonesia																		
1961	984	20	826	16	28	0	17	1	21	1	17	3	2	0	2	0	1743	34
1971	1230	24	1086	21	36	0	18	1	25	1	20	3	2	0	2	0	1919	38
1981	1480	29	1255	23	37	0	15	1	29	2	25	4	5	0	6	0	2302	45
1991	1570	31	1293	24	42	1	20	1	54	3	31	5	11	1	9	1	2379	50
2001	1587	31	1285	24	57	1	27	1	47	3	45	7	15	1	13	1	2447	53
2007	1585	32	1238	23	82	1	33	1	60	4	49	8	21	2	21	2	2538	57
Laos																		
1961	1682	39	1609	38	23	0	16	1	57	3	10	2	7	1	1	0	1951	49
1971	1700	40	1606	38	23	0	13	1	63	3	14	2	11	1	2	0	2016	51
1981	1532	36	1420	33	26	0	11	1	69	3	14	2	5	0	4	0	1966	48
1991	1587	37	1462	34	29	0	10	0	73	4	13	2	7	1	3	0	2018	49
2001	1547	36	1409	33	37	1	67	4	92	5	29	5	10	1	7	1	2108	56
2007	1567	37	1439	34	47	1	68	4	119	6	35	5	14	1	7	1	2240	61

continued

Table A3 *continued*

	All cereals		Rice		Fruits		Vegetables		Meat		Fish & seafood		Poultry meat		Eggs		Total	
	Calories	Protein	Calories	Protein	Calories	Protein	Calories	Protein	Calories	Protein	Calories	Protein	Calories	Protein	Calories	Protein	Calories	Protein
Malaysia																		
1961	1391	26	1187	21	90	1	14	1	93	4	40	6	16	1	9	1	2427	47
1971	1467	28	1233	22	91	1	17	1	102	5	44	7	29	2	26	2	2540	51
1981	1345	26	1072	19	79	1	17	1	154	8	68	11	40	3	35	3	2753	59
1991	1132	23	792	14	73	1	24	1	234	14	82	13	91	8	52	4	2678	67
2001	1242	26	787	14	72	1	35	1	227	16	102	17	123	11	44	4	2858	75
2007	1346	29	755	13	74	1	43	2	236	16	90	14	135	11	49	4	2923	78
Philippines																		
1961	982	18	823	14	124	2	48	3	92	4	56	8	8	1	10	1	1738	40
1971	1012	19	800	14	99	1	49	3	118	5	73	11	10	1	13	1	1801	44
1981	1189	23	934	16	153	2	50	3	119	6	65	10	18	2	20	2	2198	50
1991	1164	23	826	14	131	2	49	3	157	7	71	11	16	1	21	2	2209	52
2001	1311	25	1024	18	114	1	47	2	206	10	60	9	28	3	24	2	2395	56
2007	1461	27	1271	22	152	2	46	2	229	10	67	10	28	3	23	2	2565	60
Thailand																		
1961	1329	23	1323	23	77	1	31	2	78	5	17	3	13	1	40	3	1843	41
1971	1464	26	1452	26	83	1	37	2	83	5	43	7	21	2	36	3	2062	48
1981	1452	26	1375	24	118	1	38	2	110	7	36	6	33	3	29	2	2262	50
1991	1291	24	1184	21	104	1	29	1	138	8	47	7	49	4	44	3	2243	53
2001	1267	24	1121	20	106	1	34	2	160	9	57	9	53	5	40	3	2451	57
2007	1205	23	1024	18	104	1	30	1	183	9	59	9	42	4	40	3	2539	56
Vietnam																		
1961	1469	30	1378	28	46	1	29	2	86	3	25	4	8	0	6	0	1876	45
1971	1563	33	1407	29	44	1	28	2	77	3	26	4	8	1	5	0	2001	47
1981	1582	34	1380	28	56	1	27	2	88	4	17	3	9	1	4	0	2064	48
1991	1585	33	1505	31	55	1	28	2	121	5	20	3	11	1	5	0	2086	48
2001	1788	37	1643	34	61	1	50	3	211	8	34	5	21	2	9	1	2537	63
2007	1832	39	1629	33	72	1	55	3	337	13	44	7	28	2	10	1	2816	74

Source: FAOSTA⁻ 2010; Calories are given in kcal/capita/day, and protein intake is indicated in gm/capita/day.

Table A4   Global rankings of selected Southeast Asian crop productions and exports, 1961–2007

(Data are highlighted in grey when Southeast Asian countries are ranked among the world's top ten)

	Burma				Cambodia				Indonesia				Laos				Malaysia				Philippines				Thailand				Vietnam			
	Production		Exports		Production		Exports		Production		Exports		Production		Exports		Production		Exports		Production		Exports		Production		Exports		Production		Exports	
	1961	2007	1961	2007	1961	2007	1961	2007	1961	2007	1961	2007	1961	2007	1961	2007	1961	2007	1961	2007	1961	2007	1961	2007	1961	2007	1961	2007	1961	2007	1961	2007
Rice	8	6	1	11	13	14	6	59	5	3	–	69	23	21	–	–	19	24	22	96	11	8	60	88	6	7	2	1	7	5	8	3
Maize	74	54	15	24	54	75	12	31	14	8	29	28	86	72	–	40	101	103	43	75	17	15	24	81	32	24	6	15	43	17	25	94
Fresh fruits	45	79	NA	NA	81	109	NA	NA	21	10	NA	NA	113	122	NA	NA	53	60	NA	NA	16	11	NA	NA	22	18	NA	NA	32	30	NA	NA
Vegetables	47	25	NA	NA	52	91	NA	NA	22	15	NA	NA	100	67	NA	NA	84	83	NA	NA	19	20	NA	NA	26	28	NA	NA	20	16	NA	NA
Poultry meat	44	26	–	–	85	110	–	–	26	10	–	100	80	114	–	–	38	16	–	42	24	30	–	56	13	14	40	6	25	37	23	110
Pig meat	50	29	–	–	61	50	–	–	33	24	–	63	63	69	–	–	39	41	28	43	23	12	–	52	29	19	–	–	19	6	–	23
Palm fruit	–	–	NA	NA	–	–	NA	NA	3	1	NA	NA	–	–	NA	NA	6	2	NA	NA	33	18	NA	NA	32	4	NA	NA	–	–	NA	NA
Palm oil	–	–	–	–	–	–	–	41	3	1	3	2	–	–	–	–	4	2	4	1	33	18	–	37	32	4	–	6	–	–	–	37
Rubber*	12	15	–	–	8	17	9	16	2	2	2	1	–	–	–	–	1	3	1	3	16	7	–	9	3	1	3	2	5	5	5	4
Coffee	64	47	–	88	62	60	–	106	8	4	9	4	55	27	68	30	44	24	35	64	23	14	–	81	70	20	–	28	39	2	64	2
Tea	16	15	41	55	–	–	–	–	5	5	4	5	–	40	–	–	20	29	17	37	–	–	–	57	–	24	34	41	12	7	18	6
Coconut†	33	11	–	–	39	32	–	–	1	1	2	2	–	–	–	–	5	9	1	3	2	2	2	1	7	5	36	18	16	6	11	54
Cocoa	–	–	–	–	–	–	–	–	31	3	46	4	–	–	–	–	36	14	40	14	20	22	–	53	–	44	–	69	–	–	–	–
Sugar‡	41	21	–	146	56	78	–	–	10	11	–	116	85	73	–	–	72	59	59	17	6	10	2	33	27	4	64	3	32	16	–	73
Bananas	–	–	–	–	32	44	–	–	6	6	–	62	77	65	–	–	17	22	23	30	4	3	53	3	10	9	42	34	18	12	32	47
Cassava	74	43	–	14	59	21	–	14	2	4	2	3	62	47	–	–	43	35	8	25	19	22	–	27	8	3	1	1	14	7	–	2
Hen eggs	58	33	–	–	91	117	–	–	52	8	–	87	117	118	–	–	56	25	32	7	27	22	–	–	38	21	7	16	35	31	26	41

Source: FAOSTATS 2010.   * Production: natural rubber; Exports: dry natural rubber   † Production: coconut; Exports: copra oil   ‡ Production: sugar cane; Exports: sugar

Bibliography

Adas, Michael. *The Burma Delta: Economic Development and Social Change on an Asian Rice Frontier, 1852–1941*. Madison: University of Wisconsin Press, 1974.

Akiyama, Takamasa, and Akihiko Nishio. "Sulawesi's Cocoa Boom: Lessons of Smallholder Dynamism and a Hands-Off Policy". *Bulletin of Indonesian Economic Studies* 33, no. 2 (1997): 97–121.

Andersson, Magnus, Anders Engvall and Ari Kokko. "Regional Development in Lao PDR: Growth Patterns and Market Integration". In *Working Paper*, 56. Stockholm: Stockholm School of Economics, 2007.

Anonymous. "Indian Labour in Ceylon, Fiji and British Malaya". *International Labour Review* 42, no. 1 (1940): 57–73.

Arancon, Romulo N. Jr. *Asia Pacific Forestry Sector Outlook: Focus on Coconut Wood*. 42. Rome and Bangkok: FAO, 1997.

Asri, Dail Umamil. "Participatory Planning toward an Integrated Transportation Masterplan for Jabodetabek". *Proceedings of the Eastern Asia Society for Transportation Studies* 5 (2005): 2308–19.

Baird, Ian, and Bruce Shoemaker. "Unsettling Experiences: Internal Resettlement and International Aid Agencies in the Lao PDR." *Development and Change* 38, no. 5 (2007): 865–88.

Balisacan, Arsenio M., and Nobuhiko Fuwa, eds. *Reasserting the Rural Development Agenda: Lessons Learned and Emerging Challenges in Asia*. Singapore: Institute of Southeast Asian Studies, 2007.

Banerjee, B., and T.C. Chaudhuri. *Therapeutic Effects of Tea*. Enfield, N.H.: Science Publishers, 2005.

Barker, Randolph, Robert W. Herdt and Beth Rose. *The Rice Economy of Asia*. Washington, D.C. [Baltimore, Md.]: Resources for the Future; Distributed by Johns Hopkins University Press, 1985.

Barker, Randolph, and Mark Rosegrant. "Establishing Efficient Use of Water Resources in Asia". In *Reasserting the Rural Development Agenda: Lessons Learned and Emerging Challenges in Asia*, ed. Arsenio M. Balisacan and Nobuhiko Fuwa. Singapore: Institute of Southeast Asian Studies, 2007, pp. 227–65.

Barlow, Colin. "Growth, Structural Change and Plantation Tree Crops: The Case of Rubber". *World Development* 25, no. 10 (1997): 1589–607.

Beers, Howard W. *Indonesia: Resources and Their Technological Development*. Lexington: University Press of Kentucky, 1970.

Bello, Walden F., Herbert Docena, Marissa De Guzman and Mary Lou Malig. *The Anti-Development State: The Political Economy of Permanent Crisis in the Philippines*. Diliman, Quezon City: Dept. of Sociology, College of Social Sciences and Philosophy, University of the Philippines, Diliman, Focus on the Global South, 2004.

Bernard, Stéphane, and Jean-François Bissonnette. "Oil Palm Plantations in Sabah: Agricultural Expansion for Whom?" In *Borneo Transformed: Agricultural Expansion on the Southeast Asian Frontier*, ed. Rodolphe De Koninck, Stéphane Bernard and Jean-François Bissonnette. Singapore: NUS Press, 2011, pp. 120–51.

Binswanger, Hans P., and Mark R. Rosenzweig. "Behavioral and Material Determinants of Production Relations in Agriculture". *Economic Development and Cultural Change* 26, no. 1 (1987): 73–99.

Blench, Roger. "Fruits and Arboriculture in the Indo-Pacific Region". *Bulletin of the Indo-Pacific Prehistory Association* 24 (2004): 31–50.

———. "A History of Fruits on the Southeast Asian Mainland". In *Occasional Paper in Linguistics*. Kyoto: Archaeology and the Human Past. Research Institute for Humanity and Nature, 2008.

Bond, Russell, Gil Rodriguez and Jammie Penm. "Agriculture in Indonesia, a Review of Consumption, Production, Imports and Import Regulations". In the 13th Meeting of the Australia-Indonesia Working Group on Agriculture, Food and Forestry Cooperation (WGAFFC). Gold Coast, Queensland, 2007.

Booth, Anne, *Agricultural Development in Indonesia*. Sydney: Allen & Unwin, 1988.

Borja, Luis J. "The Philippine Coconut Industry". *Economic Geography* 3, no. 3 (1927): 382–90.

Bray, Francesca. *The Rice Economies: Technology and Development in Asian Societies*. Oxford [Oxfordshire] and New York: Blackwell, 1986.

Brocheux, Pierre, and Daniel Hemery. *Indochine, la colonisation ambiguë, 1858–1954*. Paris: La Découverte, 1995.

Bruinsma, Jelle. *World Agriculture: Towards 2015/2030, an FAO Perspective*. 444. London: Food and Agriculture Organization, 2003.

Burger, Kees, and Hidde P. Smit. "International Market Responses to the Asian Crisis for Rubber, Cococa and Coffee". In *Agriculture in Crisis: People, Commodities and Natural Resources in Indonesia, 1996–2000*, ed. Françoise Gérard and François Ruf. Montpellier and Richmond: CIRAD and Curzon, 2001, pp. 31–48.

Burling, Robbins. *Hill Farms and Padi Fields: Life in Mainland Southeast Asia*. Englewood Cliffs, N.J.: Prentice-Hall, 1965.

Cadilhon, Jean-Joseph, Andrew P. Fearne, Paule Moustier and Nigel D. Poole. "Modelling Vegetable Marketing Systems in South East Asia: Phenomenological Insights from Vietnam". *Supply Chain Management: An International Journal* 8 (2003): 427–41.

Carson, Rachel. *The Sea around Us*. New York: Oxford University Press, 1951.

Chenais, Jean-Claude. *La population du monde de l'Antiquité à nos jours*. Paris: Bordas, 1991.

Cherniguin, Serge. "The Sugar Workers of Negros, Philippines". *Community Development Journal* 23 (1988): 187–95.

Clarete, Ramon, and James A. Roumasset. *An Analysis of Economic Policies Affecting the Philippine Coconut Industry*. Philippine Institute for Development Studies, 1983.

Clement, Floriane, and Jaime M. Amezaga. "Linking Reforestation Policies with Land Use Change in Northern Vietnam: Why Local Factors Matter". *Geoforum* 39, no. 1 (2008): 265–77.

Cohen, Paul T. "The Post-Opium Scenario and Rubber in Northern Laos: Alternative Western and Chinese Models of Development". *International Journal of Drug Policy* 20 (2009): 424–30.

Cornia, Giovanni Andrea, and Julius Court. "Inequality, Growth and Poverty in the Era of Liberalization and Globalization". In *Policy Brief*, UNU World Institute for Development Economics Research (UNU/WIDER), Helsinki: UNU/Wider, 2001.

Côté, Denis. *Successful Strategies for the Implementation of Land Reform: A Peasants' Account from the Philippines*. Unpulished MA thesis, Université de Montréal, 2010.

Courtenay, P.P. *Plantation Agriculture*. London: G. Bell & Sons, 1965.

———. "Commercial Agriculture". In *South-East Asia, a Systematic Geography*, ed. Lin Sien Chia and R.D. Hill. Kuala Lumpur and New York: Oxford University Press, 1979, pp. 108–32.

Cramb, Rob A. *Land and Longhouse: Agrarian Transformation in the Uplands of Sarawak*. Copenhagen: NIAS, 2007.

———. "Agrarian Transitions in Sarawak: Intensification and Expansion Reconsidered". In *Borneo Transformed: Agricultural Expansion on the Southeast Asian Frontier*, ed. R. De Koninck, S. Bernard and J.F. Bissonnette. Singapore: NUS Press, 2011, pp. 44–93.

De Koninck, Rodolphe. "The Peasantry as the Territorial Spearhead of the State in Southeast Asia: The Case of Vietnam". *SOJOURN: Journal of Social Issues in Southeast Asia* 11, no. 2 (1996): 231–58.

———. *Deforestation in Vietnam*. Ottawa: International Development Research Centre, 1999.

———. "Le dynamisme agricole malaysien", *Revue Tiers Monde* 51, no. 162 (2000): 389–409.

———. "Southeast Asian Agriculture since the Sixties: Economic and Territorial Expansion". In *Southeast Asia Transformed: A Geography of Change*, ed. Lin Sien Chia. Singapore: Institute of Southeast Asian Studies, 2003, pp. 191–230.

———. "The Challenges of the Agrarian Transition in Southeast Asia". *LABOUR, Capital and Society* 37 (2004): 285–8.

———. "On the Geopolitics of Land Colonization: Order and Disorder on the Frontiers of Vietnam and Indonesia". *Moussons* 9, no. 10 (2006): 33–59.

———. *Malaysia: La dualité territoriale*. Paris: Belin, 2007.

———. "Des raisons de remettre en question, de fond en comble, notre façon d'habiter la planète". In *Une seule terre à cultiver, les défis agricoles et alimentaires mondiaux*, ed. Jean-François Rousseau and Olivier Durand. Québec: Presses de l'Université du Québec, 2009, pp. 161–7.

De Koninck, Rodolphe, and Stéphane Bernard. "Les transformations récentes du monde rural malaysien". *Archipel* 60 (2000): 217–34.

De Koninck, Rodolphe, Stéphane Bernard and Jean-François Bissonnette, eds. *Borneo Transformed: Agricultural Expansion on the Southeast Asian Frontier*. Singapore: NUS Press, 2011.

De Koninck, Rodolphe, and Modesto Capataz. "Le continent indonésien et l'archipel brésilien". *Mappemonde* 4 (1992): 14–18.

De Koninck, Rodolphe, and Claude Comtois. "L'accélération de l'intégration du commerce extérieur de l'ASEAN au marché mondial". *Études internationales* 11, no. 1 (1980): 43–64.

De Koninck, Rodolphe, and Steve Déry. "Agricultural Expansion as a Tool of Population Redistribution in Southeast Asia". *Journal of Southeast Asian Studies* 28, no. 1 (1997): 1–26.

De Koninck, Rodolphe, Guy Dorval, Jacques Charlier and Danielle Charlier-Vanderschraege. *Le grand atlas du Canada et du monde*. Saint-Laurent; Bruxelles: ERPI; De Boeck, 2005.

De Koninck, Rodolphe, and Terry G. McGee. "Du miracle économique à la crise financière en Asie du Sud-Est: érosion des acquis sociaux et retour de la pauvreté?". *Revue internationale de politique comparée* 8, no. 3 (2001): 1–26.

Delvert, Jean. *Le paysan cambodgien*. Paris: Mouton, 1961.

Dobby, Ernest Henry George. *Southeast Asia*. 7 ed. London: University of London Press, 1960.

Douglas, Ian. "The Local Drivers of Land Degradation in South-East Asia". *Geographical Research* 44, no. 2 (2006): 123–34.

Dove, Michael R. "Theories of Swidden Agriculture, and the Political Economy of Ignorance". *Agroforestry Systems* 1, no. 2 (1983): 85–99.

Duby, Georges. *L'économie rurale et la vie des campagnes dans l'Occident*. 2 vols. Paris: Flammarion, 1977.

Dumont, René. *La culture du riz dans le delta du Tonkin: étude et propositions d'amélioration des techniques traditionnelles de riziculture tropicale*. Paris: Société d'Èditions géographiques, maritimes et coloniales, 1935.

Durand, Frédéric. "Farmer Strategies and Agricultural Development: The Choice of Cocoa in Eastern Indonesia". In *Cocoa Cycles: Economics of Cocoa Supply*, ed. François Ruf and P.S. Siswoputranto. Abington: Woodhead, 1995, pp. 313–8.

Easterly, William. "What Did Structural Adjustment Adjust? The Association of Policies and Growth with Repeated IMF and World Bank Adjustment Loans". *Journal of Development Economics* 76 (2005): 1–22.

Elson, R.E. *The End of the Peasantry in Southeast Asia: A Social and Economic History of Peasant Livelihood, 1800–1990s*. New York: St. Martin's Press, 1997.

Etherington, Dan Maxwell. "The Indonesian Tea Industry." *Bulletin of Indonesian Economic Studies* 10, no. 2 (1974): 83–113.

Evrard, Olivier, and Yves Goudineau. "Planned Resettlement, Unexpected Migrations and Cultural Trauma in Laos". *Development and Change* 35, no. 5 (2004): 937–62.

Fa, John. "The Protein Gap". *Conservation in Practice* 6, no. 3 (2006): 117–23.

FAO. *Fertilizer Use by Crop in Malaysia*. Rome: FAO Corporate Document Repository, Natural Resources Management and Environment Department, 2004.

———. *Fertilizer Use by Crop in Indonesia*. Rome: Food and Agriculture Organization of the United Nations, Land and Plant Nutrition Management Service, 2005.

Feeny, David. *The Political Economy of Productivity: Thai Agricultural Development, 1880–1975*. Vancouver: University of British Columbia Press, 1982.

Fisher, Charles A. *South-East Asia: A Social, Economic, and Political Geography*. 2nd ed. London; New York: Methuen; Dutton, 1966.

Fortunel, Frédéric. *Le café au Viêtnam: de la colonisation à l'essor d'un grand producteur mondial*. Paris: L'Harmattan, 2000.

Fox, Jefferson M. "How Blaming 'Slash and Burn' Farmers Is Deforesting Mainland Southeast Asia". In *AsiaPacific Issues* 47. Honolulu: East-West Center, 2000.

Geertz, Clifford. *Agricultural Involution: The Process of Ecological Change in Indonesia*. Berkeley and Los Angeles: University of California Press, 1963.

Gibbons, David S., Rodolphe De Koninck and Ibrahim Hasan. *Agricultural Modernization, Poverty, and Inequality: The Distributional Impact of the Green Revolution in Regions of Malaysia and Indonesia*. Westmead, England: Gower Pub., 1980.

Godfrey, Martin, Chan Sophal, Toshiyasu Kato, Long Vou Piseth, Pon Dorina, Tep Saravy, Tia Savora and Soso Vannarith. "Technical Assistance and Capacity Development in an Aid-Dependent Economy: The Experience of Cambodia". *World Development* 30, no. 3 (2002): 355–73.

Goldemberg, José. "Ethanol for a Sustainable Energy Future". *Science* 315, no. 5813 (2007): 808–10.

Gourou, Pierre. *Les paysans du delta tonkinois*. Paris: École française d'Extrême-Orient, 1936. (Reprinted by Mouton in 1965 with a new preface by the author.)

———. *La terre et l'homme en Extrême-Orient*. Paris: Flammarion, 1947.

———. *Les pays tropicaux*. Paris: Presses Universitaires de France, 1947.

———. *L'Asie*. Paris: Hachette, 1953.

———. *Riz et civilisation*. Paris: Fayard, 1984.

Gregor, Howard F. "The Changing Plantation". *Annals of the Association of American Geographers* 55, no. 2 (1965): 221–38.

Hall, Derek. "Where the Streets Are Paved with Prawns: Boom Crops and Migration in Southeast Asia". *Critical Asian Studies* 43, no. 4 (2011): 507–30.

Hall, Derek, Philip Hirsch and Tania Murray Li. *Powers of Exclusion: Land Dilemmas in Southeast Asia*. Singapore: NUS Press, 2011.

Härdter, Rolf, Woo Yin Chow and Ooi Soo Hock. "Intensive Plantation Cropping, a Source of Sustainable Food and Energy Production in the Tropical Rain Forest Areas in Southeast Asia". *Forest Ecology and Management* 93 (1997): 93–102.

Hardy, Andrew. *Red Hills: Migrants and the State in the Highlands of Vietnam*. Honolulu: University of Hawaii Press, 2003.

Hass, Hans H. "Structural Problems of West African Cocoa Exports and Options for Improvement". *African Development Perspectives Yearbook* 11 (2006): 245–63.

Hayami, Yujiro. "An Ecological and Historical Perspective on Agricultural Development in Southeast Asia". *World Bank Policy Research*, 41. Washington, D.C.: World Bank, 2000.

Hishamunda, Nathanael, Pedro B. Bueno, Neil Ridler and Wilfredo G. Yap. *Analysis of Aquaculture Development in Southeast Asia. A Policy Perspective*. FAO Fisheries and Aquaculture Technical Paper, 2009.

Hung, Nguyen Tri. "The Inflation of Vietnam in Transition". In *CAS Discussion Paper*, ed. Centre for International Management and Development, Antwerp Centre for ASEAN Studies, 16. Antwerp, 1999.

Hüsken, Frans. "Cycles of Commercialisation and Accumulation in a Central Javanese Village". In *Agrarian Transformations: Local Processes and the State in Southeast Asia*, ed. Gillian Patricia Hart, Andrew Turton and Benjamin White. Berkeley: University of California Press, 1989.

Jegatheesan, S. "Contribution of Economic Research to Rice Mechanization in West Malaysia with Specific Reference to the Muda Irrigation Scheme". In *Farm Mechanization in East Asia*, ed. Herman McDowell Sowthworth. New York: Agricultural Development Council, 1972, pp. 376–401.

Jones, Gavin W. "The Population of Southeast Asia". *Working Papers in Demography*, 81. Sydney: Australian National University, 1999.

Kaur, Amarjit. "The Origins of Cocoa in Malaysia". *Journal of the Malaysian Branch, Royal Asiatic Society* (JMBRAS) 68, no. 1 (1995): 67–80.

Kay, Cristobal. "Why East Asia Overtook Latin America: Agrarian Reform, Industrialisation and Development". *Third World Quarterly* 23, no. 6 (2002): 1073–102.

Kerkvliet, Benedict J. *The Huk Rebellion: A Study of Peasant Revolt in the Philippines*. Berkeley: University of California Press, 1977.

Kosonen, Kimmo. "Vernaculars in Literacy and Basic Education in Cambodia, Laos and Thailand". *Current Issues in Language Planning* 6, no. 2 (2005): 122–42.

Kristiansen, Stein, and Purwo Santoso. "Surviving Decentralisation? Impacts of Regional Autonomy on Health Service Provision in Indonesia". *Health Policy* 77 (2006): 247–59.

Kummer, David M. *Deforestation in the Postwar Philippines*. Chicago: University of Chicago Press, 1992.

Lazaroff, Cat. "Indonesian Wildfires Accelerated Global Warming". *Environment News Service*, http://www.ens-newswire.com/ens/nov2002/2002-11-08-06.asp.

Le Billon, Philippe. "Logging in Muddy Waters: The Politics of Forest Exploitation in Cambodia". *Critical Asian Studies* 34 (2002): 563–86.

Leblond, Jean-Philippe. "The Retreat of Agricultural Lands in Thailand". *Working Paper* no. 1, 31. Montreal: The Challenges of the Agrarian Transition in Southeast Asia, 2008.

———. *Vers une transition forestière en Thaïlande*. Unpublished PhD thesis, Université de Montréal, 2011.

Li, Hui-Lin. "The Origin of Cultivated Plants in Southeast Asia". *Economic Botany* 24, no. 1 (1970): 3–19.

Lim, Joseph Y. "The Effects of the East Asian Crisis on the Employment of Women and Men: The Philippine Case". *World Development* 28, no. 7 (2000): 1285–306.

Lindberg, Lena, and Claes G. Alvstam. "The National Element in Regional Trade Agreements, the Role of Southeast Asian Countries in Asean-EU Trade". *ASEAN Economic Bulletin* 24, no. 2 (2007): 267–75.

MacDonald, Scott B., and F. Joseph Demetrius. "The Caribbean Sugar Crisis: Consequences and Challenges". *Journal of Interamerican Studies and World Affairs* 28, no. 1 (1986).

Maillet, Gilles. *Living and Fishing in a Marine Protected Area: Balancing Traditional Fisheries with Conservation in Karimunjawa National Park*. Unpublished MA thesis, Université de Montréal, 2012.

Manivong, Vongpaphane, and R.A. Cramb. "Economics of Smallholder Rubber Expansion in Northern Laos". *Agroforestry Systems* 74 (2008): 113–25.

Matassan, Zainal A. *The Malaysian Fertilizer Market*. Kuala Lumpur: Fertilizer Industry Association of Malaysia, 2008.

May, Tim. *Social Research: Issues, Methods and Process*. Buckingham and Philadelphia: Open University Press, 1997.

Meyfroidt, Patrick, and Eric F. Lambin. "The Causes of the Reforestation in Vietnam". *Land Use Policy* 25, no. 2 (2008): 182–97.

———. "Forest Transition in Vietnam and Displacement of Deforestation Abroad". *Proceedings of the National Academy of Sciences* 106, no. 38 (2009): 16139–44.

Mitchell, Donald. "Sugar Policies: Opportunity for Change". In *World Bank Policy Research Working Paper*, ed. Development Prospects Group. Washington, D.C.: World Bank, 2004.

Morgan, Joseph, and Mark J. Valencia. *Atlas for Marine Policy in Southeast Asian Seas*. Berkeley: University of California Press, 1983.

Mortimer, Rex. *The Indonesian Communist Party and Land Reform, 1959–1965*. Clayton, Vic.: Centre of Southeast Asian Studies, Monash University, 1972.

Mukherji, Aditi, Thierry Facon, Jacob Burke, Charlotte de Fraiture, Jean-Marc Faures, Blanka Fuleki, Mark Giordano, David Molden and Tushaar Shah. *Revitalizing Asia's Agriculture: To Sustainably Meet Tomorrow's Food Needs*. Colombo and Rome: IWMI and FAO, 2009.

Murray Li, Tania. "Centering Labour in the Land Grab Debate". *Journal of Peasant Studies* 38 (2011): 281–98.

Myrdal, Gunnar. *The Challenge of World Poverty: A World Anti-Poverty Programme in Outline*. Harmondsworth: Penguin, 1971.

Neilson, Jeff. "Global Private Regulation and Value-Chain Restructuring in Indonesian Smallholder Coffee Systems". *World Development* 36, no. 9 (2008): 1607–22.

Nelson, Gerald C., and Martin Panggabean. "The Costs of Indonesian Sugar Policy: A Policy Analysis Matrix Approach". *American Journal of Agricultural Economics* 73, no. 3 (1991): 703–12.

Neville, Warwick. "Population". In *South-East Asia, a Systematic Geography*, ed. Lin Sien Chia and R.D. Hill. Kuala Lumpur and New York: Oxford University Press, 1979, pp. 52–77.

Nguyen, Hoa, and Ulrike Grote. "Agricultural Policies in Vietnam: Producer Support Estimates, 1986–2002". In *Discussion Papers on Development Policy*. Bonn: Zentrum fur Entwicklungsforschung Center for Development Research and International Food Research Institute, 2004.

Nguyen, Thu Lan T., Shabbir H. Gheewala and Savitri Garivait. "Full Chain Energy Analysis of Fuel Ethanol from Cane Molasses in Thailand". *Applied Energy* 85 (2008): 722–34.

O'Brien, Timothy G., and Margaret F. Kinnaird. "Caffeine and Conservation". *Science* 300 (2003): 587.

Padilla-Fernandez, M. Dina, and Peter Leslie Nuthall. "Technical Efficiency in the Production of Sugar Cane in Central Negros Area, Philippines". *Journal of the International Society for Southeast Asian Agricultural Sciences* 15, no. 1 (2009): 77–90.

Page, Susan E., Florian Siegert, John O. Rieley, Hans-Dieter V. Boehm, Adi Jaya and Suwido Limin. "The Amount of Carbon Released from Peat and Forest Fires in Indonesia During 1997". *Nature* 420, no. 6911 (2002): 61–65.

Pascual, Francisco G., and Arze G. Glipo. "WTO and Philippine Agriculture: Seven Years of Unbridled Trade Liberalization and Misery for Small Farmers". *Development Forum* no. 1 (2002): 1–14.

Peluso, Nancy Lee. *Rich Forests, Poor People: Resource Control and Resistance in Java*. Berkeley: University of California Press, 1992.

Pelzer, Karl J. *Pioneer Settlement in the Asiatic Tropics: Studies in Land Utilization and Agricultural Colonization in Southeastern Asia*. New York: American Geographical Society, 1945.

Pirard, Romain, and Christian Cossalter. *The Revival of Industrial Forest Plantations in Indonesia's Kalimantan Provinces*. Bogor: CIFOR, working paper, 2006.

Pluvier, Jan M. *Historical Atlas of South-East Asia*. New York: E.J. Brill, 1995.

Pouchepadass, Jacques. "Colonisations et environnement". *Revue française d'histoire d'outre-mer* 72, no. 268 (1993): 5–22.

Poupon, Roland. *Alternatives agricoles en Thaïlande: de la riziculture à la globalisation*. Bangkok: Editions Kailash and IRASEC, 2010.

Prasso, Sheridan. "Condom Kingdom". *Fortune*, 7 Aug. 2006.

Ramankutty, Nevin, and Jonathan A. Foley. "Estimating Historical Changes in Global Land Cover: Croplands from 1700 to 1992". *Global Biogeochemical Cycles* 13, no. 13 (1999): 997–1027.

Ramsay, Ansil. "The Political Economy of Sugar in Thailand". *Pacific Affairs* 60, no. 2 (1987): 248–70.

Rigg, Jonathan. *More Than the Soil: Rural Change in Southeast Asia*. Harlow: Prentice-Hall, 2001.

———. *Southeast Asia: The Human Landscape of Modernization and Development*. London: Routledge, 2003.

———. "Poverty and Livelihoods after Full-Time Farming: A South-East Asian View". *Asia Pacific Viewpoint* 46, no. 2 (2005): 173–84.

Rigg, Jonathan, and Sakunee Nattapoolwat. "Embracing the Global in Thailand: Activism and Pragmatism in an Era of Deagrarianization". *World Development* 29, no. 6 (2001): 945–60.

Rigg, Jonathan, and Peter Vandergeest, eds. *Revisiting Rural Places: Pathways to Poverty and Prosperity in Southeast Asia*. Singapore: NUS Press, 2012.

Robequain, Charles. *Malaya, Indonesia, Borneo, and the Philippines: A Geographical, Economic and Political Description of Malaya, the East Indies, and the Philippines*. London and New York: Longmans; Green, 1958.

Sauer, Carl Ortwin. *Agricultural Origins and Dispersals*. New York: American Geographical Society, 1952.

Scott, James C. *The Art of Not Being Governed: An Anarchist History of Upland Southeast Asia*. Yale Agrarian Studies Series. New Haven: Yale University Press, 2009.

Sepehri, Ardeshir, and Haroon Akram-Lodhi. "Transition, Savings and Growth in Vietnam: A Three-Gap Analysis". *Journal of International Development* 17 (2005): 553–74.

Sikor, Thomas. "The Allocation of Forestry Land in Vietnam: Did It Cause the Expansion of Forests in the Northwest?" *Forest Policy and Economics* 2, no. 1 (2001): 1–11.

Sodhi, Navjot, Mary Posa, Tien Lee, David Bickford, Lian Koh and Barry Brook. "The State and Conservation of Southeast Asian Biodiversity". *Biodiversity and Conservation* 19, no. 2 (2010): 317–28.

Spencer, Joseph Earle. *Shifting Cultivation in Southeastern Asia*. Berkeley: University of California Press, 1966.

Tachibana, Satoshi. "Impacts of Log Export Restrictions in Southeast Asia on the Japanese Plywood Market: An Econometric Analysis". *Journal of Forest Research* 5, no. 2 (2000): 51–7.

Taiganides, E. Paul. *Pig Waste Management and Recycling: The Singapore Experience*. Ottawa: International Development Research Centre, 1992.

Taillard, Christian. "Les transformations de quelques politiques agricoles socialistes en Asie entre 1978 et 1982 (Chine, Vietnam, Cambodge et Laos)". *Études rurales* no. 89/91 (1983): 111–43.

Tan, Stan B-H. "Coffee Frontiers in the Central Highlands of Vietnam: Networks of Connectivity". *Asia Pacific Viewpoint* 41, no. 1 (2000): 51–67.

Thrupp, Lori Ann, Susanne Hecht and John O. Browder. *The Diversity and Dynamics of Shifting Cultivation: Myths, Realities, and Policy Implications*. Washington, D.C.: World Resources Institute, 1997.

Tiensin, Thanawat, Prasit Chaitaweesub, Thaweesak Songserm, Arunee Chaisingh, Hoonsuwan Wirongrong, Chantanee Buranathai, Tippawon Parakamawongsa, Sith Premashthira, Alongkorn Amonsin, Marius Gilbert, Mirjam Nielen and Arjan Stegeman. "Highly Pathogenic Avian Influenza H5n1, Thailand, 2004". *Emerging Infectious Diseases* 11, no. 11 (2005): 1664–72.

Timilsina, Govinda R., and Ashish Shrestha. *Why Have CO_2 Emissions Increased in the Transport Sector in Asia? Underlying Factors and Policy Options*. Washington, D.C.: World Bank, 2009.

Tran, Xuan Thiep. *Eucalyptus Plantations in Vietnam: Their History and Development Process*. Hanoi: Forest Inventory and Planning Institute, Ministry of Forestry, Vietnam, n.d.

Transparency International. *Global Corruption Perceptions Index 2009*. 2010. http://media.transparency.org/imaps/cpi2009/.

Trébuil, Guy, and Mahabub Hossain. *Le riz: enjeux écologiques est économiques*. Paris: Belin, 2004.

USDA. "Gain (Global Agricultural Information Network) Report". In *MY002 Malaysia Grain and Feed Annual USDA*, Foreign Agriculture Service, 2010.

Van den Top, Gerhard. *The Social Dynamics of Deforestation in the Philippines: Actions, Options and Motivations*. Copenhagen and London: NIAS and Taylor & Francis, 2003.

Van Zalinge, N., N. Thuok and S. Nuov. "Status of the Cambodian Inland Capture Fisheries Sector with Special Reference to the Tonle Sap Great Lake". In *Fisheries Technical Paper Series*: 10–7. Phnom Penh: Inland Fisheries Research and Development Institute of Cambodia, 2001.

Warr, Peter. "Export Taxes and Income Distribution: The Philippines Coconut Levy". *Review of World Economics* 138, no. 3 (2002): 437–58.

Wickizer, V.D. *Coffee, Tea, and Cocoa*. Stanford: Stanford University Press, 1951.

Xu, Jianchu, and Andreas Wilkes. "Biodiversity Impact Analysis in Northwest Yunnan, Southwest China". *Biodiversity and Conservation* 13 (2004): 959–83.

Yap, Wilfredo G., Simon Funge Smith, M. Rimmer, M.J. Phillips, Sih Yang Sim, H. Kongkeo and Pedro B. Bueno. *Aquaculture in Asia-Pacific and the Outlook for Mariculture in Southeast Asia*. http://library.enaca.org/NACA-Publications/Overview_of_Aquaculture.pdf, 2007.

Yusuf, Shahid. "About Urban Mega Regions: Knowns and Unknowns". In *World Bank Policy Research Working Paper*, 25. Washington, D.C.: World Bank Development Research Group, 2007.

Databases, websites

Central Bureau of Statistics (Indonesia). *Census 2010*. 2010. http://www.bps.go.id/65tahun/SP2010_agregat_data_perProvinsi.pdf, accessed 13 Feb. 2012.

Department of Statistics (Malaysia). *Preliminary Count Report, Population and Housing Census*. 2010. http://www.statistics.gov.my/portal/index.php?option=com_content&view=category&id=97%3Apreliminary-count-report-population-and-housing-c&Itemid=61&layout=default&lang=en, accessed 13 Feb. 2012.

Food and Agriculture Organization. *FAOSTAT*. FAO, 2010. http://faostat.fao.org/default.aspx, date accessed 13 Feb. 2012.

Food and Agriculture Organization. *Fisheries and Aquaculture Department*. FAO, 2010. http://www.fao.org/fishery/statistics/en, accessed 13 Feb. 2012.

Food and Agriculture Organization. *Glossary of Aquaculture*. FAO, 2010. http://www.fao.org/fi/glossary/aquaculture/, accessed 13 Feb. 2012.

Instituto Brasileiro de Geografia e Estatistica. *IBGE Database*. IBGE, 2010. http://www.ibge.gov.br/english/presidencia/noticias/noticia_visualiza.php?id_noticia=1409&id_pagina=1, accessed 13 Feb. 2012.

NASA. *The Shuttle Radar Topography Mission* (SRTM). 2010. www2.jpl.nasa.gov/srtm/, accessed 13 Feb. 2012.

National Statistics Office (Philippines). *Census-Based Population Projection in Collaboration with the Inter-Agency Working Group on Population Projections*. 2000. http://www.census.gov.ph/data/sectordata/popproj_tab3r.html, accessed 13 Feb. 2012.

Nelson Institute for Environmental Studies. *SAGE Database*. N.I.E.S., 2010. http://www.sage.wisc.edu/, accessed 13 Feb. 2012.

United Nations Conference on Trade and Development. *UNCTADstat*. UNCTAD, 2010. http://unctadstat.unctad.org/UnctadStatMetadata/Documentation/AboutUNCTADstat.html, accessed 13 Feb. 2012.

United Nations Educational, Scientific and Cultural Organization. *UNESCO Institute for Statistics*. UNESCO, 2010. http://www.uis.unesco.org/ev.php?ID=2867_201&ID2=DO_TOPIC, accessed 13 Feb. 2012.

United Nations Environment Programme. *UNEP Geo Data*. UNEP, 2010. http://geodata.grid.unep.ch/, accessed 13 Feb. 2012.

United Nations Population Programme. *World Population Prospects*. UNPOP, 2010. http://esa.un.org/unpp/ [site discontinued].

United Nations Statistics Division. *National Accounts Main Aggregates Database*. UNSTATS, 2010. http://unstats.un.org/unsd/snaama/selbasicFast.asp, accessed 13 Feb. 2012.

World Bank. *World dataBank*. World Bank, 2010. http://databank.worldbank.org/ddp/home.do, accessed 13 Feb. 2012.

Index

Challenges of the Agrarian Transition in Southeast Asia (ChATSEA)

Previously published ChATSEA titles:

Borneo Transformed: Agricultural Expansion on the Southeast Asian Frontier, edited by Rodolphe De Koninck, Stéphane Bernard and Jean-François Bissonnette, 2011

Powers of Exclusion: Land Dilemmas in Southeast Asia, by Derek Hall, Philip Hirsch and Tania Murray Li, 2011

Upland Transformations in Vietnam, edited by Thomas Sikor, Nghiêm Phương Tuyến Tuyến, Jennifer Sowerwine and Jeff Romm, 2011

Revisiting Rural Places: Pathways to Poverty and Prosperity in Southeast Asia, edited by Jonathan Rigg and Peter Vandergeest, 2012